The Dynamics of Change

University of Northumbria at

'This is an important and useful contribution to change which seeks to introduce a scientific understanding of the subject.'

Professor J.D.R de Raadt, *Lulea University, Sweden*

'This book should have a very broad appeal to systems thinkers in many different fields.'

Professor G.A. Swanson, *Tennessee Technological University, USA*

Organisational change is a core area of interest in business and management yet most of the literature on the subject ignores the fundamental question of what change actually *is*. This original and groundbreaking work explores the fundamental question of what change really is rather than just describing how it can best be managed.

The book investigates how systems thinking and interdisciplinary insights from the natural sciences, philosophy and sociology can greatly enhance our understanding of change. Features of the work include:

*   a detailed introduction to systems thinking and General Systems Theory
*   a critique of the traditional mechanistic views of change
*   an excellent overview of the main approaches and theories of organisational change
*   key building blocks drawn on metaphors and analogy from natural and physical sciences which describe the essential components and underlying dynamics of change

Written in a highly accessible style and extensively illustrated throughout, *The Dynamics of Change* is a fascinating and provocative work which will be of great interest to students, researchers and practitioners in the field of organisational change.

Francis Stickland is a consultant within the Organisational Effectiveness Practice at Hewitt Associates, a global management consulting firm specialising in human resource solutions. He has lectured in organisational behaviour, quality and systems thinking and holds a Ph.D. in Organisational Change from City University, London.

The Dynamics of Change

Insights into organisational transition
from the natural world

Francis Stickland

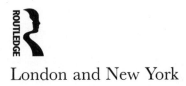

London and New York

First published 1998 by Routledge
11 New Fetter Lane, London EC4P 4EE

Simultaneously published in the USA and Canada
by Routledge
29 West 35th Street, New York, NY 10001

Typeset in Baskerville by Keystroke, Jacaranda Lodge, Wolverhampton
Printed and bound in Great Britain by Redwood Books, Trowbridge,
Wiltshire

British Library Cataloguing in Publication Data
A catalogue record for this book is available from the British Library

Library of Congress Cataloguing in Publication Data
Stickland, Francis, 1967–
    The dynamics of change: insights into organisational transition
    from the natural world / Francis Stickland.
    p.   cm.
    Includes bibliographical references and index.
    1. Organisational change. I. Title.
    HD58.8.S78   1998
    658.4'063–dc21   98–4008
                    CIP

ISBN 0–415–18415–0 (hbk)
ISBN 0–415–18416–9 (pbk)

To
Sally Jayne

One thing that is new is the prevalance of newness, the changing scale and scope of change itself, so that the world alters as we walk on it, so that the years of a man's life measure not some small growth or rearrangement or moderation of what he learned in childhood, but a great upheaval.

(J. Robert Oppenheimer 1955)

Not in his goals, but in his transitions man is great.

(Ralph Waldo Emerson, 1803–82)

Swift to its close ebbs out life's little day,
Earth's joys grow dim, its glories pass away;
Change and decay in all around I see
O Thou who changest not, abide with me.

(H.F. Lyte, 1793–1847)

Contents

Figures

Tables

Preface

Soon after the triumphs of leading the people of Israel safely through the Red Sea and out of the clutches of Pharaoh, Moses finds himself called to the summit of Mount Sinai to meet with God. The Israelites were about to embark on an incredible journey that would take them over fifty years to reach the Promised Land. During that time they would learn how to live and survive as a vast community: a moving city of tents and humanity. So long was the road ahead that many would go from the womb to the grave before reaching their destination. Therefore, God wanted to introduce a set of rules and laws that would not only help provide some order and continuity in their nomadic life, but also institute a moral and spiritual code by which they should live. Leaving aside their clear spiritual connotations for a moment, these laws were to provide a fixed, immutable reference point offering some stability and continuity for what was going to be a constantly changing life style.

Moses was duly summoned up the mountain to hear the laws imparted – among them the Ten Commandments. Shortly after the great patriarch vanishes from sight up the mountain, the people become impatient and tired of waiting for the words of wisdom and guidance that he will bring on his return. Life must move on they reason. A focus must be found to balance the uncertainties of their wandering existence. So they turn to their temporary leader – Aaron – and insist that he make them a god to worship and sacrifice to. The old man has been gone too long, they argue. Their restless hearts seek some icon of order and structured activity in the midst of a change-filled life – with its inherent ambiguity and uncertain future.

Aaron eventually relents to their incessant cries. The Bible manuscripts record that Moses returns after forty days to a people feasting and rejoicing under the shadow of their new god – a statue of a large golden calf.

I would suggest that this salutary tale is an interesting parable through which to portray progress in the field of change management. Today's managers and business leaders are in great need of some guiding principles and words of wisdom from the academic community in their quest to tame and understand change.

Responses vary. For some, what has emerged from the research literature is perceived as inaccessible – wrapped in the mists of obscurity and jargon. For others, the researchers have been up the mountain for too long, and have yet to appear from their lofty heights bearing rigorous, comprehensive change management methodologies with which to impart some order to the swirling complexity and uncertainty of today's organisation. But patiently they wait, making good use of the many excellent change models and approaches that have emerged over the years. Nevertheless, the golden age of organisation development in the 1960s is long gone and the need is pressing. Many are not able to dig back into the change management literature of that era for inspiration. Their urgent need forces them to chase from management fad to business guru and back again – creating short-lived golden calves from which to seek some measure of comfort.

This book has been born out of three things: a professional interest in better understanding change within organisations; a fascination with the science of the physical world; and a frustration with the many 'golden calves' and mechanistic approaches to change in popular use. For many years now scholars and practitioners have grappled with *how* to manage change effectively. Countless books and articles have been written on the subject. Indeed, many of these provide excellent instruction for the manager or consultant seeking to achieve or respond to change. This book attempts to take a step back and explore *what* change is as a phenomenon.

Of all that has been written on change, relatively little focuses on this intriguing and much neglected 'what' question. The 'how' question has dominated our thinking, being clearly more lucrative to answer and arguably more pressing in today's dynamic and fast-moving world. However, the history of scientific endeavour provides us with an unambiguous lesson. Practical application must go hand in hand with conceptual development. Before we could harness the potential and energy of the atom, science first had to learn what an atom was, how it behaved and what it consisted of. Whether it is nuclear power, gravity, electricity, cancer or genetics, successfully resolving the 'how' question requires simultaneous research into the 'what' – one feeds off the other in a constant cycle of discovery and application. So it must be with change if we are ever to learn to live with it in our organisations.

The motivation for writing this book is the belief that gaining a deeper understanding of what change is and the underlying dynamics that drive it will significantly enhance our ability to manage it more effectively. These pages present no grand theory of change or comprehensive framework to apply instantly to the next organisational change situation you encounter. Indeed, one may well question the feasibility of constructing some unifying scheme. Neither does this book pretend to take the reader on a 'climb up the mountain', but merely to highlight a pressing need and to offer some guide points. Nevertheless, it is my sincere hope that through the questions that are posed this book may in some small way inspire more creative thinking about the way we manage, model, measure and respond to change and transition.

Francis Stickland

Paris

February 1998

Acknowledgements

There are many who have contributed to the thinking and energy that went into making this book possible. I owe much to Ray Jowitt whose intellectual curiosity and eagerness to explore other subject domains rubbed off on me many years ago. Several people encouraged me to write up my thinking on change and publish this work, with words of support and endorsement at critical times either during the early stages of the work or towards the end – in particular G. A. Swanson, Ralph Stacey, Linda Peeno, Diane Taylor, Robert Flood, Thomas Mandel and Donald de Raadt. A big thank-you goes to John Beckford, Elaine Cole and Sionade Robinson for reviewing major parts of the manuscript and for numerous helpful comments. Many others have fielded questions or freely offered constructive advice and support along the way, including Neville Osrin, David Humphreys, Simon Spiller, Jennifer Wilby, Paul Smith, Jonathan Papier and Ed Gubman. Special thanks to Lawrie Reavill who oversaw much of the original research from which this book grew. My sons Jonathan and new arrival Ryan saw a little less of me during the preparation of the book and I am grateful to them for their patience and long-suffering.

The author and publisher would like to thank the following for permission to reproduce copyright material:

Table 2.2 is reprinted by permission of the Proceedings of the 39th Annual Meeting of the International Society for the Systems Sciences, Club of Budapest, Hungary, September, 1995. The extract from 'Footnotes to organisational change' by J.G. March, published in *Administrative Science Quarterly*, vol. 26: 575 is reprinted by permission of *Administrative Science Quarterly*. Table 2.3 is adapted by permission of the Academy of Management Review. From *Revolutionary Change Theories*, vol. 16(1): 10–36 © 1991 by C.J. Gersick, Academy of Management Review, New York. Figure 3.1 is adapted by permission of Joe Peppard. From 'The content, context and process of business process re-engineering', in G. Burke and J. Peppard (eds) *Exploring Business Process Re-engineering: Current Perspectives and Research Directions* © 1994 by Joe Peppard, Kogan Page, London. Figure 4.1 is adapted by permission of W. Warner Burke. From *Organisational Development* © 1992 by W. Warner Burke, Addison-Wesley, New York. The extracts from *Leadership and the New Science* © 1992 by M.J. Wheatley are reprinted with permission of Berrett-Koehler Publishers, Inc., San Francisco, CA. All rights reserved.

While the author and publisher have made every effort to contact copyright holders of the material used in this volume, they would be happy to hear from anyone they were unable to contact.

I am delighted to acknowledge the professional manner and close attention to detail of my Routledge editorial team. The final thank-you must go to John and Edna Stickland for ultimately making this intellectual adventure possible.

Glossary

Analogy A specific relational comparison between two subject domains. It is a subset of a *metaphor* and breaks down the general level description of a metaphor into specific analogical statements. For example, 'adjusting culturally to large-scale organisational change is like adjusting emotionally following a house move', or 'the unpredictable responses and behaviour of specific individuals within an organisation, is like the erratic flight motion of individual bees in a swarm'.

Central Limit theorem Based upon the sampling distribution of the mean, it provides the foundation for statistical inference according to the following three distributions (Kurtz, 1983):

1 The distribution of the sampling mean will approximate to a normal distribution curve, regardless of the distribution of the variable in question in the original population.
2 The mean of the sampling distribution of the mean will be equal to the population mean.
3 The standard deviation (SD) of the sampling distribution has a constant relationship to the SD of the population.

Entropy A measure of disorder and disorganisation within a system (often expressed as a measure of a system's ability to do work). Within a closed system, entropy is said to increase over time, culminating in system death and loss of identity.

Epistemology A philosophy term to describe theories of knowledge, how it is created and acquired.

Feedback The change in a given variable or system component caused by its own output. Negative feedback will close the gap between the actual state and the base or reference state. Positive feedback will increase the gap (see Beishon and Peters, 1981).

Homomorphism A 'many-to-one' mapping between concepts or objects in the source domain and the target domain. For example, the structure of the solar system can be mapped onto the structure of the atom. Not all mappings correspond, such as size and temperature, so these are dropped.

Hence, homomorphic mapping is a simplification process which ensures that key structural information is preserved (Tsoukas, 1991).

Isomorphism A 'one-to-one' mapping between concepts or objects in the source domain and the target domain, for example, a model aircraft that is designed to correspond to the full-scale version in every respect, but in miniature.

Metaphor The transference of information from one subject domain to another where it is not applicable literally. For example, 'the corporate policy department is the brain behind the recent performance improvement' or 'the powerful subterranean change processes occurring within the business threaten to erupt like a volcano at any moment'.

Metonymy The direct replacement or substitution of a word (name or attribute) with that of another, for example, *crown* for *king* (Oxford Dictionary, 1984).

Negentropy Short for *negative entropy*, and is a measure of the degree of order (or information) a system possesses. Negentropy is likely to increase if a system is able to receive energy from its environment, or self-organise through bidirectional environmental exchange.

Ontology A philosophy term to describe theories of reality or being.

Possibility space The notional area which constitutes all the possible future states for a system, through which it charts a course as it moves through time. Clearly only a limited, finite number of states are actually realised.

Stochastic process Simply put, any process which contains a random variable.

Synergetics The science of co-operation, coined from the Greek by Hanken (1981, 1983). Synergetics describe how within certain systems (particularly those which demonstrate self-organisation), internal rules, and initial conditions can determine eventual outcomes, and 'choose' for the good of the system as a whole.

1 Managing change

The problem redefined

> The world is changing faster than ever before. We are living in times of far reaching and profound transformations in the perceptions and structures of the world's politics, economics, demography, technology, ecology and ethics. These changes are evolving at a striking pace, and societies must now evaluate them and make the necessary adjustments.
>
> (Kirdar, 1992: 8)

These changing times

Most books published in recent years on the subject of change management open with the assertion that there is a lot of it about. And indeed there is. The ubiquity of change has long been acknowledged, as Engles (1959: 82) noted 'nothing remains what, where and as it was, but everything moves, changes, comes into being and passes away'. According to Whitehead (1925: 179) change is inherent 'in the very nature of things'. It has increasingly become an important topic which is fashionable to write about. Across a wide range of disciplines attention is turning to issues of change: how can change be more effectively initiated, managed, implemented and responded to? A general survey across the social sciences (including business, organisation and management fields) revealed that the literature concerned with change has been expanding rapidly in many directions. Between 1984 and 1995 the number of journals containing the word 'change' in their title more than doubled.[1]

As numerous commentators have observed, the rate of change seems to be accelerating in many spheres of human activity, and is now reaching unprecedented levels within our technological and industrial systems.[2] It is difficult to say whether this is due to an actual increase in the occurrence of change as a phenomenon or whether we are merely becoming more aware of change activity and the problems associated with it. In the field of international relations, Keohane and Nye (1989) note that the political, economic, technological and social affairs of mankind have become highly interdependent over the past two centuries – to the extent that a given change cannot be easily isolated and confined, but its effects can be felt faster and further afield than before. Coupled with the increasing interconnectedness of the world in which we now live, this makes change phenomena arguably more significant now than at any point in the past. Whatever the case, the impact on our conceptual understanding of the world is not insignificant, as Goodman and Kurke (1982: 2) have observed 'the concept of change pervades all our intellectual endeavours'.

> 'Managers are now confronted with a bewildering array of approaches, techniques and strategies to assist them in changing some aspect of their business for the better.'

Perhaps nowhere is the pace and scale of change being more keenly felt than in the organisation. Persistent downward pressures on cost and progressive deregulation in many industries around the world, coupled with the transformation that information technology has brought to our daily work, are just three of a multitude of variables driving change in organisations. On the surface, this need not worry us unduly, except that even a cursory glance through the management literature or business press will reveal that we are a long way from managing change well.

Reasons why change initiatives fail

Many change ventures fail to meet the expectations of their champions, or deliver the additional bottom line value proclaimed at the outset by their architects. Consider the following comments:

*   Results from large scale change programmes are 'seriously underwhelming' (Dr Richard Pascale, author of *Managing on the Edge*).
*   Two-thirds of companies that attempted to implement Total Quality had not seen any significant change (Arthur D. Little, management consultancy).
*   Implementation of many complex change initiatives rarely deliver the benefits anticipated (Neville Osrin, Head of Organisation Effectiveness Practice, Hewitt Associates, UK).
*   70 per cent of business process re-engineering efforts ultimately fail (Michael Hammer, co-author of *Reengineering the Corporation*).

Numerous factors are at work here, but a few reasons constantly seem to be given, in both the academic literature and the 'with hindsight' case studies of the more popular management press:

*   *Imagination*: adopting or being sold somebody else's solution due to a lack of creative effort.
*   *Repetition*: death by a thousand change initiatives.
*   *Fear*: ignoring critical issues because they may generate threat or embarrassment.

- *Sensitivity*: not taking account of 'emotional cycles of transition'.
- *Ownership*: delegating solutions without achieving prior acknowledgement of the problems or engaging the people concerned.
- *Culture*: not anticipating the influence and durability of culture (both national and organisational).
- *Leadership*: insufficient personal skills development by the champions and architects of the change.
- *Learning*: not translating operational learning into strategy learning and vice versa.
- *Communication*: announcing a radical change and then changing incrementally.

This is a very selective list and no doubt readers will be able to add to each heading from their own personal experience of change management. Upon closer inspection of these nine culprits, we see a whole range of subject domains represented: from culture, psychology, leadership development, communications through to corporate strategy. Change it seems, manifests itself in numerous ways and comes in many guises, most of which are intricately interdependent. As a result, a very rich conception of change and transition[3] is essential if we are to better understand the interdependencies and become more effective at change management – thereby avoiding some of these pitfalls.

But surely are we not already well equipped to tackle change? To some extent, the answer must be yes. The business and management shelves of most bookshops groan under the weight of titles in this area. From organisational development and systems science through to information technology and total quality, methodologies for achieving change across a range of problem situations have emerged over the past fifty years. Managers are now confronted with a bewildering array of approaches, techniques and strategies to assist them in changing some aspect of their business for the better.

However, the main thrust of much of this work has been to answer the practical *how* questions – how change can be effectively dealt with. The more fundamental 'what' questions have yet to be seriously asked at a generic level: What is the *nature* of change? What characteristics and attributes does change possess? What structural features, interactions and processes define change? What basic principles govern change, if any? What marks the beginning and end of a given change? What perception and measurement issues are associated with change? Vickers alluded to the need for such a basic understanding of the nature of change:

> The view of entities as both systems and constituents of systems raises intriguing questions about identity and continuity. When does something, or somebody, retain its identity and continuity through change? When by contrast does it cease to be its old self and either vanish or become something new or different? The question is not frivolous or merely metaphysical but may be of great practical concern.
>
> (Vickers, 1980a: 20)

These and other such probing questions need to be asked if we are better to understand the nature of change. Despite the plethora of approaches and tools for managing organisational change, theoretical frameworks for exploring and describing its complexities and dynamics have been slow to emerge and disappointingly few in number.

> 'Models of organisational change management based upon the assumption that change is merely a carefully planned transition from A to B still dominate corporate change programmes.'

The need for something more

Practitioners may point to the apparent success of certain well-established applied research techniques and strategies for dealing with organisational change, and query why such a fundamental look at change is being proposed here. However, as Golembiewski *et al.*, 1976: 133) have observed: 'There is a truism about applied research that an inadequate concept of change leads to diminished or misguided applied research.'

As we shall see later in the book, theorists have historically viewed change within organisations mainly in terms of *planned* interventions, up until the late 1960s. Even with this somewhat limited view of change, several writers noted the uneasy relationship that existed between theoretical researchers and practitioners: 'We seem, quite often, to become lost at the cross-roads of a false dichotomy; the purity and virginity of theory on the one hand and the anti-intellectualism of some knowledge-for-what adherents on the other' (Bennis *et al.*, 1970: 4). It would seem that in the intervening years, we have passed this crossroads, having chosen to tread with vigour the practical path – down which we are now making great strides. Sadly, relatively few have ventured out upon the theoretical path:

> It would be desirable to be able to justify our definition of planned change by *carefully researched knowledge of processes of changing*. But, for the most part, this research base has yet to be developed. We hope and believe that it will develop in the future.
>
> (Bennis *et al.*, 1970: 61; emphasis added)

In a similar vein, Clarke and Ford writing around the same time bemoaned the lack of theoretical endeavour: 'such scholarship and research as does exist is primarily directed to the needs of the action oriented social scientists promoting planned organisational change . . . published accounts are written for either administrators or consultants' (Clarke and Ford, 1970: 29).

As the thinking about change broadened during the 1970s and other strands of organisational change research developed with the rise of the biological and other metaphors, the 'what is change' question remained for the most part unexamined. While exploring the concept of change within organisations, Berg (1979) came to the conclusion that the task of understanding change itself had been seriously neglected. He argued 'that much of the present confusion and ambiguity in the field stems from the fact that we actually know very little about the nature of change' (Berg, 1979: 19).

March (1981) also highlighted the weak theoretical base of the organisational change literature at that time. In his discussion of broad theoretical notions about organisation action, he states that 'a comprehensive development of managerial strategies . . . requires a more thorough understanding of change in organisations, *not a theory of how to introduce any arbitrary change*' (March, 1981: 575; emphasis added). Here again we see concern expressed at the apparent overemphasis on answering the how question.

More recently Morgan (1986) has identified the need for a deeper comprehension of the fundamentals of change. He argues that 'we need to try and understand how the discrete events that make up our experience of change are generated by a logic unfolded in the process of change itself' (Morgan, 1986: 267). His work will be examined in more detail later.

Even as we entered the 1990s, the phenomenon of change within the organisation was still seen as under-conceptualised. Wilson (1992: 3) lamented, 'much of the current vogue in management theory is for delineating the steps through which successful change can occur'. He goes on to highlight the explosion of such change recipes 'which have little empirical or theoretical foundation [and] should give cause for grave concern amongst all who work in organisations of every type' (Wilson, 1992: 120). The problem with recipe approaches is that they often assume change is simply a question of moving smoothly from point A to point B by achieving prespecified intermediate goals (see Beckhard and Harris, 1977; Nadler, 1988). Experienced change management practitioners will be aware, however, that Point B is either continually moving, and thus harder to reach with a rigid predetermined change plan, or the environment changes significantly in the time it takes to reach B, making B out of date and inappropriate. This issue is captured well in Figure 1.1, the perpetually failing change management machine.

Models of organisational change management based upon the assumption that change is merely a carefully planned transition from A to B still dominate corporate change programmes. Clearly they have their place, and in certain scenarios are appropriate. But as any chef knows, a good recipe is rooted in a deep understanding of all the ingredients involved, flavour mixes, colour combinations, basic processes of cooking and the unique preferences of the palate he or she is attempting to delight.

Various calls then have been made over the years, right up to recent times, for greater attention to be given to understanding the *nature* of change. These appeals have largely been made in the conviction that organisational change practice would benefit considerably from such research. It would be unfair, however, to say that they have gone totally unheeded and in Chapter 4 we shall take a look at some of the few writers who have taken on the challenge of getting to grips with defining change within the organisation.

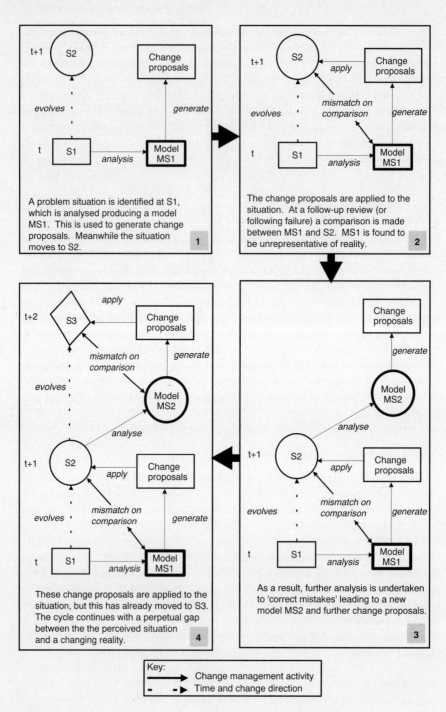

Figure 1.1 The perpetually failing change management machine (adpated with permission from Beckford, 1993)

Nonetheless, practical approaches to change management continue to proliferate, often as one-off solutions to specific problems. As one commentator has observed:

> Practice is static. It does well what it knows. It has however no principle for dealing with what it doesn't know . . . Practice is not well adapted for rapid adjustment to a changing environment. Theory is light footed. It can adjust itself to changing circumstances, think out fresh combinations and possibly, peer into the future.
>
> (Litwick, 1987: 15)

Organisational change practice – for better or worse – is well established but far from fleet of foot. It is the author's belief that greater theoretical and conceptual insight would make it far more responsive to the capricious demands being placed upon it. We desperately need more to stimulate our thinking, challenge our preconceptions about change and breathe life back into what is fast becoming a tired and well-worn subject. So, where is this deeper understanding of change going to come from? How can we break out of our prescriptive models and simplified frameworks for change management? Where can we turn for a deeper insight into the nature of change to help guide us through the next transition we encounter?

One of the main aims of this book is to help readers to dig their own wells and draw from their own creative resources when dealing with organisational change – rather than having to rely solely on the latest change management model. A good model complemented with an inquisitive and challenging outlook is a healthy balance.

Navigating through the book

On leaving Chapter 1, the reader should not feel obliged to work sequentially through the rest of the text. A summary outline is given here of the main parts of the book, allowing you to skip those sections which may be familiar to you and home in on chapters of interest.

Having defined the problem to be addressed in this chapter, Chapter 2 moves on to introduce the discipline of systems thinking. One strand of this subject domain is offered as a lens through which to examine the phenomenon of change and better understand it – General Systems Theory (GST). Some of the key tenets of GST are summarised and the chapter provides a basic introduction for readers who are new to systems thinking concepts. The power of metaphorical thinking is also covered, as this is one of the main searchlights used in later chapters to uncover insights into the dynamics of change. The chapter also reviews briefly the work of a number of authors who have pioneered the use of metaphor and analogy in exploring organisational life. For example, thinkers such as Margaret Wheatley and Gareth Morgan, writers who have stepped eagerly outside their own discipline in search of fresh ideas, which they can bring back and apply to the organisation. This chapter is crucial to understanding the cross-discipline approach and systems thinking philosophy which underpins the book. It should be read as a minimum before proceeding further.

Chapter 3 takes a rapid tour through the organisational change literature. From the late nineteenth century up to the 1960s, scientific management, human relations and contingency theory have all influenced how organisational change has been perceived and dealt with. This rich legacy is briefly examined along with some of the assumptions about change that have been carried forward from it into later change management thinking. Then attention turns to more recent developments since the 1970s, with many of the principal approaches addressing the topic of change in organisations being mapped out. The purpose is to provide a route map through the current plethora of approaches and paradigms that have emerged in organisational change thinking over the past thirty years. This is by no means a comprehensive review – merely an attempt to provide some pointers in what has become an incredibly diverse field of literature. The literature is examined in several ways, including two simple classifications. One is by root metaphor – showing how approaches are underpinned by different metaphors such as machine or organism. The other classification is made according to a spectrum ranging from theoretical focus through to practical orientation. Change approaches are plotted on this continuum and it may be no surprise to find that the theoretical end is sparsely populated. Those familiar with the organisational change literature may want to skip this chapter, as it really attempts to paint a broad-brush history of thinking in this area.

As noted earlier, there have been a few significant attempts to get to grips with *what change is conceptually* and to understand it better within organisational settings. In Chapter 4 we review the work of those who have asked the keynote question running through this book: what is this thing called change? This is very much a personal selection, but it has to be said that the field of choice is certainly not large. Names such Kurt Lewin, William Bridges or Andrew Pettigrew will be familiar to many, but others may be less well known. This review really completes the high level survey of the organisational change literature started in Chapter 3. The scene is then set for us to leave the organisation and management disciplines behind for a while and set sail for other subject domains.

In keeping with the cross-discipline systems thinking approach adopted by the book, Chapter 5 seeks to offer a whole range of alternative perspectives on change. Various philosophical change issues are explored such as the role of the observer, and his ability objectively to measure and describe what he perceives. The age-old debate of whether change is real or just an illusion is discussed, along with the question of knowledge creation and learning following change. Attention then turns to the problem of *definition*, and a range of perspectives on change is reviewed from both the social and physical sciences. Focusing in on how other discipline specialists have defined change and conceptualised it is a fascinating way of broadening one's own thinking. The review ranges from history, inter-national relations, mathematics and sociology through to quantum mechanics and classical physics. Once again, the selection of examples has to be limited. But the purpose is to sensitise the reader to some of the common themes and issue with which change scholars generally have to grapple, and how they choose to define the phenomenon as it manifests itself within their own discipline.

Chapters 6, 7, 8 and 9 take us sailing far beyond the sight of land and outside the comfort zone of organisation and management disciplines with which we may be familiar. In these chapters specific change phenomena from the natural and physical sciences are examined, in search of change insights that might be applicable within an organisational setting. In doing so, they collectively build a set of change building blocks. These are offered as a suggested initial framework for organisational change practitioners and theorists. Whether you are responding to change, designing it, trying to manage it effectively or just seeking to gain a better understanding of it as a phenomenon, it is hoped that the building blocks developed in these four chapters will aid your thinking and help you probe a little deeper. They do not constitute some prescriptive model or grand theory of change. On the contrary, the building blocks seek only to demonstrate some of the key dynamics and principles of change, thereby stimulating creative thinking for the practitioner and encouraging further enquiry by the academic.

In the process, they also demonstrate how it is possible to mine other subject domains for inspiration and insight without having to be a specialist in other fields. The change phenomena examined come from areas of physics, chemistry and biology – some of them simple phenomena you will remember from science lessons at school, others more recent discoveries in chaos theory and complexity science. In each case, examples are given showing how the general insight or principle gleaned could be applied to organisational life.

The final chapter attempts to bring things firmly down to earth by summarising how the reader can generate novel insights into organisational change for themselves – either for dealing with change practically, or as a basis for academic research. The use of metaphor is returned to with some words of caution. The question of what defines 'successful' change is also explored briefly, and whether this is a helpful adjective to use during organisational change management. The chapter concludes with a number of areas where further research is urgently needed, and some suggestions of other science domains where students of change may wish to go exploring.

A brief tour of the book has been given here to help the reader to navigate the text effectively. Table 1.1 summarises the key components. All that now remains is to begin the journey.

Summary

So we can conclude that the need to understand change as a phenomenon is becoming increasingly important, and that our capability to manage change within organisations is not as effective as it could be. Over the years we have seen organisational change scholars voice their concern that not enough effort is being spent in understanding the nature of change itself – right up to recent times. The need is arguably more pressing now than ever before. So, where is this deeper

Table 1.1 A short guide for navigating through the book

Chapter	Main thrust
1	Highlights the poor conception of change we have within organisational thinking.
2	Introduces systems thinking, in particular General Systems Theory as one route through which we can broaden our understanding of change.
3	Skim reviews the existing organisational change literature.
4	Examines some of the few authors who have attempted to explore what change is in an organisational setting.
5	Looks at the philosophical questions and issues associated with change, and offers a range of definitions from both the social and physical sciences.
6	Change building blocks: Part 1 Sources, types, methodology and foci.
7	Change building blocks: Part 2 Embedded dynamics.
8	Change building blocks: Part 3 Levels, attributes, degree and principles.
9	Change building blocks: Part 4 Resistance and endings.
10	Offers some suggestions on how readers can generate their own change insights from other subject domains.

understanding of change going to come from? How can we break out of our prescriptive models and simplified frameworks for change management? Where can we turn for more profound insights into the nature of change to help guide us through the next one we encounter? The next chapter offers one way by which we might plumb the depths of this ubiquitous phenomenon.

2 Moving beyond the conventional

Systems thinkers unite

A cosmopolitan outlook in theorising depends upon the theorist leaving at some stage, the community of practitioners with whom he or she may feel at home, to appreciate the realms of theorising defined by other paradigms, and the varieties of metaphors and methods through which theory and research can be conducted.

(Morgan, 1980: 607)

Introduction

To think about anything creatively requires some fresh input. Breaking out of the old ways, habits and thought patterns of the past demands an open mind and a willingness to view the world through a different lens. And so it is with organisational change. In this chapter we shall look at how a phenomenon such as change can be explored by tapping into the accumulated learning of other disciplines. Curiosity and imagination are the only requirements for probing what other subject domains have to offer. One branch of systems thinking will be examined which provides a basis for working across disciplines.

We shall also look at some examples of organisational practitioners and theorists who have made attempts to go beyond the established literature in their thinking. This chapter then sets the scene for our own journey of discovery into other fields of study, in search of a better understanding of organisational change.

Visionaries in search of inspiration

The term holistic – pertaining to the whole – has crept into our management speak in recent years. Thinking 'holistically' is now the order of the day. We should consider the whole organisation and not just focus on specific parts, including the wider environment with which the organisation interacts. We are urged to ponder all the alternatives before deciding upon a course of action and to understand the importance of interconnections and relationships.

Such concepts mostly find their origin in a discipline known as systems science – more popularly called systems thinking. It is not the intention here to discuss the history and roots of this discipline, as this has been done admirably elsewhere.[1] Suffice to say that many in the business and management arena discovered the power of systems thinking through Peter Senge's book *The Fifth Discipline*. On reading this work, one would be forgiven for believing systems ideas are relatively new. What he has done is to make them accessible. As a modern discipline systems thinking can in fact be traced back to the 1940s, with intellectual roots that go back as far as the Greeks. Figure 2.1 attempts to capture something of the breadth and evolution of thought that has shaped systems science as a discipline over the past fifty years.

The strand of systems science which is of particular relevance to us here is General Systems Theory or GST as it is more commonly known. During the early 1950s, a number of individuals from a variety of academic backgrounds came together to build and shape GST, including:

- a biologist: Ludwig von Bertalanffy;
- an economist: Kenneth E. Boulding;
- a mathematician: Anatol Rapoport.

Their work includes Bertalanffy (1950, 1962); Boulding (1956b), Rapoport (1966, 1988) and also to some extent Gerard (1957). Between them, they had a vision and intense passion to see the boundaries between the sciences transcended and a more open sharing of knowledge.

Theories of everything: General Systems

General Systems Theory (GST) is founded upon the notion that similarities exist between different subject domains (Waelchli, 1992).[2] GST can be described as a meta-theory, which seeks to unify science by the drawing together of common principles and laws from different disciplines. An original stated aim of GST was to 'investigate the isomorphy of concepts, laws, and models in various fields, and to help in useful transfers from one field to another' (Bertalanffy, 1968: 15). Table 2.1 outlines some of the underlying theses of GST and seeks to define what a 'system' is.

The emergence of General Systems Theory as a philosophy can be attributed to at least two clear historical reasons. First, the increasing specialisation of science over the last two hundred years has caused a fragmentation of knowledge, with communication between disciplines becoming ever more difficult as each subdiscipline isolates itself further by adopting complex vocabulary and jargon. During the 1950s and early 1960s there was a growing sense that an integration and unification of science should be attempted in an effort to redress the balance (see Mesarovic, 1964). In some ways, this was reminiscent of the philosophy of scientific endeavour prevalent during the Renaissance, when the physical, natural and social world were all viewed as one glorious whole and studied largely without artificial distinction.

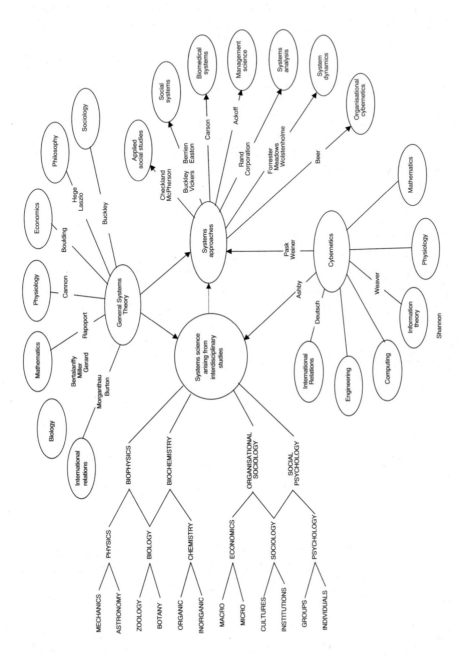

Figure 2.1 An overview of systems thinking (adapted from Beishon, 1980)

Table 2.1 General Systems Theory: some basic tenets (adapted from Waelchli, 1992)

- Nature is one unified *whole*.

- The notion of a *system* is a revealing concept through which to model nature and the world in which we live. Systems do not actually exist, but are defined by the observer.

- Simply put, a system is any organised collection of *elements* or parts, interconnected with *relationships* and contained within some identifiable *boundary*. In addition:

  - A system has an *identity* that sets it apart from its environment and is capable of preserving that identity within a given range of environmental scenarios.
  - Systems exist within a *hierarchy* of other systems. They contain subsystems and exist within some wider system. All are interconnected with the subsystems being less complex than the containing systems. For example, Kenneth Boulding (1956) described the following hierarchy of system levels:

1	Framework	6	Animal
2	Clockwork	7	Human
3	Thermostat	8	Organisations
4	Cell	9	Transcendental
5	Plant		

  - Systems at the level of the whole have *emergent properties* which do not exist within the subsystems. The whole cannot be completely defined or predicted by the properties of the parts. A tangerine is round and orange in appearance at the level of the whole. Viewed through a microscope, it ceases to be round and orange.

- The general systems thinker uses the notion of system to highlight *structural similarities* across disciplines.

- General Systems Theory provides a *meta-language* through which the paradoxes and language of individual subject disciplines can be discussed.

- Systems are often characterised by their degree of *complexity* – as measured by the *variety* of states they can occupy.

- Any attempt to change or *control* a system over time must generate at least as much variety as the system itself (Ashby's Law of Requisite Variety – Ashby, 1956).

- A *complex system* is deemed to have so much variety that it cannot be managed or changed by any approach that requires dealing with all its states sequentially.

'the problem with studying change is that it parades across many subject domains under numerous guises, such as transformation, development, metamorphosis, transmutation, evolution, regeneration, innovation, revolution and transition to list but a few.'

Indeed, there have been those throughout history who have possessed such universal interests. Shurig (1986) identifies some of them and notes that they were eager to look outside of their own specialist discipline for inspiration:

Aristotle, Leonardo da Vinci, Francis Bacon, G.W. von Leibnitz, Benjamin Franklin and J.W. von Goethe to name but a few . . . They strode through specialised disciplines like colonies of marching ants . . . They lacked the tendency, so characteristic among highly learned and disciplined academics of every age, to methodically filter out of the consciousness those ideas which do not pertain to their speciality, which threaten it in some way, or which go counter to learned, prevailing, and cherished paradigms.

(Shurig, 1986: 9)

However, historically, such individuals have always been in the minority. This may be because their breadth of interest and investigative approach seem rather daunting to the researcher, given the cognitive limits of the human brain. One person can only be aware of but a tiny part of the vast knowledge base that already exists. This is certainly more true today than it has ever been. Schrodinger foresaw this difficulty within his own subject of physics, but was not in the least dissuaded by it:

We feel clearly that we are only now beginning to acquire reliable material for welding together the sum total of all that is known into a whole; but on the other hand, it has become next to impossible for a single mind to command more than a small specialised portion of it. I can see no other escape from this dilemma (lest our true aim be lost forever) than that some of us should venture to embark on a synthesis of facts and theories, albeit with second hand and incomplete knowledge of some of them – and at the risk of making fools of ourselves.

(Schrodinger, 1944: 1)

A second reason for the rise of GST was the inherent reductionist nature of science generally, and the narrow constraints it placed upon analysis of a given phenomenon. That is, there was an implicit belief within scientific disciplines that to understand the whole, disassembly of a system's constituent parts and to identify hierarchical cause–effect relationships was all that was necessary. We even see this played out in the organisational field with developments such as Frederick Taylor's Scientific Management (1911), Henry Fayol's Industrial Administration (1916) and others. The influx of ex-military personnel into corporate management and captains of industry positions after World War II brought with it another wave of deterministic, reductionist thinking into the organisation.[3]

These two themes of increasing specialisation and reductionist thinking within the sciences provided the necessary catalyst for the birth of GST. Indeed, De Greene speaks of 'pressures to integrate similarities and relationships among the sciences, to enhance communication across the disciplines, and to derive a theoretical basis for *general* scientific education' (De Greene, 1970: 91; original emphasis).

While GST has had its critics over the years, research still continues within the movement.[4] It has broadly developed along two lines: formal systems theory and qualitative systems theory. Formal theories are based upon rigorous mathematical formulations and logical definitions of system types, attributes and dynamics. Some of the work undertaken by the Sante Fe Institute in the 'new sciences' falls into this category (see Stein, 1989; Zurek, 1990).[5]

Qualitative systems theory, on the other hand, does not use formal mathematics as a vehicle for system investigation and description, but deals in conceptual models as well as metaphor and analogy where appropriate. A good example is Peter A. Corning's work (Corning, 1983, 1995a, b).[6] He has explored the phenomenon of synergy as it is described across a range of disciplines (see Table 2.2) highlighting how synergy has become an umbrella term:

> Synergy – the combined effects produced by two or more parts, elements or individuals – is a ubiquitous phenomenon in nature and human societies alike. Although it plays a significant role in most, if not all, of the scientific disciplines, its importance is not widely appreciated because it travels under many different aliases.
>
> (Corning, 1995a: 663)

GST remains then, a conceptually insightful approach – a uniting analytical schema within which the artificial boundaries between different disciplines can be transcended:

> GST, even stripped of its substantive laws (though few), has made its mark in the scientific world by providing the framework for viewing complex phenomena as systems, as wholes, with all their interrelated and interacting parts. Herein lies one of its merits, and its justification.
>
> (Schoderbek *et al.*, 1990: 35)

Developments in both qualitative and more formal GST continue, with organisations such as the International Society for the Systems Sciences and the numerous special interest groups within it providing an ongoing focus and forum for work in this area around the world.[7]

The road to exploring change and transition

A GST approach allows us to examine a phenomenon across a range of subject domains, looking for general parallels and similarities. The phenomenon of interest here is *change*. Kenneth Boulding outlined a strategy for dealing with what he termed phenomena of universal significance: 'to look over the empirical universe and pick out certain general *phenomena* which are found in many different disciplines, and to seek to build up general theoretical models relevant to these phenomena' (1956a: 199; original emphasis). Arguably, change is just

Table 2.2 Synergy in selected scientific disciplines (Reprinted with permission from the Proceedings of the 39th Meeting of the International Society for the Systems Sciences, Club of Budapest, Hungary, September, 1995)

Discipline	Example	Associated vocabulary
Thermodynamics	Dissipative structures	emergence, low entropy, order/disorder, negentropy
Quantum physics	Quantum coherence	ordering, holism
Physics	Chaotic phenomena	emergence, attractors, order, interactions
	Self-organised criticality	interactions, holism
	Phase transitions	symmetry breaking, co-operative effects
Neurobiology	Neuronal transmission	threshold effect, co-operativity, emergence
Biophysics	Hypercycles	co-ordination, emergence interactions, co-operation
Molecular biology	DNA	co-ordination, interaction, complementarity
Developmental biology	Homeobox complex	co-ordination, organisation, co-operation
Biology	Symbiosis	co-operation, mutualism
	Co-evolution	parasitism, interactions, mutualism
	Sociobiology	reciprocal altruism, emergence, co-operation
Biochemistry	Supra-molecules	functional integration, co-ordination, interaction
Chemistry	Molecular macro-structures	symmetry, order, collective stability
Anthropology	Cultural evolution	symbiosis, co-ordination, co-operation

such a phenomenon. It is to be found in any discipline which attempts to comprehend the complexity and workings of the world. Thom referred to it as succession of form:

> It is indisputable that our universe is not chaos. We perceive beings, objects, things to which we give names. These beings or things are forms or structures endowed with a degree of stability; they take up some part of space and last for some period of time. . . . Next we must concede that the universe we see is a ceaseless creation, evolution, and destruction of forms and that the purpose of science is to foresee this *change of form* and, if possible, explain it.

> (Thom, 1975: 1; emphasis added)

Being able to explain and describe such change of form within the organisation would enhance enormously our ability to shape and manage it effectively. However, as with synergy, the problem with studying change in this way is that it parades across many subject domains under numerous guises, such as transformation, development, metamorphosis, transmutation, evolution, regeneration, innovation, revolution and transition to list but a few. Sadly, with the continuing and increasing specialisation of science into subdisciplines, the ability to step back and survey the general field of research endeavour for a given phenomenon is hampered. As one systems thinker has remarked:

> Very often researchers in a discipline have discovered aspects of the isomorphy on their own level or scale and named it in the jargon of their own discipline. When approached about the existence of the isomorphy across disciplines they tend to respond, 'Oh! that's just xxxxxxx. We've studied that for years.' The special features that each isomorphy takes on with each scalar level. . . . obscures the general features it maintains across levels.
>
> (Troncale, 1985: 188)

It is those general features which this book seeks to probe with regard to change – and inspire the reader to do likewise. Identifying and comparing similar concepts of change from across disciplines serves as a useful starting point.

The rise to prominence of chaos theory during the 1980s is an example of attempts to describe similar phenomena across a range of subject domains, as Andersen (1988), Goerner (1994) and others have observed. While not explicitly classed as a GST area of research, it does embody some of the GST ideals of cross-discipline studies, isomorphic analysis and the search for general theories. The impact it has made upon physical and natural science generally, cannot be underestimated: 'Fifteen years ago, science was heading for a crisis of increasing specialisation. Dramatically that specialisation has reversed because of chaos' (Shlesinger, 1987). Or as Gleick states:

> Chaos is a science of process rather than state, of becoming rather than being. . . . Chaos breaks the lines that separate scientific disciplines. Because it is a science of the global nature of systems, it has brought together thinkers from fields that had been widely separated.
>
> (Gleick, 1987: 5)

As a uniting field of study, chaos theory has achieved much, and clearly demonstrates that cross-discipline analysis of common or similar phenomena can be highly productive. However, to be productive, the collation and investigation of ideas, concepts and phenomena must clearly be undertaken in a structured and purposeful manner. As Rapoport (1995: 663) has noted: 'Generalisations derived from a juxtaposition of facts are not fruitful unless some conceptual, theoretical scheme guided the generalisations.' GST provides a sound underpinning philosophy for harvesting lessons and principles on change from a range of subject domains.

Like Corning's analysis on synergy, this book falls firmly into the qualitative side of GST and in true cross-discipline spirit, attempts to offer some insight into the nature of change and transition within the organisation.

Escaping the familiar: the power of metaphor

At the heart of systems thinking is the use of metaphor and analogy. Metaphor is increasingly being used within organisations for problem solving and creative management activities.[8] Individual metaphors can be a very powerful catalyst for change due to the vivid mind pictures they create – capable of dramatically highlighting inadequacies of the old and the advantages of the new much faster than persistent logical argument:

> The act of creative perception in the form of a metaphor . . . involves an extremely perceptive state of intense passion and high energy that dissolves the excessively rigidly held assumptions in the tacit infrastructure of commonly accepted knowledge.
>
> (Bohm and Peat, 1987: 17)

It is this ability of metaphor to 'dissolve' the old and create the new which makes it such a persuasive and powerful tool. As Handy (1989: 14) has stated: 'New imagery, signalled by new words, is as important as new theory; indeed new theory without new imagery can go unnoticed.' Another reason why metaphor is particularly helpful during organisation analysis is because, like most social sciences, organisation theory and management theory lack the clinical exactness of description normally associated with the physical sciences. As one observer has noted:

> We need metaphor in just those cases where there can be no question as yet of the precision of scientific statements. Metaphorical statement is not a substitute for formal comparison or any other kind of literal statement, but has its own distinctive capacities and achievements.
>
> (Black, 1962: 46)

Metaphor and analogy can have at least two potential applications. The first is to use them to generate high level abstractions about similarities and common themes among different disciplines, as a basis for constructing a general systems framework. This usage is very much in the spirit of GST.

The second use is to apply them direct to the target domain, using them as descriptive and explanatory tools within specific organisational change situations. The historical precedent for employing analogical thinking in this way has long been set, as Leatherdale notes:

The basis of progress in science is not an analogical act in the ordinary sense, but an analogical perception which involves the importation of analogues from discrete areas of experience into areas of experience under investigation, with a resultant reformulation or re-ordering of the area under investigation so that hitherto unremarked analogies are seen and novel inferences suggested.

(Leatherdale, 1974: 32)

In later chapters specific physical science phenomena will be examined, where the first usage is a means of getting to the second. In other words, each change phenomenon we shall examine is first considered for what general insights it offers. These will then be taken and considered within an organisational setting. This means that the building blocks thus generated are to some extent applicable to other system types – not just organisations. Clearly, what we are interested in here is probing change within organisations and so the systems link is not overemphasised. But it should be borne in mind that each building block is first distilled out at a general systems level.

To clarify, let us take an example of how powerful a change metaphor from another discipline can be. Consider for a moment the phenomenon of atmospheric motion. From large bodies of air and cloud systems to minute particles and molecules of water, the atmosphere is in a state of constant activity and turbulence. The standard atmosphere is generally thought to consist of four layers: the troposphere, stratosphere, mesosphere and thermosphere. Each sits at a certain average height above sea level and has its own particular composition of gases, average air pressure and temperature. However, the different general characteristics of the various layers mean that this 'standard atmosphere' is rarely stable. Interactions between layers and local differences ensure a continually fluctuating and restless system, producing perpetual movement and dynamic behaviour. Turbulence and air flows at each level interact to produce both global and local changes in weather and climate.[9]

In addition to the dynamics within the atmosphere itself, the complexity of the change processes at work is increased when one considers the interactions between the atmosphere and terrestrial ecosystems such as tropical rain forests, deserts and mountainous regions. These interactions include water, radiation, carbon dioxide and heat transfers, as Figure 2.2 illustrates. Ecosystem dynamics are the product of a large number of individual interactions resulting in complex behaviour, involving stability and change at both micro and macro levels.

There are several emerging themes from the area of atmospherics and climatology which are useful for conceptualising change. For example, they demonstrate that change can occur across a range of scales and levels, in a complex and interdependent layering of events. Within organisations, different local conditions such as training levels, resource allocations or work load between different parts can create tension and conflict at the micro level, perhaps leading to a change in culture, productivity or flexibility at the macro level. Other macro parameters like levels of investment, corporate image or organisation size may

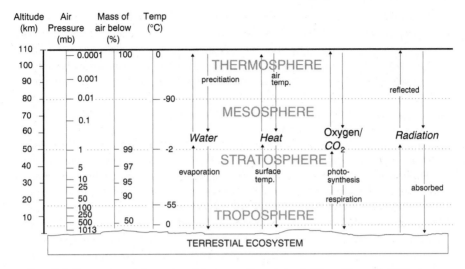

Figure 2.2 Structure and dynamics of the atmosphere (adapted from Hanwell, 1980; Scholes 1990)

remain unaffected and stable. Local imbalances can often form the basis for change and stability within a system, but at different levels.

In a study of atmospheric and climate dynamics, Scholes (1990) proposes a number of change principles which can be usefully abstracted for the analysis of system change generally:

- Multiple, locally stable states separated by transition thresholds are much more likely than global stability;
- Directional change is therefore more likely to be jumpy than smooth;
- Stability is more likely to be encountered at large spatial scales and small, very short or very long rather than intermediate time scales, and at high integrative levels rather than low;
- Environmental predictability is more important than the absolute magnitude of environmental extremes ('harshness') in determining stability and resilience.

(Scholes, 1990: 352)

Direct quotes have been used to preserve the language and vocabulary of the climatologist. These ideas have tremendous metaphoric potential for exploring the nature of organisational change. Taking just one theme from the phenomenon of atmospheric motion: there is an emerging realisation in science that it is possible for equilibrium and disequilibrium to co-exist at different scales; that change and stability are not either/or situations but can occur simultaneously at different levels.[10] This raises serious doubts about the validity of separate change-centred theories and equilibrium-centred theories of organisational behaviour. Understanding the dynamics of change means understanding the duality of change and stability. Practically, managers are now having to come to terms with this change–stability dilemma within organisations:

> How do you simultaneously 'manufacture refrigerators and, on the other hand, plan their obsolescence in order to maintain competitive advantage?' How do you do this with the same work force and the same management group? How do you keep the store running profitably while you are converting it into a supermarket?
>
> (Beckhard and Harris, 1987: viii)

Exploring change phenomena in atmospheric and climatic systems suggests, then, some useful metaphors and ideas for conceptualising change at both a general systems level and within organisations. In particular, they help us to better understand the apparent contradiction of change and stability co-existing. The generation of a new descriptive vocabulary which enables the analyst to 'step outside' of a duality such as this can often be the key to generating new ways of thinking about a problem.

> 'Individual metaphors can be a very powerful catalyst for change due to the vivid mind pictures they create – capable of dramatically highlighting inadequacies of the old and the advantages of the new much faster than persistent logical argument.'

In later chapters, we shall be taking a selective trawl through physics, chemistry and biology to see what they have to offer the organisational change thinker. Fundamentally, physics attempts to understand the interactions between energy and matter, and how matter can be changed from one form to another. It is therefore a promising hunting ground for insightful change metaphors and descriptions.

Chemistry also has much to offer. Unlike most change processes in physics, chemistry deals with changes to matter which alter its actual composition and make-up. The discipline is based upon the concept of reaction – two or more chemical elements changing and being changed by each other as they interact together. This makes it a good subject area for structural change analogies and metaphors. Consider the following statement:

> When a chemical reaction occurs, there are frequently visual signals that something has happened. Colours may change; gases may evolve; precipitates may form. Less obvious are changes in energy which almost invariably accompany chemical reactions.
>
> (Sienko and Plane, 1979: 10)

Articulated here are some common properties of change: visual and non-visual manifestations. Unseen change processes may be taking place in the heart of a system, transforming its very structure. As with physics, the concept of energy plays an important role in chemistry – that nebulous emergent property of a system which is so often overlooked and underestimated when attempting to manage change. Outwardly at the macro level, nothing appears to have changed and yet, inside, new relationships have been formed between elements, and old ones abandoned, subtly shifting the balance of power to some new equilibrium state. Failure to notice these changes can lead to inaccurate behaviour prediction and ineffectual system intervention. This highlights the role of the observer and measurement as two important issues which are crucial to understanding the nature of change. Such are the problems of chemistry.

With biology, we enter the realm of living. The somewhat mechanistic metaphors from physics and chemistry here combine with that indefinable quality of 'life' to produce biology. A whole raft of ideas becomes readily available for systems and organisational thinkers looking for inspiration. Biology has traditionally been the hunting ground for useful organisational and systems metaphors. Indeed, the whole concept of a 'system', composed of elements, relationships and boundary exchanges attempting to remain viable within a given environment is based on parallels with a biological organism. We have our old friend Ludwig von Bertalanffy partly to thank for making this valuable connection.

As we move into later chapters then, change phenomena from the natural world will form the basis of analysis for deriving a deeper insight into the nature of change. Several concepts from the 'new science' of complexity and chaos theory will be looked at, but the 'old' sciences still have much to offer us metaphorically and most of the ideas will come from traditional, well-established areas within the three core science disciplines.

But first, it is worth taking a brief look at some writers who have already started to make the connection between phenomena in the natural world and the organisation. They have to some extent already blazed a brave trail out of established organisational theorising, and in doing so may even have been frowned upon by those of a more purist disposition. Yet their work stands as a powerful precedent; an abiding testament to intellectual creativity and curiosity.

'The derivation of new and original change metaphors is a vital first step to revitalising our conception and comprehension of the nature of change within organisations.'

Examples of cross-discipline based organisational thinking

As we have seen, systems science – in particular GST – provides a basis for organisational thinkers to go in search of new ideas and concepts which may benefit their work, and move beyond the confines of their own discipline. The ideas of several who have already attempted to do just that will now be considered.

The work of Connie Gersick (1991) examines the concepts of evolutionary and revolutionary change across six different subject areas:

- adult psychology;
- group behaviour;
- organisational development;
- history of science;
- biological evolution;
- physical science.

Her work is a fascinating blend of detailed specialist knowledge and perceptive generalised observation, in which she attempts to:

> juxtapose similar theories from different research domains and . . . show how each suggests questions and insights for the others. Two premises underlie [the approach] . . . (1) that there are important commonalities in the way many systems, including human systems, *change* and (2) that we can benefit by comparing research findings from disparate areas because different facets of kindred processes may come into focus as the methodology and level of analysis vary.
>
> (Gersick, 1991: 11; emphasis added)

She examines in detail the phenomenon of change as punctuated equilibrium – periods of stability in the organisation periodically shattered by change events. Her cross-discipline approach is demonstrated in Table 2.3 and she concludes with three generic questions which she argues, are applicable to any study of organisational systems:

- Do the results indicate whether the system is in equilibrium or undergoing change?
- Is the propensity to remain in stability or undergo transition a function of the parts of the system, or a function of the forces and deep processes that organise them?
- To what extent will this propensity alter if the system undergoes a radical transformation?

Assuming that one accepts Gersick's world view of 'change as punctuated equilibrium', her approach contains much rich descriptive imagery and demonstrates well how much light other subject domains can shed on an issue.

In a similar vein, Tsoukas (1991) has argued for a cross-discipline, structured and more rigorous use of metaphor within organisational thinking. He demonstrates that knowledge is often stratified, and that a disciplined imagination is required to reach the lower levels:

Table 2.3 The phenomenon of punctuated equilibrium explored across disciplines (based on the work of Gersick, 1991, material used with permission)

Subject domain	Authors selected	Concepts of deep structure	Concepts of equilibrium	Concepts of revolutionary periods
Individual adult development	Levinson (1978, 1986)	Life structure	Structure building periods	Transitional periods
Group development	Gersick (1988), Gersick and Davis (1989)	Framework	Learning periods	Transition period
Organisational evolution	Tushman and Romanelli (1984, 1985)	Strategic orientation	Convergent periods	Reorientations
History of science	Kuhn (1970)	Paradigm	Normal science	Scientific revolutions
Evolutionary biology	Gould (1977, 1980, 1989), Wake *et al.* (1983), Eldredge and Gould (1972)	Genetic programs	Phyletic transformation	Speciation
Self-organising systems	Hanken (1981), Prigogine and Stengers (1984)	Order parameters	Stable regions	Bifurcation

Mechanisms responsible for experienced events are sought at increasingly deeper strata. In the very beginning of such a 'drilling' process of knowledge acquisition, metaphors may provide the initial insights leading to the hypothesis of plausible causal mechanisms. At subsequent strata, however, metaphorical insights and analogical reasoning need to be transformed into a literal language that expresses real mechanisms and identities.

(Tsoukas, 1991: 572)

He goes on to examine the concepts of isomorphism, metaphor and analogy and how they can be employed to explore the knowledge base of other disciplines, in order to enrich thinking and research within organisational science.

Morgan (1980, 1981, 1983, 1986) has used metaphorical thinking extensively in his analysis of organisations. Drawing from a range of subject domains he explores various facets of organisational life through an assortment of metaphors and pictures. These have been taken from fields as varied as political science, biology, psychiatry and cybernetics. As our opening quote at the beginning of this chapter demonstrates, Morgan advocates an openness and receptivity to concepts from other disciplines. Describing his own work, he states:

Frequently, the discussion ranges well beyond the confines of organisation theory, for the metaphors and ideas considered are drawn from diverse sources . . . it is important to understand that the mode of analysis developed here rests in a *way of thinking* rather than in the mechanistic application of a small set of clearly defined analytical frameworks.

(Morgan, 1986: 16; original emphasis)

Subsequent development of Morgan's work by Flood and Jackson (1991a, b) into a practical methodology for metaphor application within organisations has not stayed loyal to this exhortation to 'remain open'. Flood and Jackson took five of Morgan's metaphors and institutionalised them within a creative problem-solving approach called Total Systems Intervention (TSI):

- machine metaphor;
- brain metaphor;
- political metaphor;
- organic metaphor;
- culture metaphor.

However, what was lost in terms of creativity and freedom to draw from other subject domains was partly compensated for by providing a practical tool for managers to choose an appropriate problem-solving approach which best fits their situation. Having chosen the 'dominant' and 'dependent' metaphors, an appropriate systems approach is then selected for analysis and implementation purposes. TSI then attempts to take a cross-disciplinary approach to organisational analysis and change, by employing five rich and conceptually insightful metaphors.

In her excellent book *Leadership and the New Science*, Margaret Wheatley has explored several areas of physical and natural science in search of lessons applicable to the organisation. She speaks of the need to 'draw from the sciences to create and manage organisations, to design research, and to formulate hypotheses about organisational design, planning, economics, human nature, and change processes' (Wheatley, 1992: 6). Specifically, she examines aspects of quantum physics, chaos theory, phenomena of self-organisation and field theory, discussing some of the implications which these knowledge domains have for our understanding of the organisation. Her underlying premise is that, historically, organisational theorists have been influenced (consciously or otherwise) by the prevailing scientific view of the world and the assumptions embedded within it. With the advent of what she calls the 'new science' – typified by the emergence of disciplines such as quantum mechanics, relativity theory, complexity science and chaos theory – Wheatley argues that organisational theorists and managers need to realign themselves with the new scientific world view and the principles they contain.

Wheatley's work is not specifically aimed at exploring the phenomenon of change. Nor is it the result of a coherent and explicit cross-discipline research programme, but rather the gradual accumulation of observations and insights into some of the parallels between the 'new science' and organisational behaviour.

Nonetheless, it does represent a valuable attempt to harness the creative potential and conceptual richness offered by recent advances in the natural and physical sciences, and to apply them to organisational thinking.

Therefore, a cross-discipline approach to the study of organisations is not entirely new. A number of theorists and practitioners have already undertaken such an approach. Their work shows that they have not been afraid to venture into other subject domains in search of inspiration. The GST philosophy described in this chapter provides a conceptual basis for such constructive 'subject surfing' and comparison between disciplines.

Having set the scene then, Figure 2.3 is offered as road map to where we will head in the rest of the book. Once we have reviewed the organisational change literature in the next two chapters, we begin to explore the notion of change as it appears in both the physical and social sciences. From there a selection of change phenomena from the natural sciences will be examined, along with the theories and concepts used by the relevant specialists to describe them. Based on these a number of building blocks for thinking about organisational change are offered.

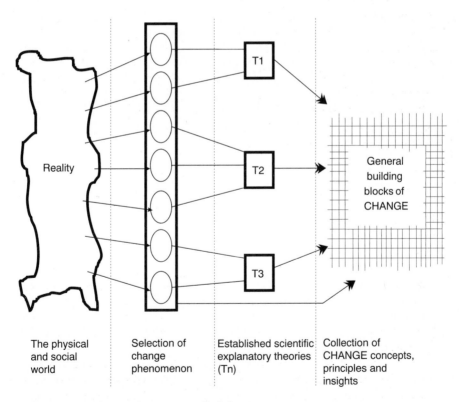

Figure 2.3 Investigating change across disciplines

Summary

This chapter has introduced General Systems Theory as one strand of systems science which offers an approach to phenomenon investigation. More specifically, a GST approach has been proposed as the means of exploring change within the organisation and to help address the urgent need for a greater understanding of the nature of change. Some examples of organisational theorists who have tried cross-disciplinary studies have been discussed, demonstrating that such research is possible and has already produced some fruitful results.

It is acknowledged that exploring the phenomena of change by using such an approach may not in the short term yield the comprehensive and robust methodologies which change management practitioners desire. The initial thrust of the approach is certainly abstract and conjectural in nature. However, as Lundberg (1984: 61) observed while discussing the notion of change within organisations:

> 'even speculative reasoning which is carefully done and which probes the pragmatic dimensions of a major, increasingly crucial phenomenon, has utility, for it begins to inform and guide practice and to stimulate inquiry.'

Pursuing such an approach, however, should open up an abundance of change concepts from across the disciplines, making them available to specialists within organisation theory and the management sciences. It is hoped that in the long run these will provide organisational change theorists and practitioners with a fresh source of rich concepts, metaphors and analogies from which they can draw inspiration and enhance their language, theories and methods. The derivation of new and original change metaphors is a vital first step to revitalising our conception and comprehension of the nature of change within organisations.

3 Organisational change thinking

A look back

Understanding organisational change requires discovering the connections between the apparently prosaic and the apparently poetic in organisational life.

(March, 1981: 575)

Introduction

In this chapter we take a look back at some of the main ideas and schools of thought that have shaped our conception of change within the organisation over the years. The three main strands of thinking up to the 1960s are examined briefly – scientific management, human relations and contingency theory schools of thought – to see what legacy they have given to those interested in organisational change. Attention then turns to some of the more recent developments in organisational change thinking. Various classifications of what has become a vast and diverse literature are offered in order to understand the current state of knowledge in this area.

Change: early thinking reviewed

Evidence of thinking about organisations can be traced back over many hundreds of years. It is not the intention here to give a detailed history of organisational and management thought as this has been done extensively elsewhere (see Claude, 1968; Wren, 1979). Views on the importance of good administration and organisation can be found as far back as the ancient Chinese and the writings of Confucius (Hsu, 1932); the early Egyptians (Lepawsky, 1949); and the Greeks (Crombie, 1963; Burnyeat, 1990). The Roman Empire was founded on clear principles of administration and military organisation. Indeed one of the most long-lived formal organisations is the Roman Catholic Church (Mooney, 1947).

However, the widespread appearance of observable, large-scale commercial organisations as entities did not take place until the industrial revolution (Ashton, 1948; Pollard 1965). It was at this time that the formal organisation of work became an issue of concern as factories sought to utilise their labour efficiently. During this period, what has become known as the classical or Scientific–Rational school of organisational management emerged.

The Scientific–Rational view of change

From the late nineteenth century up until the 1930s, western thinking on organisational structure, design and management was dominated by this approach. It was advocated by several theorists[1] but arguably the most influential writer of this period was Frederick Taylor (1903, 1911). The underlying canons of the approach were as follows:

- The organisation of human work activity is a science.
- Human work activity is motivated by financial reward.
- Organisations are rational, machine-like structures capable of efficient, output-maximizing behaviour.
- Clear definition of responsibilities and duties in the division of labour and rigid management hierarchies are essential to effective working.

Understanding of the concept of change during this period was limited. Change was seen as a planned and managed phenomenon. It was directed at increasing control over individual endeavours, ensuring they were subordinate to corporate interests. Change was functionally orientated, concerned with altering specific job actions to achieve maximum efficiency. The premise that there was a best way to perform a given task which would work equally well in all situations largely underpinned change activities. The belief that an optimum solution was achievable and maintainable at maximum efficiency at the task level resulted in change being enforced by experts on the individual. There was no conception of external sources and dynamics of change occurring in an organisation's environment, or indeed any significant internal mechanisms for adaptation. Change was centred around what was perceived to be the objective measurement of variables which could be assessed and calculated in a scientific manner. Taylor's writings (1903, 1911) suggest that there was no concept of change at more abstract, intangible and conceptual levels of an organisation such as culture or public image. Individual creativity and innovation among workers as a source

Table 3.1 The Scientific–Rational perception of change

Change focus:	Job/task
Measurement:	Micro variables, objective, quantifiable
Driver for change:	'Maximising' behaviour; belief in existence of a best way
Transformation: (direction)	Sub-optimal TO perceived optimal Individuality TO co-operation Discord TO unity Heterogeneity TO standardisation Uncertainty TO institutionalisation Variety and diversity TO complexity reduction
Methodology for change:	Scientific (technical), functionalist, planned, reductionist, institutionalising

of change seems to have been untapped. Clearly innovation was occurring, as demonstrated by the speed of technological progress at the time, but it was more of an institutionalised, professional activity undertaken by a few. Table 3.1 summarises early practice, experiences and conceptions of change within organisations.

Essentially, then, the notion of change was seen as associated with: internal, operational issues only; hard measurement and quantification; rational, maximising behaviour; subjugating individual interests to achieve standardisation and unity of purpose; scientific, reductionist analysis and methods. Hence, change was largely an internal planned affair, driven by a unitary world view and focused on the rational, mechanical nature of work at the operational level.

> 'The danger comes when we allow them [these assumptions] to become so embedded in our outlook that they remain in our thinking un-challenged – dulling solutions . . . and frustrating our attempts to grasp the complexity of the change scenario with which we are faced.'

The Human Relations view of change

From the 1930s onwards theorists began to focus more on the human individual within organisations as a reaction against the machine like regimes advocated by the Scientific–Rational writers. What emerged became known as the Human Relations approach and was founded upon the work of a number of scholars.[2] Like the Scientific–Rational approach, the Human Relations school believed that it too had found the one best way to manage and operate organisations effectively. The approach emphasised the following themes:

- the informal and social nature of organisations;
- the importance of considering human needs, attitudes and values;
- the emotional and psychological facets of the worker, not just the rational or economic aspects.

The understanding of change embodied within this approach broadened beyond the restricted Scientific–Rational paradigm but, arguably, the pendulum swung too far the other way. In moving the organisation away from the rational towards the social, changes centred upon human motivation, values, attitudes and behavioural norms. Change activities were concerned with facilitating increased emotional satisfaction. Experimental studies of group dynamics and behaviour led to an understanding of the importance of the softer aspects of organisational change. The famous Hawthorne experiments (see Roethlisberger and Dickson, 1939) highlighted the problems of attempting objective measurement and

Table 3.2 The Human Relations perception of change

Change focus:	Individual performing the job or task
Measurement:	Micro variables, qualitative
Driver for change:	Individual human needs
Transformation: (direction)	Rational TO social Theory X TO theory Y Unmotivated TO motivated Unfulfilled needs TO needs satisfied
Methodology for change:	Scientific (social), functionalist, planned, reductionist

assessment of change within social systems – an area which change management practitioners continue to grapple with. However, there was still no conception of external change dynamics influencing the organisation from without. Table 3.2 summarises the Human Relations view of change.

In short, change was now perceived as concerned with: human traits, norms and attitudes necessary for effective performance; measurement of soft variables such as motivation and emotional satisfaction; behavioural and psychological aspects of individual/group dynamics internal to the organisation.

The Contingency view of change

During the early 1960s thinking shifted once more, this time away from the notion that there needed to be one best approach to operating and managing all organisations. Instead, several theorists took the view that an organisation's operation and structure was contingent upon specific internal and external variables,[3] namely, organisational size, environment dependence and uncertainty and relevant technology.

The concept of change broadened further under the Contingency approach. It was acknowledged that the organisation existed within an unpredictable environment with which it was interdependent. This adds to the complexity of change dynamics within the organisation. However, despite the recognition of the uncertainty associated with external variables, the contingency approach remained rational and deterministic in style. Given sufficient understanding of the three key variables, it was believed that all one had to do was to implement the necessary structural changes to achieve the appropriate balance between them for smooth, efficient organisational operation. The inherent ambiguity and apparent randomness which characterise perturbations from and change dynamics within the environment were still not fully acknowledged by the approach. As with the Scientific–Rational view, the idea still persisted that to achieve predetermined goals at some point in the future required the mechanistic implementation of planned change activities.

The Contingency Approach acknowledged that there were variables external to the organisation which should influence its internal structure. However, there

Table 3.3 The Contingency perception of change

Change focus:	Organisational structure
Measurement:	Macro variables, hard and soft
Driver for change	Belief in existence of a best match between organisational structure and environment
Transformation (direction)	Unsuitable structure TO appropriate structure Ignorance of external factors TO understanding of environmental interdependence
Methodology for change:	Scientific, functionalist, planned, reductionist.

was still an underlying scientific determinism to the approach which assumed that once these environmental variables had been identified and structural changes made to take account of them, the organisation would operate efficiently and effectively. That the environment was dynamic over time and presented a continually shifting set of variables requiring a constant readiness for change, was not fully recognised. Table 3.3 captures the Contingency view of change.

Table 3.4 summarises the view and understanding of change on which each of the three approaches are based. As can be seen, common themes are evident across all three:

- *Theme 1*: organisational change is essentially a planned activity, scheduled and implemented in a deterministic and reductionist manner.
- *Theme 2*: change is enforced blind to the dynamics of an uncertain environment.
- *Theme 3*: there is a perceived 'best way' or optimum solution which a given change should seek to realise.
- *Theme 4*: change occurs in a sequential manner, and is essentially a one-dimensional phenomenon.

The extent to which these themes still influence our thinking on change today should not be underestimated. Obviously, in certain contained and highly focused organisational change situations they may remain appropriate. The danger comes when we allow them to become so embedded in our outlook that they remain in our thinking unchallenged – dulling our creativity, constraining our solutions and scope for action and frustrating our attempts to grasp the complexity of the change scenario with which we are faced.

Organisation change: recent developments

Since the 1960s many other approaches and schools of thought have emerged within management thinking and organisation theory regarding change. Table 3.5 attempts to map out many of these other strands of development. As can be seen, they cover an enormous area and some have roots which can be traced back

Table 3.4 Early perceptions of change summarised

	Scientific–Rational	Human Relations	Contingency
Focus of change	Job or task	Person performing job or task	Organisation structure
Measurement approach	Hard, objective, quantitative, micro level	Soft, qualitative, micro level	Macro variables: hard and soft
Change driver	Maximising behaviour, search for optimal way	'Satisfied' workers are better motivated and perform better	A 'best match' between the organisation and its environment is achievable
Type of change	Planned	Planned	Planned
Transformation process (direction)	Sub-optimal TO optimal Individuality TO shared purpose Discord to unity Heterogeneity TO standardisation	Rational TO social Theory X TO theory Y Unmotivated TO motivated Unmet need TO fulfilled need	Unsuitable structure TO suitable structure Ignorance of interdependence with environment TO understanding of environmental dependency
Methodological stance	Reductionist, determinist	Reductionist, determinist	Reductionist, determinist
Recognition of a dynamic environment as a change source	None	None	Partial

before the 1960s. The rise of systems thinking as a discipline is one such example, although explicit application of systems theory to the organisation has been a more recent development. Many of the approaches overlap. Indeed, the whole literature can be seen as an interconnected, evolving knowledge set which is constantly being added to. Some are more centred on specific aspects of change, for example, information technology design and implementation. Others are concerned with change at a more generic level, such as quality orientated approaches. However, what they all have in common is an underlying premise that aspects of an organisation can be changed for the better to increase overall performance. Each has its own specific focus, whether it be structure, culture or communication. Diagnosing, prescribing, designing and implementing effective change measures are common to many of them. Some have a clearly defined theoretical foundation, while others have evolved as operational and practical approaches to organisational change. A detailed and comprehensive review of them all is not possible here and, indeed, is not the purpose of this book. However, there are several ways in which this vast literature can be categorised in order to

Table 3.5 Some of the main approaches to organisational change

Strands of organisational change thought	Example authors (selected)
Adaptation and evolution	Child (1972), Miller and Friesen (1980b)
Business process change	Kaplan and Murdock (1991), Davenport (1993), Hammer and Champy (1993)
Chaos theory and complexity science	Nonaka (1988), Smith and Gemmill (1991), Stacey (1992), Gaustello (1995), Kiel and Elliot (1995)
Continuous learning and self-organisation	Hedberg *et al.* (1976), Argyris and Schon (1978), Senge (1990), Fortune and Peters (1995)
Creative management and innovation	Kirton (1980), Flood and Jackson (1991a), Henry (1991), Morgan (1993)
Culture and corporate identity	Schein (1983), Sathe (1985), Hofstede (1991)
Ethics and values	Jacobs (1992), Salomons (1992), Hall (1994), Simons (1995)
Information technology approaches	Bemelmans (1984), Tozer (1985), Martin (1989), Scarbrough and Corbett (1992), Sprague and McNurlin (1993)
Miscellaneous popularist approaches	Peters and Waterman (1982), Handy (1989), Kanter (1989)
Organisational development	French and Bell (1984), Cummings and Huse (1989), Burke and Lithin (1989)
Population ecology	Hannan and Freeman (1977), Rundall and McClain (1982)
Quality approaches	Crosby (1979), Deming (1982), Taguchi (1986), Juran (1988)
Phenomenological approaches	Zucker (1977), Ranson *et al.* (1980)
General change frameworks	Lewin (1951), Nadler (1988), Meyer *et al.* (1993)
Philosophical paradigmatic analysis	Nisbet (1970), Burrell and Morgan (1979)
Social theory	McKinney and Tiryakin (1970), Zald and Berger (1978)
Systems approaches	
Soft systems	Checkland (1972, 1981), Churchman (1979), Ackoff (1981), Mason and Mitroff (1981)
Systems engineering and operations research	Hall (1962), Jenkins (1969), Daellenbach *et al.* (1983)
Systems dynamics	Forrester (1971), Wolstenholme (1990), Sterman (1994)
Open systems	Miller and Rice (1967), Scott (1987), Mullins (1989)
Organisational cybernetics	Beer (1985), Robb (1985), Espejo (1987)

highlight similarities, differences, common themes and unexplored gaps in the existing knowledge base. Several will be described in the following section, starting with a look at how root metaphors can be used to cut this enormous body of knowledge.

Classification by metaphor

Metaphors can provide alternative lenses through which to view the organisation. Many authors have invoked the use of metaphor over the years to describe developments in organisational theory and management thinking: Burns and Stalker (1966); Thomas and Bennis (1972); Ackoff (1974); Berg (1979); Morgan (1986), to name but a few. Some of the most common metaphors to emerge which describe the underlying characteristics of particular approaches and strategies for organisational change are:

- machine;
- organism;
- brain;
- culture.

An approximate placing of approaches within these four metaphors is illustrated in Figure 3.1. The metaphors span a range of paradigms from the hard, scientific world of the machine to the soft and abstract language of culture. Like any tool for creative thinking and theory development, metaphor and analogy can be overused and abused. Over-extending comparisons, stretching the perceived similarity beyond what is reasonable and insensitivity to where a metaphor ends and reality starts are all dangers of which to be wary. In exploring what the natural sciences have to teach us about change in later chapters, extensive use is made of metaphor and analogic comparison. It is left for the reader to judge whether any of these traps have been fallen into. One of the most powerful strengths of metaphor is to help break thinking out of the established, open up novel and intriguing lines of thought and trigger creative hypotheses. If they achieve this, the more rigorous dotting of 'i's and crossing of 't's can take place during later theory proposition, development and testing. The role of metaphor in helping us to get that initial insight which radically alters the way we see the world is what is so important.

Classification by theory–practice level

Approaches to organisational change can be categorised according to their theoretical contribution at one extreme and practical application on the other. In attempting to analyse the many different orientations to patient behaviour change within clinical psychology, Goldfried (1980) has suggested several levels of abstraction useful for charting developments in his field. Drawing on this work, and expanding and adapting it for organisational theory and management thinking, provides an interesting way to categorise the change literature.

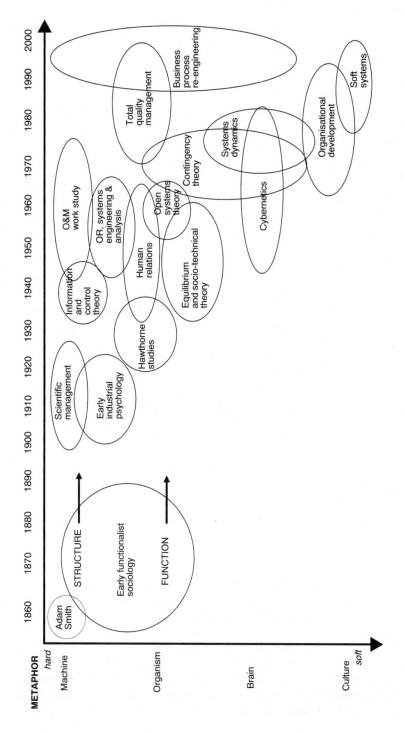

Figure 3.1 Organisational change approaches mapped according to root metaphor (based upon Peppard and Preece, 1994; material used with permission)

Level 1: Theoretical framework

This is the highest level, offering explanations as to why and how change occurs, usually accompanied by a particular philosophical stance, for example, the regulation versus radical change debate described by Burrell and Morgan (1979) as two contrasting sociologies underpinning different organisational paradigms (see Table 5.1 on p. 65).

Level 2: Guiding heuristic

This describes the underlying 'rules of engagement' and represents the practical manifestation of the change philosophy of Level 1, for example: point of stakeholder involvement; process or function orientation; autocratic or consensus-based decision-making.

Level 3: Collective strategy

This is the generic methodological approach being followed during change activity. It can often be an umbrella level for a range of different change techniques and methods – as under Level 4 described below: for example, information engineering; interactive management (Warfield and Cardenas, 1993); total quality management; business process re-engineering.

Level 4: Change technique / procedure

These are the specific tools and techniques for change management which may or may not be part of a particular collective strategy at Level 3, for example: structured interviewing; nominal group technique; process mapping or statistical process control.

Goldfried discusses the possibility of identifying useful commonalities and the potential for consensus between approaches at different levels within the field of clinical psychology. It is doubtful whether any such consensus of approach could be achieved among organisational change theorists and practitioners at Levels 1, 3 and 4. However, within Level 2 there is considerable potential for agreement and co-operative research. Table 3.6 is an attempt to place the approaches to organisational change listed earlier across the four levels. The classification is somewhat general and some of the specific placings are certainly debatable. Nonetheless, it can be seen that most of the organisational change approaches are not fully represented at all four levels. This is because very few of them have been explicitly defined and consciously documented at each level, but rather have emerged over time as organisational thinking has developed. For example, business process re-engineering currently exists at Levels 3 and 4. Systems thinking approaches to organisational change fare better with, for instance management and organisational cybernetics achieving coverage at Levels 1, 2 and 3 with a growing commitment to Level 4.[4]

Table 3.6 Classification of approaches by theory–practice orientation

Strands of organisational change thought	1. Theoretical framework	2. Guiding heuristic	3. Collective strategy	4. Technique/ procedure
Adaptation and evolution	*	*		
Business process change			*	*
Chaos theory and complexity science	*			
Continuous learning and self-organisation		*		*
Creative management and innovation			*	*
Culture and corporate identity				*
Ethics and values		*		*
Information technology approaches				*
Organisational development		*	*	*
Population ecology	*	*		
Quality approaches		*	*	*
Phenomenological approaches		*		
General change frameworks	*			
Philosophical paradigmatic analysis	*	*		
Social theory	*	*		
Systems approaches				
Soft systems	*	*	*	*
Systems engineering and operations research		*	*	*
Systems dynamics			*	*
Open systems	*	*		
Organisational cybernetics	*	*	*	

Of particular note are the number of approaches that lack significant research at Level 1, which would involve getting to grips with change at a theoretical level.

> 'The famous Hawthorne experiments (see Roethlisbeger and Dickson, 1939) highlighted the problems of attempting objective measurement and assessment of change within social systems – an area which change management practitioners continue to grapple with.'

Other miscellaneous classifications

There are numerous other ways in which the organisational change literature could be categorised, for example, the specific focus each takes. There are many aspects of organisational life which could be targeted, for example:

- *Technology*: information technology and business system implementation.
- *Human*: employee/culture focused change programmes.
- *Process*: work flows and cycles.
- *Function*: operation-specific functions and structures.
- *System*: organisation-wide change activities, focusing on the viability of the organisation within its environment.

These five categories are by no means all-encompassing and they do not reflect different levels of change activity. However, they do provide an initial broad-brush classification of many organisational change approaches.

Conner and Lake (1988) have distinguished between objects, methods and strategies of organisational change as one way of categorising the literature:

Object	*Methods*	*Strategies*
Individual tasks	Technological	Facilitative
Organisational processes	Managerial	Informational
Strategic direction	Structural	Attitudinal
Organisational culture	Human	Political

Goodman and Kurke, on the other hand, have suggested that the literature can be analysed according to recurring themes:

- Methods of intervention
- Large-scale multiple system interventions
- Assessment of change including:
  - Models of assessment
  - Techniques and instrumentation
  - Analytical procedures
- Analysis of failure
- Level of theorising

(Goodman and Kurke, 1982: 3)

Goodman and Kurke also suggest that making a distinction between what they term planned change and adaptation is a useful means of sorting the multitude of approaches to organisational change. The former relates to specific premeditated internal change programmes within a given environment; the latter to changes which keep the organisation viable and in harmony within a changing environment.

Organisational development theorists such as Harrison (1970); Schmuck and Miles (1976); Blake and Moulton (1983); French and Bell (1984) have proposed several typologies for classifying intervention and change approaches:

- unit of change (individual, group, corporate);
- depth of intervention (strategic, operational, personal);

- focus of intervention (goals, structure, expectations);
- mode of intervention (prescriptive, confrontational).

Typographical work like this is useful in distinguishing between change roles such as the intervening 'change maker' and the target of the change. A great deal of the organisational development literature is based upon techniques and methods for the practitioner (see Huczynski, 1987). However, there are exceptions such as the work of Burke and Litwin (1992) which shall be considered in the next chapter.

Summary

This chapter has attempted to provide a broad overview of the organisational change literature.[5] Change has traditionally been seen as a mechanistic, planned affair up until the 1960s. The proliferation of approaches and models since then has certainly broadened our thinking about organisational change. Many of the approaches, techniques and methods encapsulated earlier in Table 3.5 have been taken up and applied by organisational change practitioners with a good measure of success. Nonetheless, in much of this applied research and method-ological development there has been a distinct emphasis on the 'how' question: specifically, how to initiate, manage, respond to, plan for and implement change as a phenomenon – whether it be internal or external to the organisation. It has not yielded the deeper understanding of the nature and dynamics of change that some scholars and practitioners had hoped would emerge.

However, it would be unfair to say that no efforts have been made to look at the phenomenon of change itself as manifested within organisations. The next chapter reviews the work of several people who have attempted to take on this challenge.

4   Tentative beginnings

Some pioneers reviewed

Change stems from the imposition of the future on the present.
Engines for the process are in the conception of destinies and
necessary steps toward their fulfilment.

(March, 1994: 40)

Introduction

Having perused the vast literature on change within organisations, we look here at
the relative few who have attempted to address head on the 'what is change'
question. Most readers of this book will have their own preferred models, frameworks and writers on organisational change to whom they turn for inspiration
– those that challenge their perspective and force a new line of thinking through
the change problem which they face. If we scan our personal bookshelves with
honesty, we would probably be forced to admit that there are not many such
writers represented. This chapter offers a personal selection from those who have
attempted to dig a little deeper into change and explore how it works. However,
first it is worth taking a step back to outline the main strands of change theory that
have emerged over the years.

Theoretical foundations

As Burnes (1992) has noted, organisational change theory can be summarised
according to three perspectives:

- theories of change that focus on the whole organisation;
- theories that are based upon the dynamics of groups or teams;
- theories that are centred on individual behaviour.

These bear many similarities to Allison's three models of decision-making (1971):
different perspectives and explanations of reality, from three different standpoints.[1]

Organisation level

Theories based at the level of the organisation see change originating from two sources: interactions between the subsystems of which they are composed; and interactions and exchanges across their boundary with an external environment. Child (1972) emphasises the latter, proposing three key external factors which may determine the degree of change experienced by an organisation: environmental complexity, variability and illiberality. Zey-Ferrell (1979) proposes three similar classifications: the rate, variability and instability of environmental change. Change analysis and intervention tends to be holistic in nature, with an acknowledgement of synergistic change phenomena occurring at the level of the whole. There have been many proponents of this macro, systemic theoretical view of organisational change.[2] However, while widely supported and firmly rooted in the Contingency school of thought, this perspective on organisational change does have its limitations. Internal change is often seen as reactive and driven by environmental disturbances in a homeostatic manner. As we shall see later, recent advances in the natural sciences suggest that even inanimate systems do not all respond to external stimuli in such a deterministic manner. There is also a tendency to focus on complex cause–effect relationships in attempting to describe and explain organisational change (Butler, 1985), rather than searching for underlying change patterns and emergent themes at the level of the whole. Furthermore, while systems theories of organisational change are able to describe macro change phenomena such as changes in culture, corporate structure or high level business process, they are not so effective in explaining lower level transitions such as changes in individual behaviour, operational procedure or personal performance.

Group level

The second strand of organisation change theory considered here concerns group and team behaviour. Here change dynamics are viewed in terms of group values, norms and roles (Smith *et al.*, 1982) and if effective change is to be achieved then, according to this view, these group characteristics should be identified and understood prior to attempting planned change. This theoretical perspective on organisational change draws heavily upon the social psychology literature (see, for example, Swanson *et al.*, 1958). In describing change, a distinction is made between formal and informal groups. Examples of the former include task groups, technological groups, decision-making groups and problem-solving groups (Dubin, 1958; Arglye, 1974). Organisational change is seen in terms of interactions, conflicts and relationships between groups, with particular functional or task groups exhibiting cohesive resistance to change (Blau, 1961; Tajfel and Fraser, 1981). However, this strand of organisational change thinking is limited in its ability to describe wider, more macro level dynamics such as technology change. It tends to underplay external and environmental sources of change and is not fully capable of describing transformations of a revolutionary nature that occur across several organisational groupings (for example, corporate downsizing due to market recessions). Nevertheless, group dynamics based change theories remain a mainstream area of organisational change research, as Smith (1980) and Brown (1988) have shown.

Individual level

The third broad area of organisational change theory is centred upon individual behaviour. Similar to the group-based theories, there is an emphasis on understanding individual needs and motivations, in an attempt to unlock human resistance to change. Some theorists take a decentralised view, arguing that individuals are best able to cope with and facilitate change if they are involved and empowered to design and initiate it (Kanter, 1984). Emancipation, participation and ownership are considered key concepts to understanding effective change management. On the other hand, others take a more Scientific–Rational view, arguing that change is best understood in terms of control and manipulation – initiating change by providing specific change sources to reinforce or discourage certain actions or propensities to change (see Porter *et al.*, 1975). Whether one takes the empowerment or control stance, however, theories of change based upon the individual have been severely criticised because they assume a certain rationality about human nature – based on what Schein (1980: 52) has termed rational–economic assumptions. Decisions about the future are invariably based on knowledge from the past, and partial perception of the present. Hence, there is inherent uncertainty embedded within all seemingly rational decisions.[3] Individualist theories of organisational change therefore have little conception of counter-intuitive, illogical change within human activity systems.

These three strands of theoretical development in organisational change complement each other well, as they each take change as a phenomenon from a different perspective. However, even taken together, they fail to provide a deep, unifying insight into the nature and dynamics of change within organisations. The group and individual theories tend to err on the side of change management, providing justification for specific change tools, techniques and methods. The organisation-based change theories can be rather abstract and difficult to apply practically to the operational realities of day-to-day business management, as Beach (1980) has observed. While perhaps conceptually richer than the individual and group theories, organisation level theories have historically been tied to the biological organism metaphor.

With this theoretical backdrop, the rest of this chapter moves on to look at some of the relatively few attempts to understand what change is and the dynamics that drive it.

What is this thing called change?

Modelling the transition

One of the most influential attempts to describe the phenomenon of change within the organisation was the Force Field approach of Kurt Lewin (1947, 1951,

1958). Lewin maintained that changing some aspect of an organisation involves manipulating the social forces which influence it. His classic three-stage approach is well known: unfreezing the current state, moving to the new state and, finally, refreezing at the new state. The metaphorical use of a change phenomenon from the natural sciences is of particular interest here, offering a conceptual richness which has inspired many authors to develop Lewin's work further (see, for example, Schein, 1964, 1980, 1987; Rubin, 1967; Kahn, 1974; Zand and Sorensen, 1975). This foundational work by Lewin demonstrates that the natural sciences have much to offer both the organisational scholar and the change practitioner. It should be noted that practical change management thinking has moved on a long way from the concept of refreezing. Change practitioners and management consultants are increasingly seeking to leverage the uncertainty of change and promote it as a continuous process.

The popular work of William Bridges (1980) describes the processes of personal transition through which we all go at various points in our lives. In modelling transition, he outlines three natural phases:

- *Endings*: emphasising the need to be recognised and celebrated;
- *Neutral zone*: a period of emotional disconnection and reorientation;
- *New beginning*: focusing on new priorities and being alert to what the future has to offer.

These stages have some obvious overlaps with Lewin's unfreeze, change, freeze cycle, but the focus of Bridges is on the psychology of change and how individuals can attempt to cope with it in the workplace. The principles have been applied to broad change management initiatives within organisations, but the emphasis is firmly on helping the individual to cope with and adjust to change.

Views on planned change

Bennis (1963, 1966a, b) described three approaches to planned change, each of which embodies a different change perspective. All are concerned with changes in behaviour and are arguably influenced by the Human Relations orientated thinking of the day. The first is based upon a *system of opposing forces* which dictates the energy available for a given change, and has its roots in Lewin's work. Change is enabled via tension reduction. This approach is called the Equilibrium Model and is based upon the research of Jacques (1951) and Sofer (1961) among others.

The second approach describes change in terms of reconstructing mental models, in a manner not unlike that outlined by Senge (1990) and the organisational learning approaches to change. However, the means of achieving mental model change is different. Cognitive maps are altered via a process of *power redistribution* within the organisation involving the promotion of openness and trust through participation in laboratory and T-Group exercises. Examples of this

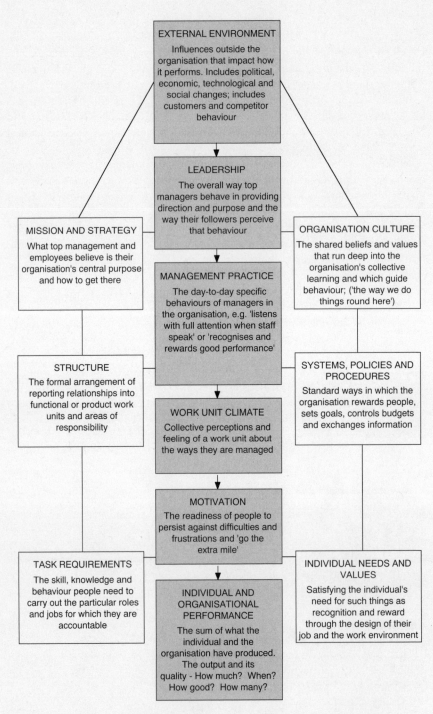

Figure 4.1 The Burke–Litwin model (adapted with permission from Burke, 1992)

approach include the work of Shepard and Blake (1962). It is described by Bennis as the Organic Model.

The third approach views change in terms of the *interrelationships between individuals*. The underlying premise here is that enhancing interpersonal competence is essential to effective organisation. This was labelled the Developmental Model and is exemplified by the work of Argyris (1962). Other theorists have outlined phases or models of planned change including Lippitt *et al.* (1958). The above merely demonstrates that some thinking on the planned process of change has been undertaken, largely by the Organisation Development community.

Burke and Litwin (1989, 1992) have developed a model of organisational change and performance, shown in Figure 4.1. It attempts to show three main things. First, it highlights the key components of organisational life. Doubtless there are some who will want to debate the number, placing and meaning of the various components. Nonetheless, collectively they are fairly comprehensive and cover most domains of change activity within an organisation. The shaded central core represents the critical path for translating some leadership response to an external stimulus *into* effective performance at the individual and organisational level.

Second, the model demonstrates well the interdependent nature of the components. As Burke and Litwin themselves confess, a two-dimensional representation is not really adequate. They suggest a holographic version with multiple relationships would be better. In this regard, the model is conceptually far richer than the McKinsey 7S framework (see Waterman *et al.*, 1980). Every component of the model is in reality connected to all the others in a web of complex, multilayered interaction across both time and space.

Third, the model attempts to show those interrelationships which cause radical and transformational change, and those which result in change of a more incremental and transactional nature. The transformational components include the external environment, leadership, organisation culture, mission and strategy – all affecting performance and output. According to Burke and Litwin, transformational change can be best achieved by altering any of these elements. They are the components that will have the most impact on performance in the long run. All the others are classed as transactional because targeting them will only achieve change at more operational levels lower down within the organisation. Changes aimed at transactional components will, by definition, not be effective if the root problem lies higher up the model with a transformational component.

Attributes of change

Glick *et al.* (1990) have attempted to define change at an operational level in more pragmatic terms. Their work is concerned with 'the process of reducing open-ended descriptions of change into a parsimonious set of attributes for theory testing and building' (Glick *et al.*, 1990: 305) They describe four such attributes:

- the type of change: whether it is designed or not;
- the impetus for the change: was it proactive or reactive;
- the ability to distinguish ongoing processes from discrete change events;
- the relative importance of the changes – determined by value judgements made by the participants.

Ferlie and Pettigrew (1990), in a similar vein, highlight another four attributes, discussing change in terms of speed, quantity, process and quality.

March (1981: 575) has examined a range of factors which he suggests must be considered in any investigation of the 'fundamental adaptive processes by which change occurs'. He argues that theories of organisational change must:

- not be based upon simple responses to specific forces such as economic and demographic factors;
- be capable of encompassing both change and stability;
- accommodate the surprise, non-linear aspects of change.

Here we see an attempt to look beyond the obvious triggers and drivers of change. These constitute useful ground rules and the ideas will be returned to in later chapters.

Change as flux and transformation

Within the social sciences, Morgan (1986) has realised the need for a more profound understanding of the concept of change. He examines the organisation through what he terms the metaphor of flux and transformation, considering how organisations may exist within deep structures and processes which possess their own logics of change. He proposes three such 'logics' and discusses them in detail. The first has to do with self-organisation principles drawn from biology, such as autopoiesis – the ability of an organism continually to renew itself while maintaining structural integrity and identity. Second, he looks at concepts of mutual causality taken from cybernetics, such as interconnected circular loops of positive and negative feedback. Morgan's third logic of change concerns dialectics and the notion of opposites. Here he examines Tao philosophy and the work of Marx as examples of dialectical thinking.

All three logics of change are discussed in the context of organisations, in an attempt to encourage new ways of thinking about and dealing with change. Morgan (1986) argues strongly that future research in organisation theory must begin to examine ways to influence the nature of the changes which organisations actually experience, as opposed to just describing and classifying different types of change. This implies a proactive approach to change which has in part been adopted in recent years by the organisational learning school (see, for example, Senge, 1990) and the application of system dynamics modelling tools within the organisation.

Order of magnitude

Levy (1986) has added to the debate by highlighting the distinction that has emerged in the literature between First Order and Second Order change. First Order change is characterised as a slow and incremental process that does not challenge the organisation's core structures. Conversely, Second Order change is typically radical, multidimensional and revolutionary in nature, altering fundamentally the organisation's world view and design. While Watzlawick *et al.* (1974) seem to have been the first explicitly to describe these two types in detail, various writers on organisations have identified some of the basic characteristics of each:

Author	First Order change	Second Order change
Vickers (1965)	Executive change	Policy-making change
De Bono (1971)	Vertical change	Lateral change
Greiner (1972)	Evolutionary change	Revolutionary change
Putney (1972)	Linear quantitative changes	Non-linear qualitative changes
Argyris and Schon (1978)	Single loop learning	Double loop learning
Sheldon (1980)	Normal change	Paradigm change

(Adapted from Levy, 1986: 8)

This distinction is a useful one in that it highlights two very broad sets of defining attributes for change, and uncovers some of the dynamics perceived to be operating at deeper levels which often go unrecognised. Lundberg (1984) has observed, however, that there is a dearth of suitable analytical frameworks within which to develop further the concept of Second Order change. Krovi (1993) has added to the taxonomy by introducing the concept of Middle Order change in discussing information technology and organisational change. This sits somewhat uneasily between Levy's two categories: 'Middle order change represents a compromise; the magnitude of change is greater than first order change, yet it neither affects the critical success factors nor is strategic in nature' (Krovi, 1993: 331). Others have explored the theoretical roots of the distinction, illustrating it with examples of change behaviour (see, for example, Bartunek and Louis, 1988). Torbert (1989) has gone even further, arguing that First Order changes within organisations are often planned, while those of the Second Order tend to be unplanned and unpredictable.

More recently, Meyer *et al.* (1990, 1993) have taken the concepts of First and Second Order change and applied them at two levels: that of the organisation, and the industry in which it exists. This produces a two-by-two matrix illustrated in Figure 4.2, within which they classify various approaches to incremental and radical change. Their work clearly distinguishes between the mode of change (First or Second Order) and the level at which the change is manifest (industry or firm). They also recognise that modes and levels of change are fundamental concepts found in both the natural and physical sciences.

	First order change		Second order change	
Firm level	ADAPTATION		METAMORPHOSIS	
	Focus:	*Incremental change within organisations*	Focus:	*Frame breaking change within organisations*
	Mechanisms:	*- Resource dependence* *- Strategic choice*	Mechanisms:	*- Strategic reorientation* *- Life cycles*
Industry level	EVOLUTION		REVOLUTION	
	Focus:	*Incremental change within established industries*	Focus:	*Emergence, transformation and decline of industries*
	Mechanisms:	*- Institutional isomorphism* *- Natural selection*	Mechanisms:	*- Environmental partitioning* *- Quantum speciation*

Figure 4.2 Mode and level change (adapted from Meyer *et al.*, 1993)

Putting change into context

Pettigrew (1990a, b) argues there has been an overemphasis on prescriptive writing in the literature, leading to underconcern with descriptive analysis and conceptualisation. He highlights the contextual nature of change within organisation theory, emphasising:

- embeddedness: acknowledging interdependent levels of analysis;
- interconnectedness of change over time;
- how the change context shapes and is shaped by action;
- the multi-causation and non-linear nature of change.

(Pettigrew, 1990a: 269)

Pettigrew's research identifies the need to study change across different levels of analysis and different time periods and goes a considerable way towards refuting the simplistic, one-dimensional and discontinuous view of change within early management and organisational thinking. He believes that each researcher should define what they mean by change within their own theoretical framework, thereby emphasising the particular facet of change upon which their theory is focused.

Van de Ven has defined change as 'an empirical observation of differences in time on one or more dimensions of an entity' (1987: 331). His conception of change is closely associated with the passage of time and physical observation. Expanding this definition further, he says:

Mobility, motion or activity in themselves do not constitute change, although each is in some degree involved in change. Certain dimensions or categories of an entity are the objects being transformed. Change without reference to an object is meaningless.

(Van de Ven, 1987: 331)

Here we see an attempt to define change by describing what it is not, and this is a useful start in placing broad limits around the concept. He goes on to draw a distinction between this definition of change, identified by direct empirical observations over time, and the process of change. The latter he argues can only be indirectly perceived as 'conceptual inferences about the temporal ordering of relationships among observed changes' (Van de Ven, 1987: 331). Conner and Lake allude to a similar distinction, highlighting the difference 'between change as a phenomenon, and changing, as a set of actions' (Conner and Lake, 1988: 7).

Change as relationship

Smith (1982) has attempted to analyse some of the philosophical problems that cloud our thinking about organisational change. He comes to the conclusion that an organisation consists essentially of 'relations among parts and relations among relations' (Smith, 1982: 318). Therefore any concept of organisational change must be founded upon changing relationships. These, he argues, can only be altered by changing the metaphors, analogies and metonymies used to describe them. He discusses the notion of boundary as the place where change occurs and emphasises that it too is a relation, and not part of the structure of the organisation. Drawing heavily on the language of biology and other life sciences to explore the concept of change, he makes a clear distinction between the rules which govern internal structure changes and those which determine changes of order at the level of the whole.

As we have seen, Gersick (1991) has attempted to explore the nature and dynamics of evolutionary and revolutionary change. She discusses the concept of deep structures: fundamental choices and resource configurations which shape organisation structure and environmental interaction. These she argues represent fundamental drivers and controllers of change within organisations, which can lie hidden and often unrecognised. We will return to her work in Chapter 7.

Types of change

Golembiewski *et al.* (1976) have made the important link between the perception of change and how we measure it. They propose three broad classifications:

- *Alpha change*: variation within a given state as measured by an instrument whose calibrations remain fixed.
- *Beta change*: variation within a given state where the intervals of calibration on the measuring instrument have shifted.

- *Gamma change*: a complete change of state as opposed to variation within a given state, making the use of measurement instruments from the original state inappropriate.

They argue that these different types of change have serious implications for designing, assessing and interpreting organisational change interventions. Specifically, they suggest that gamma changes are the most prevalent in organisational development interventions. Aware of the problems in trying to distinguish between the three types of change, they describe various statistical techniques for identifying evidence of gamma change in organisational change projects. Two of their conclusions are worth noting:

- Many studies assume that only alpha change is relevant to organisations, and make no distinction between different types of change.
- The measurement and interpretation of organisational change interventions 'is chancey in the absence of knowledge about types of change, which is seldom available' (Golembiewski *et al.*, 1976: 153).

While acknowledging that there remains much further research to be done in this area, their contribution represents a significant attempt to explore the nature of change by asking what kind of change is being measured before tackling the problem of how actually to measure it. Other writers have explored their taxonomy further and attempted to apply it as a measurement framework during change interventions.[4]

Stacey (1992, 1993) identifies three distinct types of change – closed, contained and open-ended – within organisational systems. These apply to what he terms equilibrium, near to equilibrium and far from equilibrium systems respectively. Closed change is considered predictable and deterministic in the Newtonian sense and governed by specific cause–effect chains. He quotes changes within the popular music market as an example, with demand and supply moving within known limits.

Contained change relates to situations where prediction is only possible based upon laws of probability. Because the system is near equilibrium, certain underlying cause and effect chains can be identified which produce regularity. However, due to the variability of the environment, elements of irregularity result in behaviour which is not completely deterministic or predictable. Continuing Stacey's organisational example, this corresponds to changes in trends and patterns identified through market research activities for specific types of product.

Open-ended change is described as being typified by ambiguity and uncertainty, where 'it is not possible to predict long-term consequences because the connections between cause and effect are lost in the detail of the interactions that occur over time' (Stacey, 1993: 251). He suggests diversification or company mergers as examples of open-ended change, because the long-term consequences are inherently unknowable due to the complex interdependence of the environmental variables involved. Stacey then, uses predictability over the short, medium and long term as a means of classifying change within organisations.

Table 4.1 Summary of selected authors from Chapter 4 who have attempted to understand change within organisations

Author focus	Author	Theory/description of change
Modelling the transition	Lewin (1947, 1951, 1958) Bridges (1980)	• Thaw – change – refreeze • Endings – neutral zone – beginnings
Views on planned change	Bennis (1963, 1966a, b)	• System of opposing forces • Power redistribution • Inter-relationships
	Burke and Litwin (1989, 1992)	• Interdependencies and interconnections • Transformational versus transactional
Attributes of change	Glick *et al.* (1990)	• Designed or not • Proactive versus reactive • Discrete versus continuous • Judgement of relative importance
	March (1981)	• More than just simple responses to external triggers • Encompass both change and stability • Accommodate the surprise and non-linear
Change as flux and transformation	Morgan (1986)	• Logics of change • Self-organisation • Mutual causality • Dialectics and opposites
Order of magnitude	Levy (1986) Krovi (1993) Meyer *et al.* (1990, 1993)	• First order versus second order • Middle order • Adaptation and evolution versus metamorphosis and revolution

continued

Table 4.1 continued

Author focus	Author	Theory/description of change
Putting change into context	Pettigrew (1990a, b)	• Embeddedness • Interconnectedness • Change context
	Van der Ven (1987)	• Multi-causality and non-linearity • More than mobility and motion • In relation to some reference point
Change as relationship	Smith (1982)	• Changing relationships • Change occurs at the boundary
	Gersick (1991)	• Evolutionary and revolutionary change • Deep structure: choices and resource configurations
Types of change	Golembiewski *et al.* (1976) Stacey (1992, 1993)	• Alpha – beta – gamma change • Closed – contained – open change • A function of predictability
	Miller and Friesen (1980a)	• From the onset of imbalance to equilibrium • Nine archetypes of transition

Miller and Friesen (1980a) have sought to identify various archetypes of organisational change, focusing on the transition processes which organisations undergo in adapting to their environment. They define a transition as 'a package of changes that occur between the onset of the imbalance or stress and the time when some equilibrium or tranquil interval is reached' (1980a: 271). Their study of the histories of thirty-six firms led them to propose nine archetypes of organisational transition including: entrepreneurial revitalization; consolidation; boldness and abandon; maturation; fragmentation; initiation by fire; formalisation and stability. These categories represent particular modes of adaptive behaviour in response to environmental disturbances and provide an insight into the cause–effect aspect of change. That is, they describe some of the common patterns of change which emerge in given scenarios, and reoccur over time.

From their analysis, Miller and Friesen argue that there do not seem to be many common transition types and, as a result, conclude that 'it might eventually be possible to discover the fundamental building blocks or response behaviours constituting the elementary dynamics of change' (Miller and Friesen, 1980a: 288). Their conception of organisational change is somewhat similar to that of Greiner (1972) and Gersick (1991): general stability with minor adaptation for most of the time, punctuated by periods of acute instability – enabling revolutionary transitions to take place which help maintain viability.

Summary

This chapter has demonstrated that some efforts have been made to define and explore what change is within organisations. Some excellent work has already been undertaken in this area, but it is only a small proportion of the organisational change literature. Table 4.1 provides a summary overview of the main authors who have been reviewed here and the valuable ideas they have contributed to our understanding of what change is. These tentative beginnings are but first steps on the road to further uncovering the mysteries of change and much still needs to be done. The next chapter begins to broaden out into more general definitions and perspectives on change from both the social and physical sciences. This will start to take us outside of the organisational domain into the territory of the sociologist, historian and philosopher – and on into the world of the physical and natural sciences.

5 Forsaking pride and prejudice

Multiple perspectives on change

To say with the ancient philosopher 'All is flux' is perhaps too obvious. But to say 'All is change' is far from obvious. There are, on the surface at least, too many clear evidences of fixity and persistence.

Nisbet (1970: 177)

Introduction

In this chapter we examine some of the philosophical ideas that surround change. From the Greeks through to modern times, a multitude of perspectives and descriptions of change have emerged. History has left us with a rich literature of comment, views and opinion on the subject of change: is it real or imaginary? Can it be assessed and measured? How should we describe it? Can change be reversed? How is change best defined? When does one change stop and another start? Here we shall look at a few areas of thought on the subject of change, to provide a conceptual backdrop to later chapters. In keeping with the systems thinking ideas presented in Chapter 2, these will be drawn from both the physical and social sciences. Much insight can be gained from understanding how various scholars and specialists across the sciences have grappled with change as it reveals itself in their own area of study. Some of the commonalities are surprising – others somewhat predictable. The chapter concludes by drawing out a number of recurring themes raised by this review. Leaving the comfort zone and prejudices of our own subject domain – the organisation – can be both liberating and challenging. Apart from enriching our language and vocabulary, learning how others view change can enable us to better conceptualise it.

In looking at some of the philosophical issues associated with change, it should be noted that various terms have been used in the literature to describe different schools of thought. These have been outlined for both the physical and social sciences by a number of authors[1] and so we will not descend into a plethora of confusing labels here. However, several specific terms are used to introduce some important concepts. These are shown in italics.

Reality: real or imagined?

We all make assumptions about the world in which we live and how we interact with it. Many of these are often taken for granted and lie so deeply ingrained in the way in which we see the world that we are scarcely aware of them. For example, does the world we inhabit actually exist 'out there' independent of our awareness of it or does it cease to exist when we are asleep? A naive and strange question perhaps, but one which has engaged many serious minds down the years.

According to the *objectivist* position, change can occur regardless of our perception of it, and can therefore take place beyond human influence or control. This view of the world assumes that a changing reality exists 'out there' as a seamless dynamically interacting whole, regardless of the labels and vocabulary used to portray it. Take, for example, the terms we use to describe change in organisations such as transformational, radical, second order, incremental. According to the objectivist, these are merely descriptive terms employed to try and define specific dominant attributes which are of interest and relevance to the enquirer and his time frame. Whether such terms are accurate and representative, fully capturing the actual dynamics of the change, is inherently difficult to assess. For the objectivist, there could well be aspects of the change occurring beyond the scope of human perception and measurement of which the observer is completely unaware.

An alternative view of change is offered by the *individualist* position. As the term suggests, this view is based upon one's own individual perspective. Accordingly, change does not occur independently of human cognition. Hence, a changing reality cannot exist outside of the mind as individual perception essentially creates it. Clearly here, concepts and labels are key to expressing and giving actual substance to a particular change being perceived. As a result, a dearth of suitable descriptive language can severely restrict the individualist's awareness and understanding of the change phenomena which he encounters. For the individualist then, the use of metaphor and analogy represents a useful palette from which to draw images and descriptions to explain the change events and processes they experience.[2]

Another aspect of this debate concerns the nature of reality itself. On the one hand, it can be considered to be one of perpetual flux and change as the Greek philosopher, Heraclitus, believed: 'You cannot step into the same river twice; for fresh waters are always flowing in upon you' (Heraclitus, 500 BC) Indeed, if you hold this view, even stepping once into the same river becomes an impossibility, as Cratylus (500 BC) observed. One event, one moment in time immediately follows those preceding. Extreme adherents to the Heraclitian view believe that capturing the constant flux of events in words becomes impossible due to the inadequacy of language.

On the other hand, reality can be viewed as fixity and permanence of form, as Parmenides (450 BC) suggests. Nothing actually changes, only the appearance of change convinces us that things do not remain the same. In later life, Einstein took this latter view. He used the analogy of a film to describe what he believed to be the unchanging, predetermined nature of reality: 'in the eyes of God, the film was just there, and the future was there as much as the past: nothing ever happened in this world, and *change was a human illusion*, as was also the difference between the future and the past' (Einstein, 1950: 90; emphasis added).

How then do we perceive an organisation? Is it some virtual entity composed entirely of a network of individual relationships which shift and gyrate over time? Is it merely a defined legal concept that only exists on paper? Or is the organisation in which I work the total of my daily experience of it – which could well be different from that of my boss's understanding of what constitutes his workplace? Checkland (1972) offers us a way of exploring the various conceptions which people have of a given organisation, focusing on the purpose we believe it exists to serve. For example, is a hospital a healthcare delivery system, a clinical training provider for healthcare professionals or an allocation system for community services? For some, no doubt, it is all of these things, but each definition implies a different perception of reality. As a researcher or consultant, attempts to achieve change within a hospital can be a fraught exercise. Often the key actors and stakeholders will see the function, purpose and identity of the organisation slightly differently. How we perceive a given organisational reality then – in objectivist or individualist terms – can have a significant effect on the way in which we choose to interact with it and manage change within it.

Knowledge: acquired or experienced?

The process of learning something about a given change is critical to change management endeavours. How we measure and capture information in order to increase our knowledge of a specific phenomenon will often determine how we subsequently interact with it. According to the *rationalist* view, knowledge about change can be acquired in an objective manner. Change phenomena are deemed to be inherently measurable and therefore descriptions and explanations of them can be verified or falsified. A common understanding of a particular change event or process can be obtained and communicated. For the pure rationalist, change is fundamentally an explicable and predictable phenomenon because of the belief that objective measurement is possible, and that a cumulative knowledge base can be constructed to describe it. Based on the assumption that all the necessary information is 'out there' for the taking, cause and effect relationships are believed to be identifiable.

On the other hand, the *relativist* takes a very different position. Here, knowledge and understanding of change phenomena cannot be objectively acquired, only experienced. Accordingly, any knowledge derived comes from individual perception and interpretation via direct contact with the change itself. As a result, there is no common knowledge base shared between observers, as all see the change from differing perspectives. The notion of change here then is subjective and intangible in nature, with consensus and effective communication inherently difficult to achieve.

The nature of reality and the way in which we choose to extract knowledge from it are intimately linked. Knowledge is capable of changing the way in which we perceive the world and (depending upon one's philosophical stance) able actually to change reality itself through application. This in turn will promote changes in how one attempts to gain further knowledge. In this respect, the social sciences are fundamentally different from the natural sciences as Vickers (1983) has convincingly argued. He uses the following illustration. Copernicus and Ptolemy had very different theories about the structure and workings of the solar system. Whether one believed in one theory or the other did not change the actual structure in the slightest. On the other hand, Marx produced a theory of history and social development: belief in that theory by some has fundamentally changed the course of human history. Clearly, this difference between the social and natural sciences is based upon the degree to which the theorist is part of the system he is attempting to describe, and presents serious philosophical dilemmas for the individualist.

Exploring the knowledge–reality relationship further, if we take a Heraclitian perspective, the language and knowledge available at time t is only capable of describing things in the past, and how they have changed up to that point in time t (see Figure 5.1). To understand future change dynamics at $t+1$, the language and knowledge available must evolve to a higher level. The part of the river we stepped into has now flowed on downstream and we are experiencing a different river. In other words, to describe change and the emergent properties it produces, new descriptions must continually be generated. Accordingly, an evolving or changing system therefore requires an evolving language to describe it. Lofgren (1980) has called this 'linguistic complementarity'.

What does this mean for those concerned with change in the organisation? Simply this: that how we decide to measure, model and describe change will ultimately determine our view of how it 'works' and should be managed. A

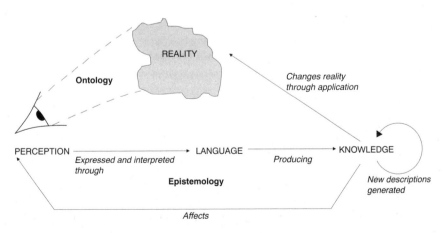

Figure 5.1 Evolving language to describe change

business process re-engineering specialist may approach change with an objective, rational perspective. An organisational psychologist may well have an individualist, relativist perspective. Having both involved on the same team for a particular change project presents some unique challenges when it comes to scoping and designing the change initiative – as the author knows only too well from personal experience.

Change and the outside world

Here we are concerned with issues of individual creativity and human ability to influence the magnitude and direction of change activities within a system. There are broadly two schools of thought here.[3] The first believes that human activity systems are dictated by their environment, both in the immediate and long term. Change phenomena in human behaviour are therefore viewed as mechanistic and deterministic in nature, caused and shaped by external forces beyond the control of individuals inside the system. The second offers an alternative view: human systems are viewed as largely autonomous possessing free will. As a result, internal change is within the control and influence of the system. Change behaviour is individually created and spontaneous in origin. Therefore, the potential exists for immense variety and unpredictability. Taking this view allows for the possibility of emergent behaviour and change at the level of the whole which could possibly affect the external environment over time.

Practice often lies somewhere between the two, with some changes being imposed from outside and others seemingly initiated and determined from within the organisation. However, from personal consulting experience, it is hard to find specific examples of changes which cannot be traced back to some external trigger. Logic demands that for an organisation to remain viable in the long term, it must ensure all internal changes ultimately support long-term survival in the environment in which it operates. For example, a change in corporate strategy is usually undertaken to exploit some perceived change in the external market. Changes in organisation structure or culture, in the normal course of events, should be alignment actions to ensure they support the strategy. Business process re-engineering, although on the surface a purely inward-looking cost reduction and corporate restructuring exercise in its infancy, is normally triggered by competitive pressures and the need to remain efficient in a hostile market. Even changes in areas such as pay and benefits should ultimately be made to reinforce and encourage behaviours and practices which will help a business achieve its corporate strategy and remain viable. Whether or not such connections are valued and actively sought by senior managers and consultants is another matter.

We shall explore sources and causes of change in more detail in the next chapter, where this internal versus external change debate will be resumed. In keeping with our cross-discipline approach, the next sections review a range of definitions for change from across the social and natural sciences.

'The challenge facing consultants, researchers and managers alike is to become capable of discerning when, for example, a change has started and when it has ended; or knowing when something of substance has changed and not being lured by frenetic activity and background noise.'

Problems of definition

The Oxford English Dictionary defines *change* as 'making or becoming different; difference from previous state; substitution of one for another'. This captures two contrasting attributes: first, that of 'making' or 'becoming' which implies process and activity over time; second, 'substitution', suggesting that change can also be more of an instantaneous event, in which a physical switch-over takes place at a discrete moment in time. Dissecting the definition further, 'making' can imply a planned and directed change endeavour, whereas 'becoming' suggests a more natural, unconscious change which is intrinsically part of the life cycle of the entity or system concerned. This basic definition serves as an initial working description for change and, as we shall see, the themes it contains play out across a range of different disciplines.

A social science perspective on change

Researchers across the social sciences have grappled with defining the concept of change within social systems such as organisations. Thomas and Bennis (1972) describe it in terms of conflict, revolution, uprising and rebellion. Deutsch (1966), on the other hand, discusses change in terms of feedback through active goal-seeking and perpetual learning, while Oliga (1990) argues that change and stability are functions of ideology and power. Confused? It is hardly surprising, given the variety of ways in which change manifests itself within social systems. As Berg (1979) has noted, the problems of definition are due in part to the fact that there is a multitude of concepts that can and have been used to describe change phenomena. Depending upon their focus and level of study, researchers also tend to emphasise different aspects of change. As we saw in Chapter 3, the diversity of perspective just within organisational thinking is enormous. The use of different vocabularies and the problem of finding the right descriptive concepts to use which have agreed meanings further complicates the issue. This problem has its roots in the philosophical debate discussed earlier between the objectivist and individualist. Unable to reach any definite conclusions, Berg arrives at a simple and somewhat thesauratic definition: 'Change belongs to a set of concepts (such as development, growth, evolution, transition, renewal, progress, revolution, transcendence, etc.) that are used to describe similar phenomena' (Berg, 1979: 19).

Let us peruse a selection of definitions from social scientists. Each of the definitions which follow have been chosen because they highlight a particular aspect of change, and attempt to put some parameters around the concept.

Coleman (1968) focuses on the perception and measurement aspects of change, defining it as a concept which:

> is based on a second order abstraction, created through a comparison or difference between sense impressions of two component states, while simultaneously comparing the time positions when those two impressions took place. Thus the concept of change requires an extra intellectual leap beyond the mere formation of concepts that reflect a state of the world.
>
> (Coleman, 1968: 428)

Here we see the importance of time, as the continuum on which change occurs. Coleman's definition also emphasises the role of perception and cognitive processing in identifying change, as well as the position of one observer relative to another. As Albert Einstein (1921, 1952) has shown, simultaneous experience of a given event does not hold true for all observers. Indeed, Einstein's Special Theory of Relativity shows that even the passage of time is relative to individual observers. By necessity, this introduces a subjective and pluralistic aspect to the definition of change. Because of this, Coleman argues that mathematics is the only language which can measure and define the attributes of change in social research, without unduly complicating it.

Building on the work of Dahrendorf (1959a, b) and Hernes (1976), Van de Ven (1987: 339) suggests that a good, robust theory of change in social structures should satisfy four basic requirements:

- It should explain how change, behaviour and structure are interconnected at both macro and micro levels of analysis.
- It should describe how change is a function of internal and external factors.
- It should account for both change and stability.
- The theory should incorporate time as the 'key historical metric'.

These are excellent guide points for any scholar of change. The interplay between internal–external and macro–micro is critical to understanding the dynamics of change and transition. Van de Ven's ideas suggest that we should not think of change as occurring in a straight line. For example, interconnections between different departments and hierarchical levels of an organisation mean that change is rarely sequential or predictable.

In describing the history of ideas and events, Foucault (1972) outlines a similar multi-layered, non-linear view of change, with change processes moving at different speeds across different levels of analysis. He argues that our understanding of the nature of change is not sophisticated or subtle enough to identify the slower, silent and deep moving, underlying change processes at work, that 'history has covered with thick layers of events' (1972: 3), with the consequence that events get lumped together and labelled according to the more discernible and obvious changes: 'as if time existed only in the vacant moment of the rupture, in that white, paradoxically atemporal crack in which one sudden formulation replaces another' (Foucault, 1972: 166).

This aggregation of events, while perhaps serving as a useful approximation, implies that the key dynamics of change can often be missed or ignored. How often do we see top management hold a distorted, idealised view of what the workforce really think and feel, and how decisions are made lower down – unaware of the subtle interdepartmental dynamics and power plays that are part of any organisation? Or consider the example of political parties going into elections blissfully unaware of true grassroots sentiment, deteriorating goodwill, fluctuating moods and constantly shifting expectations across the electorate. Come polling day, it is these that will ultimately determine political fortunes.

The extent to which this is a failing of the measurement abilities of the observer depends partly on the situation in question. However, if we acknowledge the existence of these deeper forces for change, it may be that empirical approaches for diagnosing them within social systems are not as holistic and sophisticated as they need to be for change management practitioners.

Lauer (1971) argues that research into the nature of change within social systems has been constrained and 'neutralised' by certain misleading common-sense assumptions. These he calls *fallacies* and suggests that they have gained such scientific legitimacy as to impede further study into the nature of change:

1 Change represents some deviance from the norm.
2 Change is associated with trauma and crisis, to be regarded as foreign and unwanted.
3 Change is considered to be unidirectional and deterministic, converging inevitably towards some predestined end.
4 The difference between theories of change and theories of stability constitutes a semantic illusion.

Lauer concludes that these fallacies need to be turned on their head. This he argues, would serve to inspire further theoretical exploration into the nature of change:

> Specifically . . . that change is normal; that change carries with it no intrinsic trauma; that diverse patterns of change and a range of future alternatives are open to any society; and that whether one assumes change or persistence as the basic reality has both theoretical and practical consequences of import.
>
> (Lauer, 1971: 887)

Here again we see the importance of the distinction between the Heraclitian and Parmenidian positions discussed earlier on the nature of 'basic reality'. It is worth noting that Lauer's proposition that change is not inherently traumatic is somewhat arguable: there is little doubt that the implementation of change within social systems can often be very disturbing for the individuals concerned. Whether it need necessarily be that way is the key question. Nevertheless, Lauer's analysis represents an attempt to explore the nature of change in a social context, by examining some of the common misconceptions which often distort our under-standing of the phenomenon.

Within the field of sociology, Nisbet (1970) has defined change as 'a matter of observation; it is something experienced, something that we are justified in referring to as empirical. We become aware of change through our perception of differences in time within a persisting identity' (Nisbet, 1970: 177). From this definition, he clearly identifies three key components of change:

- the passage of time;
- the maintenance of identity;
- the perception of differences.

However, the idea that change cannot be said to have occurred if there is no continuation of identity, is open to debate. Nisbet's belief that identity must persist for change to occur can be challenged, as it would appear to confine the concept of change to first order, minor variations.[4] It can be argued that in the event of system identity not being maintained, change has still occurred but of a distinctly different type. Major structural change often brings about a shift in identity, but nonetheless still constitutes change. For example, the privatisation of a utility can result in a change of management, strategy and structure to enable the organisation to face its new environment with confidence. As with UK electricity companies such as National Power, the transition from public to private sector over the first three years can constitute nothing less than a transformation. Even change within non-commercial, broader social systems can imply an evolving identity. Philosophically, there must be something which does not change over the time scale in question, in order for other changes to be identified. However, in suggesting that constant should be 'identity' may exclude the possibility of radical, terminal or catastrophic change.

Discussing social change specifically, Nisbet makes six assertions:

1   Persistence, stability and inertia are as real as change and movement.
2   Major structural change is usually initiated by some trigger external to the system.
3   Social change does not result from emergent evolution, i.e. change from the current state to some future state is not connected by some causal linkage.
4   Social change is not autonomous or automatic. It does not occur by default.
5   Social change and historical events are inseparable over time.
6   No grand theory describing both social change and stability can ever be developed.

Several of these points are intriguing. Point one suggests an interesting position which is both Heraclitian and Parmenidian. Nisbet argues that change is fundamentally spontaneous, punctuating social existence sporadically over time (point three) in a similar manner to that proposed by Miller and Freisen (1980b) and Gersick (1991). He disagrees with Van de Ven's position discussed earlier, by suggesting that change and stability can only be explained by separate theories, and should not be considered together (point six).

Burrell and Morgan (1979) take a similar stance to Nisbet on the issue of change and stability. Building upon the opposing social theories of order and conflict developed by Dahrendorf (1959b), they propose two philosophical frames of reference: the sociology of radical change, and the sociology of regulation, illustrated in Table 5.1.

They argue that to conflate the two models of social behaviour ignores the fundamental philosophical differences between them:

> We conceptualise these two broad sociological perspectives in the form of a polarised dimension, recognising that while variations within the context of each are possible, the perspectives are necessarily separate and distinct from each other.
>
> (Burrell and Morgan, 1979: 19)

While such a mutually exclusive distinction is helpful when examining human motivation, decision-making regimes and social goal seeking, at another level of analysis, radical change and regulation are merely reciprocal concepts – two sides of the same coin. Over time the equilibrium of regulation may be disturbed and the social system may move to a sociology of radical change. Therefore a system could exhibit both separately over a period of time. Moreover, examined historically, the phenomenon of 'radical change' in social systems cannot be identified and understood without the occurrence of stability and regulation with which to compare it. Furthermore, it can also be argued that at different levels it is possible for both to exist simultaneously. The occurrence of change across levels will be discussed in Chapter 8.

Table 5.1 The sociologies of regulation and radical change as proposed by Burrell and Morgan (1979: 18); table adapted

Regulation	Radical change
• Status quo	• Radical change
• Consensus	• Modes of domination
• Solidarity	• Emancipation
• Actuality	• Potentiality
• Social order	• Structural conflict
• Need satisfaction	• Deprivation
• Social integration and cohesion	• Contradiction

'How then do we perceive an organisation? Is it some virtual entity composed entirely of a network of individual relationships which shift and gyrate over time? Is it merely a defined legal concept that only exists on paper? Or is the organisation in which I work the total of my daily experience of it?'

Bahm (1979) takes a philosophical view of change, stating simply: 'A thing may change by gaining a part, by losing a part, or by exchanging parts. A thing can change completely only by ceasing to be' (1979: 132). This is in total contrast to Nisbet's definition discussed earlier, where 'ceasing to be' would mean a loss of identity and therefore would not constitute change. Bahm argues that change is interdependent with the concept of permanence, the two notions being complementary and polarly related. He suggests that for change to have occurred there has to be an element of permanence to it. Otherwise change becomes an instantaneous thing, where any difference or alteration created immediately ceases to exist. On the other hand, impermanence and temporality are required for change to occur in the first place. He goes on to examine change as the product of cause and effect relationships, emphasising that change can be conceptualised as multilevel causality over time.

Widaman (1991) explores various ways of representing and measuring change within the field of psychology, making a distinction between qualitative and quantitative changes. The former he defines as 'change in the organized form of behaviour that the subject exhibits' (Widaman, 1991: 205). Quantitative changes, on the other hand, are viewed more in terms of the analysis of static differences. However, there can be a degree of interdependence between the two definitions, with qualitative changes being expressed in terms of relationships between quantitative changes. Nonetheless, Widaman acknowledges that the distinction between qualitative and quantitative change is not clear and poses several exploratory questions as to the nature of change: 'How are we to conceive of change? What changes? Why does change occur? How does change occur? How much change occurs?' (Widaman, 1991: 205). He concludes that much research into change is reductionist, examining variations in specific parts and relationships of a system and from the results trying to infer something about the nature of change at the level of the whole.

In an examination of change within human behaviour, Nesselroade (1991) has stated that 'change can (and should) be defined across a complex of observations, the dimensionality and nature of which are carefully chosen to reflect the various phenomena of interest to the investigator' (Nesselroade 1991: 93). In attempting to define change, he makes two interesting distinctions. The first is between change and variability: that is, those changes which are relatively permanent and those which are more short-term reversible fluctuations. Nesselroade describes variability as constant background noise or steady state 'hum' which constitutes minor fluctuations around some basic state or condition, but does not constitute change, for example, human moods. The second examines slow, more regular change that is typified by learning and development, for example, trait and character change. This notion of background noise change will be returned to in Chapter 7.

Discussing the concept of change from the perspective of the historian, Krieger (1992) defines change in terms of purpose. He denies that there is or ever has been some coherent, progressive purpose to change, defining it as 'a sequence of way-ward accidents, each subject only to local forces and not a rationalized, timeless pattern' (Krieger, 1992: 12). In analysing major change throughout history, there are certainly change events which could arguably be described as purposeless in the sense that they were not designed or planned with specific goals to be achieved: for example, the climatic changes which brought about the ice age, the evolution of language and social behaviour, or the advent of the Great Plague in England (Bell, 1994). On the other hand, the rise and fall of empires or the advancement of technology over the centuries could be classed as purposeful – the result of human ambition, intellect and creative ability. This issue of purpose highlights the distinction between planned and designed change on the one hand, and arbitrary, unexpected change on the other.

A physical science perspective on change

The concept of change within the physical sciences has been significantly influenced by the prevailing scientific world view. The perceptions Newton had of the universe were markedly different to those of Einstein and his contemporaries in the so-called quantum age. As Davies (1980: 21) has noted, 'Newton's mechanics is a description of change, the reorganisation of the world according to the passage of time.' Quantum theory, on the other hand, has no room for the notion of universal time, and the concept of change takes on a new identity, becoming inherently indeterministic and associated with uncertainty. Table 5.2 highlights the main differences between these two perspectives:

The shift in thinking is quite dramatic. The view of the world swings from being objectivist to individualist. With quantum theory comes the realisation that change at a microscopic level cannot be understood, examined or measured 'independently'. As Prigogine has noted:

> Quantum mechanics is a microscopic theory in the sense that it was introduced with the primary purpose of describing the behaviour of atoms and molecules. Thus, it is surprising that it has led to the questioning of the relation between the micro world we seek to observe and the macro world to which we ourselves and our measuring devices belong.
>
> (Prigogine 1980: 48)

It is the author's belief that the new way of thinking associated with quantum theory has not yet been fully accepted by the systems and organisation theory communities – particularly with regard to the notion of change. Zohar (1990)

Table 5.2 Quantum versus Newtonian perspectives of change

Newtonian view of change	Quantum view of change
• Change is deterministic and predictable assuming initial conditions are known.	• Knowledge of initial conditions is *not* sufficient to predict change.
	• Quantum laws only permit prediction based on probabilities about possible outcomes.
• Chance = ignorance of initial conditions	• Chance = genuine unpredictability
• Describes reality assuming the observer is independent of the phenomenon being observed and measured.	• Describes reality assuming the observer is *not* independent of the phenomenon being measured.
• Assumes a closed universe.	• Assumes an open universe.
• Past, present and future are clearly definable in the 'now'.	• No concept of universal time – past, present or future.
• Change at the macroscopic level governed by Newton's laws.	• Change at the macroscopic level approximately concurs with Newton's laws.
• No concept of irreversible change.	• Irreversible change believed to occur.
• Change at the microscopic level assumed to be governed by Newton's laws.	• Change at the microscopic level proved *not* to be explained by Newton's laws.

has made a useful start in applying basic quantum concepts to social and organisational behaviour, exploring the conceptual implications of quantum indeterminism: 'At the level of analogy, quantum physics is rich with imagery that almost begs application to the experiences of daily life' (Zohar, 1990: 4).

Wheatley (1992) has also suggested some interesting parallels between quantum mechanics and human behaviour. However, much remains to be done. Certainly, the open system concept has been embraced with its notions of complexity and dynamical behaviour. Nonetheless, the interconnected and problematic issues of measurement, micro–macro levels of description and irreversibility have yet to be given adequate attention. In attempting to understand fully the nature of change, both in natural inanimate systems and human activity systems, these concepts have much to offer. Recognising their existence and building them into the fabric of our models of change will make them more representative of the phenomenon they attempt to describe. Some of the change phenomena examined in later chapters will explore these ideas further.

Prigogine (1980, 1981) has examined the nature of change in the physical sciences, particularly physics. He outlines three basic descriptions, or levels of change: macroscopic, stochastic and dynamic change in an attempt to unravel the concept of irreversibility. At the macroscopic level, most interactions are linear; small fluctuations at the micro level average out for large systems, and a normal probability distribution applies. At the stochastic level, interactions tend to be non-linear. Instabilities arise as fluctuations at the micro level and are amplified, leading to multiple bifurcation points within the system. The Central Limit theorem as it applies to a normal probability distribution breaks down. Finally, at the dynamic level change is described by classical quantum mechanics, with all conceivable states of the system and outcome probabilities being considered within a single defined phase or possibility space.

These levels offer graduated descriptions of the complexity and nature of change. Accordingly, micro level change can be averaged out and not affect higher levels (macroscopic), or it can be amplified resulting in change at higher, macro levels (stochastic). Prigogine's work highlights different levels of change activity, and some of the defining characteristics of each level.

In Jantsch's (1980a) exploration of the basic principles of evolutionary dynamics, he also distinguishes between three types of change:

- *Ontogeny*: 'the evolution of any coherent system through a sequence of space–time structures. The logical process of organisation remains largely the same'. For example, the non-sexual reproduction of bacteria through horizontal gene transfer, with no separation of generations.
- *Phylogeny*: 'any coherent sequence of ontogenies implying a change in the logical process organisation. There may be repeated branching into a multiplicity of such sequences'. For example, the growth and expansion of cities over time.
- *Anagenesis*: 'the evolution of evolutionary dynamics, bringing into play new levels of evolving systems'. This he describes as *metaevolution*, a kind of recursive dynamics which occurs across different scales of analysis. For example, the transition of subatomic particles from independent entities to atomic nuclei, to atoms and to molecules.

In his discussion of change concepts, Jantsch makes a clear distinction between evolution and growth, the latter being merely a 'multiplication of the same space–time structure' (Jantsch, 1980a: 86). Here, change as evolution has the potential for core structure alteration, whereas change as growth does not. Elsewhere, Jantsch highlights the multidimensionality of change and states: 'Change, increasing in an absolute sense, occurs not only vertically, in a historical time, but also horizontally, in a multitude of simultaneous process' (Jantsch, 1980b: 256).

As previously mentioned, one of the earliest descriptions of change within physical systems is Newtonian mechanics: the reorganisation of reality according to the flow of time (Davies, 1980). Newton's equations of motion represent a model of change for macroscopic bodies:

- change in position relative to some origin point (displacement);
- change of displacement (velocity);
- change of velocity (acceleration).

Note that each is a subset of, and contains the previous change, in a recursive manner. In mathematical terms, all are vector quantities, that is, the change has two components: magnitude and direction. Although Newton's equations of motion only apply to one dimensional kinematic scenarios – where motion is in a straight line and has uniform acceleration – they do define some basic aspects of change:

- Change occurs at a certain rate.
- Change occurs according to the passage of time.
- Change can have a recursive quality to it.
- Change can have both a magnitude and a direction.

Prompted possibly by the conceptual advances made by quantum theory, Trifogli (1993) has examined what he calls the instant of change: the moment in time when 'two successive temporal parts join' (Trifogli, 1993: 93). He explores the concept of change within the framework of continuous time and ponders what constitutes the intrinsic duration of a given change. Is it possible for an entity, in changing from one state (or condition) to another, simultaneously to coexist in both states at the moment of change, or is there some instant during which it is in neither the original state or the destination state? He defines this duration as 'divided into two contiguous motions, and within them both a last instant of the first condition and a first instant of the later are given' (Trifogli, 1993: 107).

Trifogli's work highlights one of the most problematic aspects of change: attempting to determine where the change begins and ends over a given time scale *t*. While this is partly a philosophical question, it does raise an important measurement issue. The inability to measure at *every value* of *t* means that determining the instant of the change is inherently difficult within certain systems. To use a photographic metaphor, however advanced a camera is, it is only capable of capturing a finite number of frames per second. There are values of *t*, and locations on the time–space continuum which exist between those frames, and within which change events can take place 'unobserved'. The camera may never lie but, like the human eye, it can also never capture the total stream of events which fall within the view of the lens, because they are taking place outside the time frame of the camera. This is similar to Foucalt's argument that deep, slow-moving processes of change within social systems often lie undetected partly as a result of inappropriate measurement tools.

'Logic demands that for an organisation to remain viable in the long term, it must ensure all internal changes ultimately support long-term survival in the environment in which it operates.'

Thom (1975) has explored the paradox of change and stability in nature. He argues that, historically, the role of science appears to have been to reconcile this apparent contradiction by removing indeterminism from our understanding of change phenomena. This is partly a perception issue, with stability occurring at one time scale or level of analysis, and change occurring at another. Thom's work highlights this and explores examples of 'change of form' in an attempt better to understand it. Nonetheless, it is possible for change and stability to co-exist on the same scale, and this presents difficulties for planned change management within social systems such as organisations. In 1997, British Airways undertook one of the most high-profile organisation image changes in corporate history. To say that it was logistically challenging would be an understatement. Meticulously planned for, prepared to the last detail, the change was not just an event that happened at a moment in time. While the new image was revealed with much publicity, repainting an entire fleet of aircraft in the new logo designs was estimated to take five years. Running an airline and keeping existing customers satisfied with an acceptable level of service while converting the entire fleet into the new livery is a good illustration of change and stability in action. Running the local corner shop while you convert it into a hypermarket, and still keeping your regular customers happy, is another way to put it. This is one defining attribute of a transition: being able to hold one element constant to preserve identity and continuity within the organisation, while changing some other element – and in so doing maintaining a creative tension between stability and change.

Advances in theoretical physics since Einstein have led Bohm (1957, 1978, 1980) to propose a conceptual scheme which views change and flux as the hidden foundation to the physical reality which we experience. He refers to this as the *implicate order*, and argues that it gives rise to the *explicate order* of perceivable events, objects and processes which we encounter in everyday existence. Not unlike Heraclitus, Bohm argues that within the explicate order, stability and 'solidness' are illusions which spring from a quantum world of continual flux, uncertainty and discontinuous change. The subatomic particles of which matter is composed are all at various stages of birth and decomposition into yet smaller and more short-lived entities, whose fleeting existence give the appearance of stone, water and flesh, etc. As Bohm expresses it:

> The notion of continuity of existence is approximated by that of very rapid recurrence of similar forms, changing in a simple and regular way (rather as a rapidly spinning bicycle wheel gives the impression of a solid disc, rather than a sequence of rotating spokes). Of course, more fundamentally, the particle is only an abstraction that is manifest to our senses. *What is* is always a totality of ensembles, all present together, in an orderly series of stages of enfoldment and unfoldment, which intermingle and inter-penetrate each other in principle throughout the whole of space.
>
> (Bohm, 1980: 183)

Other theorists in the fields of particle and quantum physics – including Nobel laureate, B.D. Josephson (Josephson *et al.*, 1985; Josephson, 1990) – have proposed a similar view of reality, arguing that change is not a phenomenon of the world in which we live, but rather gives form, shape and substance to it.[5] According to this view, researchers should be seeking to identify and understand the underlying dynamics of flux and change upon which physical reality is based.

Summary

This chapter has explored some of the philosophical debates and stances concerning change, providing a context within which to explore further the nature of change in the rest of this book. It has also reviewed briefly some of the diverse viewpoints and definitions for change which have emerged within the social and physical sciences. Of necessity, the selection of authors and aspects of change considered in this chapter have been limited. Nonetheless, it is hoped they do provide a diversity of description and opinion, and give the reader cause to ponder their own conception of change.

A number of recurring themes become evident from this very limited cross-discipline foray into change and how it is perceived. These are summarised in Table 5.3.

Associated with these themes, a number of measurement issues can be drawn out from the chapter (Table 5.4).

These distinctions are important for anybody attempting to measure change within organisations. The challenge facing consultants, researchers and managers alike is to become capable of discerning when, for example, a change has started and when it has ended; or knowing when something of substance has changed and not being lured by frenetic activity and background noise. The announcement by the CEO on 1 January of a new organisation chart to lift the business, containing some new faces and a few amended reporting lines, may constitute a change of sorts. But what has really changed? At some levels of analysis and for most employees, nothing changes at that point in time. However, a year later the leadership style of the new managers and the additional relationships created by the new reporting lines could potentially have transformed the fortunes of the business. It is only then that the desired changes in staff morale, expectations and behaviour would become evident.

Table 5.3 Emerging themes from Chapter 5

- The role and position of the observer relative to the change phenomenon.
- The multi-level nature of change and interconnected levels of analysis.
- Historical time as the continuum upon which change may or may not be said to occur.
- The dialectic of change and stability and the tension this generates.
- The teleology of change, and extent to which a given change is regarded as purposeful or purposeless.
- The deterministic and non-linear qualities of change.
- The 'degree' and extent of a given change, and how this is described or labelled.

Table 5.4 Measurement distinctions facing the change practitioner

• Mere motion, activity and movement	• Actual structural, behavioural or process change
• The start of a given change	• The end of that change
• The *reality* of underlying flux and dynamics within a system	• The *illusion* of apparent stability and solidity that it can create at other levels
• The background noise of reversible, impermanent changes	• The slow, irreversible, deep-moving changes which are more durable

Our measurement tools clearly need to become more sophisticated if we are to monitor, manage and shape change better through planned interventions. The same holds true for researchers undertaking longitudinal studies, perhaps observing without direct involvement in a change process. Whether it is through survey feedback instruments, focus groups or structured interviewing, we must be thinking deeper and broader in our measurement and detection of change within organisations. Against the backdrop of the somewhat philosophical examination of change made in this chapter, the next four chapters explore a selection of change phenomena and core concepts. Many of the themes and issues raised here will be seen at work within the natural and physical world as we examine some specific examples.

6 Building blocks of change
Part 1: The basics

How do we come to think of things, rather than processes in this absolute flux? By shutting our eyes to successive events. It is an artificial attitude that makes sections in the stream of change, and calls them things. . . . Life is no thing or state but a continuous movement or change.

(Radhakrishnan, 1925: 155)

Introduction

Having looked at a range of change perspectives and definitions up to this point, we shall now attempt to pull together many of the ideas and common themes into a number of building blocks. It must be stressed that the building blocks being proposed in the following chapters are by no means considered complete, comprehensive or fully defined. Collating together recurring themes, issues and unifying ideas about change is an enormous undertaking, and this text can only but scratch the surface. Nonetheless, they do offer considerable insight into the nature of change at a generic level, and together constitute a powerful analytical frame of reference with which to explore organisational change specifically. In keeping with the ideals of General Systems Theory discussed in Chapter 2, many of the building blocks have their roots in change phenomena from other subject areas – principally the physical sciences. Where this is the case, a brief technical description of the phenomenon will be given to provide some technical context.

Figure 6.1 illustrates all the building blocks to be covered in the next four chapters. As can be seen highlighted, this chapter takes a look at sources, types and foci of change – arguably the most basic and foundational aspects of change. Along the way we shall also look briefly at change methodology as a means of achieving planned change.

Sources and causes of change

There has long been a debate about whether causal links for change can be identified and traced at all levels of analysis, particularly with the rise of quantum mechanics. However, regardless of the measurement and philosophical issues, logically change has to be caused by some agent or interrelationship, whether or

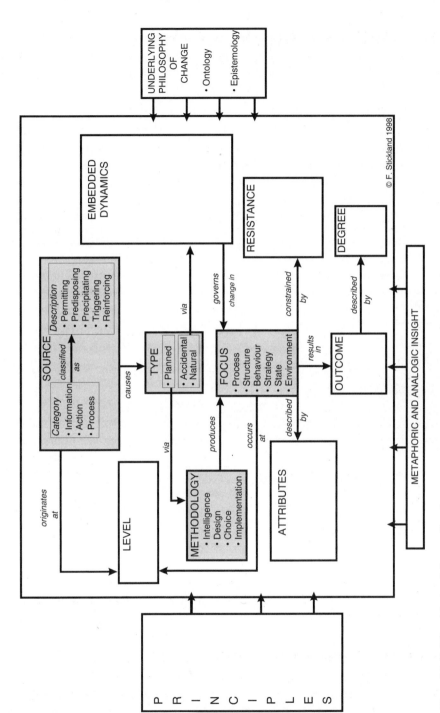

Figure 6.1 Building blocks of change: Part 1

not it can be identified and manipulated. Sources and causes of change have traditionally been classified as originating inside the system or outside the system as Van de Ven and Poole (1987) have noted. Certainly within social systems, this internal–external distinction stems historically from the nature versus nurture debate within biology and other life sciences. To what extent does the environment drive changes within a system and to what extent is the system in control of its own change processes? Nisbet (1970) has traced this debate back through philosophy and the life sciences, discussing in detail the implications for understanding change – particularly within social systems. As we saw in the previous chapter, changes within a system can be categorised in two ways: those which are driven by influences from outside, and those which are generated from within.[1]

Furthermore, incongruencies between reality as it actually exists and reality as it is perceived to be or 'ought to be' can also constitute a major source of change as Drucker (1986) has noted. For example, if our customer survey tells us service levels are poor and sales staff are not listening enough, and we assume the survey is an *accurate reflection of the actual situation*, we will want to improve things. Our vision of how sales staff ought to behave and what the desired level of service should be will cause us to want to close the gap between actual and desired. This is one of the main origins for change in many organisations, and at its heart it assumes an objectivist outlook – that there is a real, commonly agreed situation that can be accurately measured and diagnosed.

It is questionable whether the precise cause(s) of a given change can always be identified – indeed some would argue against such endeavours:

> Arguments over the true or single source of change, while interesting and worthwhile in the sharpening of academic egos, are ultimately pointless. For the analyst interested in the theory and practice of changing, the task is to identify the variety and mixture of causes of change, and to explore through time some of the conditions and contexts under which these mixtures occur.
>
> (Pettigrew, 1990a: 269)

Nonetheless, there may well be occasions when the actual source(s) of change are obvious or can be accurately determined. Also, as Pettigrew rightly suggests, the mixture of causes and sources of change still need to be articulated and clearly defined, even in general terms. Hence the issue of change sources cannot be completely ignored.

'some social systems possess very slow moving, deep change events and processes, that exist far below the gaze of the most discerning eye. These can often pass unobserved until they cause a ripple or change phenomenon on the "surface" of the system at the macro level.'

Given that change sources can originate both inside and outside an organisation, there would appear to be at least three fundamental source categories of change: information, action and process.

Information

Access to and the availability of information can be a cause of change – often unseen and taking place at a micro level between organisational units, or between entire organisations. Rapid information transmission and communication can cause cascading change within large composite systems. For example, the Stock Market crash of October 1987 represented change at a number of levels, including buying behaviour, expectations and confidence, stock structure, financial positions, share price, etc. Such changes have been attributed to the advanced level of information technology, capable of relaying information to traders in different parts of the market virtually simultaneously (see Kamphuis *et al.*, 1988; Skolmli, 1989; Teweles *et al.*, 1992).

Action

This represents a specific act attributable to a particular part of the organisation and locatable at a given fixed moment in time. The ensuing change caused could affect the organisation in which the action originated, or another external to it. For example, the action of terminating a worker's employment will have change repercussions for both the individual concerned and the discharging organisation. Decision-making falls under this category, as it can be seen as both a cognitive act in and of itself, as well as resulting in specific behavioural actions.

Process

This can be defined as a connected series of actions attributable to one or more parts of an organisational system, or the whole, occurring over time. For example, viewed over several years, periodic internal audit reviews within an organisation can be seen as an ongoing process, causing minor incremental changes to working practices and procedures. Similarly, a recruitment process actively to hire new staff to meet a particular psychological profile will eventually have a cumulative affect on the culture of the organisation, as the new people settle in and begin to influence others in the way in which business gets done.

It can be argued that over time there may be a causal link from information to action and on to process. Nonetheless, each category can also represent a specific, individual source of change. Together, they are proposed as a simple analytical base from which to describe both internal and external change sources within organisations. To take this initial classification further, there is a range of ways in which these three change sources can be brought to bear. The build-up to a given change is a critical period and one in which the seeds of the final outcome are often sown. In managing change programmes, the potential for this pre-change phase to have a deep, unseen influence on the nature of the ensuing transition is often overlooked. Let us examine it in more detail.

Drawing from the work of Miller (1993) in clinical psychology, Coleman *et al.* (1984) in behavioural psychology, and Levy (1986) in organisational theory, information, action and process sources of change can each be further described as follows.

Permitting: necessary but not sufficient

These are the factors which must be present in order for the change to happen, but not necessarily sufficient. For example, a given level of experience and operational knowledge is necessary within a particular management role before that manager will feel able to introduce effective changes to working practices and improve performance in his area. Such pre-change honeymoon periods are often only as long as it takes for the permitting factors to come into force.

Predisposing: leanings in the right direction

These are the factors that can increase propensity towards change. For example, a low overall age profile of a workforce may make it easier to restructure the business or introduce radical changes to working practices than a high average age, as younger staff will find it easier to retrain and adapt to a new situation. Identifying and exploiting those variables, which are likely to play in your favour before a change management initiative begins, should be an important first step for any manager planning change.

Precipitating: symptoms to watch out for

These are the factors that directly precede the onset of change. They often manifest themselves as pre-change symptoms. For example, just prior to a top management reshuffle the informal organisational grapevine can begin to hum louder than normal with rumours and speculation. Share prices can rise briefly or take a short tumble. A drop-off in corporate communications from senior management in the weeks immediately before the change is another indicator. Rarely do precipitating factors constitute actual change sources themselves. This category is therefore helpful in distinguishing between what is a cause of change and what is in fact only a pre-change symptom.

Triggering: the straw that breaks the camel's back

These are the factors which actually initiate the change, following the build-up. For example, a memorable speech by the CEO which fires the imagination and endears employees to her can be a turning point in staff motivation, attitudes and morale. A senior management resignation could be all that was needed to activate a long-awaited succession plan, elevating a rising star to a key role in the business.

A major production line breakdown can be the trigger for a major change in the way maintenance schedules are drawn up. Some triggering sources will be planned and others will be just natural or random sources that are part of normal organisational life.

Reinforcing: keeping the show on the road

These are the factors which increase the likelihood of perpetuation following the onset of change. For example, ensuring the effective ongoing roll-out of a new computer system across an organisation will be helped by reinforcing factors such as adequate training, broadcasting success stories ahead of the roll-out from satisfied staff and responsive query handling.

Feedback processes may be at work within and between any of these five descriptions, but particularly in reinforcing change sources where the change in question feeds on itself and external stimuli in order to keep going. Often, sources of change are analysed in an attempt to build up a deterministic model of cause and effect, in the hope that it may yield some predictive utility. Noble as this endeavour is, cause and effect chains are not always identifiable, particularly within social systems and if they are, they are rarely complete. Organisational decision-making based upon the fallacy that such models allow the future to be anticipated and planned for with accuracy is fundamentally misplaced. Nevertheless, this should not be seen as justification entirely to neglect an analysis of change sources. The source categories and descriptions proposed here are intended as a means of stimulating and guiding management enquiry – not in the first instance for facilitating prediction. Taken together, it is hoped that they provide sufficient conceptual variety to begin exploring the complex web of interconnected sources which can combine over time to produce a given change.

> 'There can be a tendency to talk about change only in terms of the business objectives or improved performance that is being sought. Those specific foci which must be changed to achieve these desired outcomes must also form a critical part of the debate when planning change.'

Source examples

Rosabeth Moss Kanter (1984) has identified several forces which she argues are basic sources of change within an organisation. These are worth reviewing briefly as examples of the source categories introduced earlier:

Departures from tradition: precipitating

Staff who challenge the established protocols, circumvent corporate policies or who deviate from the collective preferences and expected behaviour of the organisation can all be signs that something is fundamentally misaligned within the organisation and that change is on the horizon. As we shall see later with change phenomena in the physical world, minor perturbations to the norm such as these at one level can disturb overall equilibrium to the point of causing change at another level. Hence, in some situations the minor perturbation can become an actual change source and not just a pre-change symptom.

Crisis or galvanising event: triggering

Kanter defines those moments in an organisation's history where a response or change is demanded in order to limit damage or maintain corporate viability as coming from both inside and outside the organisation. They often demand a new way of operating or fresh look at how the organisation has traditionally been run. A stock market crash, the loss of a key supplier or the sudden revolt by the production workforce over health and safety will all force a re-examination of the business. Subsequently, change is rarely far away.

Strategic decisions: permitting

When senior management vision and leadership produce a 'top–down' statement of where the organisation should be heading and how it is going to get there, Kanter argues it is often at this point that potential sources for change originating at lower levels are given the legitimacy and energy they need to prevail. It is here that the strategy planning process finally acknowledges the 'departures from tradition' or the crisis that has yet to happen – and seeks to harness the potential they represent by building them into some strategic statement or action plan. However, while strategic decisions are a necessary component of achieving large-scale corporate change, they are certainly not sufficient on their own. Hence they are a good example of a permitting source.

Individual prime movers: predisposing

These are the personnel in positions of authority who are able to help transform the change idea into a changed reality. The management literature has long recognised the importance of champions who will doggedly push through an initiative and make it happen. For many, this is one of the essential criteria for holding a leadership position.

Action vehicles: reinforcing

These are the means by which the change idea actually starts to get implemented. Kanter talks of integrating and institutionalising mechanisms which reiterate the change message, demonstrate commitment to it and help bring the cynics on board.

This first building block of sources is foundational to our understanding of change. A number of techniques from the field of systems dynamics such as signed digraph and causal loop modelling can be helpful in gaining an understanding of the various sources of change present in a given situation.[2] Diagnosing these before introducing one's own changes into the situation is an essential step in change management and should be an integral part of the planning phase. At the same time, there needs to be a clear definition of what new sources will be brought to bear on the situation and how these will interact with those already present.

Types of transition: did he jump, was he pushed or did he fall?

The second basic building block we shall consider is change type. Organisational changes typically fall into two basic types. These are defined by the degree of conscious intervention and predictability they each engender: *planned* and what we shall call *natural* change.

Orchestrating the future: planned change

Planned change constitutes a deliberate and premeditated intervention designed to alter some aspect of organisational life. Planned change endeavours are usually achieved via some methodology, whether it be explicit or implicit. Oliga (1990: 161) has defined a methodology as 'a method of methods that examines systematically and logically the aptness of all research tools', that is, how a given set of problem-solving techniques, methods and modes of inquiry are ordered and applied to a particular target domain. Planned change usually involves some methodological approach or set of steps which the change initiator will go through. These are often explicit and predefined, as in, for example, Total Quality Management approaches to change. Airport book stalls groan under the weight of 'Seven Steps To Successful Change' type books. There is undoubtedly a need for some shape and rigour to any change intervention. In general, methodologies typically go through four broad stages, identified by Simon (1960) as essential planned methodological activities:

- *Intelligence*: identifying, defining, shaping and structuring problems – understanding the context of the planned change.
- *Design*: generation and synthesis of alternative options, solutions and designs – designing the content alternatives of the planned change.
- *Choice*: decision-making to compare, assess and choose between the alternatives generated – deciding upon the change option to implement.
- *Implementation*: bringing about the change decided upon and making it happen, followed by monitoring and feedback to assess how successful the change was – making adjustments where necessary.

As Chapter 3 highlighted, methodologies for achieving planned organisational change can take many forms. At a general level, Burrell and Morgan (1979) have identified two underlying philosophical stances with which to describe intervention methodologies in the social sciences: *nomothetic* and *ideographic*. Here we shall consider them in terms of their implications for understanding the nature of change.

Nomothetic methodologies for effecting change are based on the identification of similarities and patterns within a system. Once identified, they become the basis for generating change options and alternatives, from which a 'best fit' decision can be taken. Such approaches embody a belief that an optimal change strategy exists which must be found. Therefore, the design phase is often preoccupied with seeking to identify the optimal, 'correct' change action to pursue. Of necessity, this clearly requires a unitary world view: the key players involved all see the change problem in the same way and agree on the objectives that have been set. Rigorous analysis of the various options for achieving the desired change is considered vital. The concept of change associated with this somewhat objectivist methodological position is one of direct 'interference' with the organisational system, involving analytical disassembly in a hard, reductionist manner.

Within social systems, methodologies associated with systems engineering such as Hall (1962) and Jenkins (1969) can be described as nomothetic. An organisation like NASA is an extreme example of how to deal with change in a nomothetic manner. To put a man on the moon and bring him home again requires a methodological rigour rarely encountered in normal organisational life. As many change contingencies as possible are considered with a range of responses being pre-planned. The thinking is very linear with cause and potential effect chains being planned for in enormous detail. Nothing that can be planned for is left to chance. Nomothetic methodologies for managing change usually imply a clear, unambiguous goal and purpose – which is commonly agreed by all the stakeholders involved.

Manufacturing and engineering communities have historically favoured a nomothetic methodological approach. Organisation and Methods (O&M) finds its roots in such principles,[3] as to some extent does Business Process Reengineering as an approach to organisational change. Other examples include many of the structured problem-solving methodologies from Operational Research and System Dynamics, and some of the social engineering approaches described by the National Science Foundation (1972), Boguslaw (1965) and Hoos (1976). Common targets for change with such methodologies would be organisation structure, work flow, information technology platforms or operational procedures.

An ideographic methodological approach places great emphasis on human relationships, perceptions and softer aspects of change within an organisation. Pluralist viewpoints abound and the approach towards managing or analysing change is more qualitative. Methodologies of this kind seek to drive change through the exploration and resolution of differences of opinion, paradox, contradiction and ambiguity: see, for example, Quinn and Cameron (1987). Instead of seeking to eradicate uncertainty from a potential change situation, an ideographic approach would actively seek to harness the uncertainty and use it to full advantage in managing the actual change. These methodologies tend to target for change things like organisation culture, leadership style or cross-functional communication flows between departments.

Peter Checkland's Soft Systems Methodology is a good example of an approach to organisational change which is founded on ideographic assumptions, where differences in opinion about how the organisation is viewed and what should change are actively sought. Other examples include Mason and Mitroff's (1981) Strategic Assumption Surfacing and Testing (based upon the work of Churchman, 1979), and to a lesser degree the more recent approaches of Soft Operational Research (see, for example, Lane, 1993; Forrester, 1994). It is worth noting that ideographic methodologies tend to be more systemic in nature with their focus on relationships and emergent properties at the level of the whole, while nomothetic methodologies favour a reductionist approach and are more systematic in nature.

Navigating the possibility space: natural change

The second type of organisational change proposed here is natural change. That is, an unengineered indigenous change consistent with the life cycle of an organisation.[4] As an organisation moves forward in pursuit of whatever strategy it has set itself, certain events and opportunities arise unlooked for. At best these only require a mid-course correction to be dealt with. At worst, they may demand a radical rethink of the way the business operates, for example, the sudden resignation by a middle manager. If the human resource department does not have a succession plan in place, that part of the business is likely to suffer a minor setback in productivity until the new person is appointed and becomes familiar with the role.

An important question for us here is the extent to which natural change can be predicted or whether it can be totally unexpected.

Buffeted by chance: accidental or predictable

To what extent an organisational change is an expected, logical and predictable event, or alternatively the result of 'random' interaction is worth considering for a moment. Being able to predict the successful conclusion of a hostile takeover bid, or the detrimental effect of changing the way in which employee bonuses are calculated is vital management information. Allen (1981) has suggested that there are certain types of change process which involve both random and deterministic mechanisms, citing examples in economics, urban development and international relations. These have been referred to as 'order by fluctuation' change phenomena (Nicolis and Prigogine, 1977). Leading up to the change, the system follows deterministic laws until immediately prior to the transition where triggering random fluctuations and stochastic mechanisms within the system take over, shaping the nature and direction of the ensuing change.

There are several issues here. First, there is the question of true randomness. Can a given organisational change ever be considered inherently unpredictable and random or is it merely considered random due to the complexity of inter-actions and the observers' inability to note cause and effect? Within the physical sciences the latter view was held for several hundred years from Newton until the advent of quantum mechanics. It was believed that 'the world cannot *change* in any way; the available paths for development are constrained to those that conform to the laws' (Davies, 1980: 22). In principle, observational inadequacy and the inability to measure accurately were seen as the reasons for apparent randomness. Even Einstein believed that it was ignorance of actual, true causes which give the impression that certain actions are random and that people have free will (Einstein and Besso, 1972).

Now, however, progress in the field of quantum theory has demonstrated that at the level of the atom, change does not occur in such a deterministic way. Heisenberg's famous Uncertainty Principle has been influential in reinforcing this new view. According to one prominent school of thought known as the Copenhagen Interpretation (after Niels Bohr, 1948), the role of the observer and system interventions to measure and extract information, cannot help but change the system itself. Consequently, as one physicist has noted 'the relevant entity to consider is always *system observed plus measuring instruments*, so that a change in the disposition of the measuring instruments, even without a change in the system observed, is considered to create a totally new situation' (Polkinghorne, 1984: 93). While the Hawthorne studies (Roethlisberger and Dickson, 1939) demonstrated that a similar phenomenon can occur within social settings and organisational systems, the full implications of this for human activity systems generally have yet to be fully explored. Chaos theory has also shown that dynamic feedback mechanisms within non-linear complex systems can produce apparent random-ness in behaviour, where the ability to note cause and effect is lost in the continual flux of dynamic and chaotic processes (see Bai-Lin, 1984).

The second issue relevant to the predictability question concerns the effect of the passage of time in obscuring the causes and sources of a given change phenomenon. Context and history may hide cause–effect chains leading up to the eventual change under layers of events. As we have seen, Pettigrew (1987a) argues that when analysing change within organisations, one must be aware of the extent to which the change is embedded within some environmental context – which must be fully explored, if the dynamics of the change itself are to be adequately understood.

Third, some social systems possess very slow moving, deep change events and processes (Foucault, 1972), that exist far below the gaze of the most discerning eye. These can often pass unobserved until they cause a ripple or change phenomenon on the 'surface' of the system at the macro level. Because no obvious cause–effect chain can be established, the phenomenon is likely to be described as 'random' when in fact it could well be deterministic in nature. The development and emergence of organisational culture, brand image or collective customer expecta-tions are possible examples of this within organisations. The fields of archaeology, seismology, cosmology, history and climatology also exhibit such slow-moving change phenomena, which require enormous elongations in time frame for analysis to capture the causal links and build up to the eventual observable change event. It is therefore possible that what may appear to be random change in the short term, may be shown to have been 'predictable' with hindsight when the cause and effect links have become apparent.

Fourth, a distinction is made here between the occurrence of random sources of change and random entity change. A random disturbance from the environment can set off deterministic change within an organisation in response. For example, an unexpected rise in the number of finished products failing quality checks will cause the production line manager responsible to commence established and prearranged root-cause diagnostic routines – possibly resulting in a change of component materials somewhere down the supply chain, or a re-engineered production process. The external source triggers a reflex response which results in a planned and deterministic change. Conversely, a perfectly predictable environmental source can trigger a series of random, indeterministic changes within an organisational system. Take, for example, the detonation by France of a nuclear device in Polynesia in September 1995. Although preannounced and publicised several weeks in advance, this caused a series of unpredicted behaviours such as public disorder, looting and violent protests in the short term and political isolation, diplomatic upheaval and even foreign policy changes during the months that followed. Even more traumatic, perhaps, is the year 2000 problem for many IT managers. Failure to adjust the way in which computers store a year date, from two digits to four digits, will potentially cause untold disruption and upheaval to management information systems and customers at the turn of the century. A known and predictable change source resulting in unpredictable change – from customer behaviour through to organisational state and viability.

Chapter 7 will explore in more detail some of the dynamics that drive natural change, embedded deep within the organisation.

Subject to time scale, the two types of change we have looked at here – planned and natural – can be considered either *melioristic*, leading to negative entropy (Schrodinger, 1944; Kast and Rosenzweig, 1970) and self-organising behaviour, or *pejoristic*, leading to disorder and entropic decline. Within social systems such as organisations the emphasis is on effecting changes which are deemed beneficial and in the best interests of the system. From an individualist viewpoint, however, these are essentially value judgements placed upon a given change; descriptive labels which attempt to associate the implications of the change with the future state of the organisation. At an objectivist level such descriptions are meaningless. Of concern here is whether the change has pushed the system towards disorganisation or structural cohesiveness and order. Any attribution of value judgements must be based around clear viability criteria: is the change likely to affect long-term viability or will it increase system viability over time? For an organisation, such viability criteria could be based on such things as revenue generation capability; low cost base; effective command and control structure; or efficient process flows.

Stacey (1993) has argued that the optimum positioning for an organisation is one where it can operate at the boundary between order and chaos:

> If the organisation gives in to the pull to stability it fails because it becomes ossified and cannot change easily. If it gives in to the pull to instability it disintegrates. Success lies in sustaining an organisation in the borders between stability and instability.
>
> (Stacey, 1993: 245)

At this point, it is open to both melioristic and pejoristic change – either type being of potential benefit and capable of increasing the organisation's viability, depending upon the options and choices facing management at a given point in time. Viewed in this manner, pejoristic change must not be seen as inherently bad or undesirable. On the contrary, it may be necessary to introduce an element of disorganisation and structural weakness in order to encourage creativity and innovation. Any management consultant who has been asked to examine a research and development department will have discovered this challenging paradox.

This is where organisational change practitioners need to be thinking ahead. A given change will either support the strategic direction of the business or it will not. It is either appropriate, given the purpose and objectives set by senior management, or it is dysfunctional. Alignment between strategic intent and the change in question is therefore vital. Misapprehending can spell disaster for the long-term future of an organisation.

The change focus: what actually changes

The focus of change is that part or aspect of a system upon which the change is centred or has its main impact and primary domain of influence: i.e. that which is changing. Several generic foci are suggested in this section with examples: structure, process, behaviour, strategy, environment, state.

Organised resource: structure

Organisation structure is perhaps one of the most common targets for change. The concept of organisation structure here is more than just names in boxes on a traditional organisation chart. It has to do with how a business is held together: the various configurations of people, communication channels, job roles, skills and relationships within an organisation which give it internal shape and coherence. For example, within the system of UK government, the infrastructure of local government is comprised of councils and local authorities; within a commercial organisation structure can denote functional division as well as chains of command and communication. Whether it represents spans of control, autonomous versus fully integrated business units, centralised versus decentralised operation or status-driven hierarchies, organisational structure has long been an established focus for change.

Transcending the boundaries: process

Processes have traditionally been seen as sequences of related activities within an organisation which transform inputs into outputs. In recent years this has been the domain of business process re-engineering (BPR) type change projects. For instance, within a manufacturing organisation there will be a product manufacturing process involving activities of product design, raw material procurement, product construction and assembly, packaging, distribution and sales. Such a process will typically cross several hierarchical functions, delivering some output for the end customer. Interactions with customers are often documented in process terms – the classic example being that of dealing with an insurance claim: see Figure 6.2. The wandering line charts the process for handling a customer's insurance claim following a house fire. The BPR concept of process has traditionally been very narrow, typically focusing on the items listed on the right-hand side of Table 6.1. The left-hand side shows some of the softer aspects essential to the effective working of a business process.

Table 6.1 Business processes – where hard meets soft

The hard side of process	*The soft side of process*
• Task sequencing	• Vital cultural dependencies
• Data/information flows	• Process 'memory'/corporate experience
• Ergonomics	• Core people competencies and skills
• Activity-based costing	• Acknowledgement of staff needs and aspirations
• Workflow and IT infrastructure	• Understanding of service performance expectations of customers

Other types of process that are often the target of change include:

- *Communication processes* for disseminating information and knowledge around the organisation. These can be formal information technology or procedure driven processes, as well as more informal, unarticulated processes such as the grapevine and customer feedback, or the unspoken messaging process conveying image, power posturing, leadership and management style.
- *Management processes* govern how decisions get made and the allocation of work and resources. At higher levels they will involve policy setting and environment monitoring. Further down at middle management or supervisory levels, they will be more concerned with other things such as co-ordination, project management and staff monitoring.
- *Learning processes* which shape how an organisation learns from its past through its customers, its competitors and its staff. Traditionally this has been where survey–feedback tools, staff appraisals and continuous improvement regimes

Dealing with an insurance policy claim

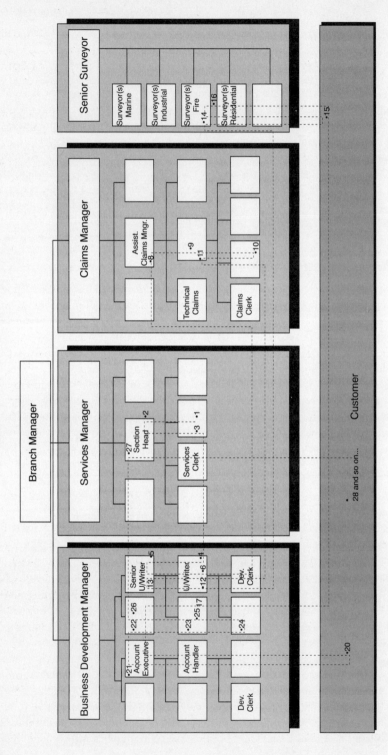

Figure 6.2 A simple business process flow

such as Total Quality Management (TQM) have sought to harness and direct the creative potential within the organisation. More recently, concepts such as 'knowledge management', 'soft systems dynamics' and 'action learning' have sought to deepen our conception of organisational learning.

These three types of processes are much harder to identify and change than traditional activity-based processes. They form part of the very fabric of an organisation and can give a business a distinct 'look and feel' from a staff and customer perspective. Nevertheless, they are fundamental to effective operation and need first to be identified and then given periodic health checks thereafter. However one views processes within the organisation, the key requirement is that they are appropriately aligned with the direction and needs of the business, and are helping to make strategic intent a reality.

The human factor: behaviour

The third change focus being proposed here is behaviour. This is defined in terms of patterns of action and reaction within the organisation, at the level of the whole or interactions between individual elements. An obvious example is organisation culture: the collective preference or shared mind set which determines 'the way things get done' day to day. Others examples include individual behaviours such as the manner in which an employee deals with uncertainty, reacts to a demanding customer or treats a new member of staff. Changing consumer buying behaviour or customer expectations are often the focus of much change effort. For our purposes here then, behaviour is an umbrella term for a range of traditional change targets such as values, needs, practices, expectations and attitudes.

Journeying into the future: strategy

Crucial to any organisation are its corporate objectives, strategic goals and the basis on which it will compete in a given market, for example, a market penetration strategy that defines how a business will differentiate itself from competitors. Periodic review of strategic intent is clearly vital for an organisation if it is to stay aligned with market needs and shareholder expectations. The organisational literature is awash with strategy models (see Mintzberg and Quinn, 1996) and it is not appropriate to cover them here.[5] Needless to say, the need to create or adjust strategy over time and occasionally undergo a radical strategic repositioning exercise makes strategy one of the most critical change foci.

The turbulent world outside: environment

At any given moment, most organisations are actively trying to change something in their environment. It could be shareholder expectations, customer buying habits, or something more fundamental such as the future shape and direction of an industry sector. These are largely planned changes with management proactively looking to manage the future of their organisation. On the other hand, an organisation can cause change in its immediate environment without deliberately seeking to engineer it. For example, poor financial results will move the share price; deteriorating performance may trigger a hostile takeover by a competitor. Shell's decision to tow the Brent Spar – a decommissioned oil storage vessel – out into the ocean for disposal caused an enormous reaction from conservationists and public bodies which was both unforeseen and unintentional.

Vital signs: state

All of the change foci suggested so far will – if they do undergo some change – affect the overall state or condition of the organisation. An organisation's state is measured by that set of parameters and variables which define its condition or 'mode' at the level of the whole. Analogous with the state of the human body being determined by parameters such as blood pressure, pulse rate and respiratory rate, an organisation's state is often assessed by such measures as cash flow, annual turnover, share price, return on capital employed, or market share. Taken collectively, a set of macro measures like these will provide some indication of whether changes to other change foci further down have in fact occurred. Kaplan and Norton's (1992, 1996) work on the concept of a Corporate Balanced Scorecard provides a good framework for assessing change at the level of the whole. They propose that an organisation should attempt to set up a measurement regime to monitor organisational performance in four key areas:

- business processes;
- innovation and learning;
- finance;
- customer satisfaction.

Making changes in any of these areas should then be reflected in the measures adopted. Taking the concept of 'state' measurement further, the organisation could have a set of measures across a wider range of change foci, as Figure 6.3 illustrates. Developing measures for assessing change of organisation state which cover structure, processes, behaviour, strategy and targets in the environment would give management a powerful metric and compass for navigating through organisational transformation and managing transition within their business.

These focus categories are somewhat broad, but do capture the main domains of change within the organisation.[6] There is a danger in any planned change initiative that we do not fully articulate what it is we are attempting to change, and perhaps of equal importance, what else is likely to change in the process. All too often in consulting, the author hears phrases like 'we need to re-engineer the organisation to improve business performance' or 'radical transformation is required if this business is to survive in the long term'. There can be a tendency to talk about change only in terms of the business objectives or improved

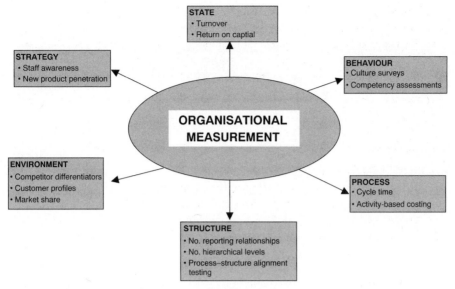

Figure 6.3 Assessing the vital signs of the business: some simple measures

performance that is being sought. Those specific foci which must be changed to achieve these desired outcomes must also form a critical part of the debate when planning change.

Table 6.2 Summary of Chapter 6 building block concepts

Building block	Description	
Sources	*Category*	*Description*
	• Information	Permitting
	• Action	Predisposing
	• Process	Precipitating
		Triggering
		Reinforcing
Types	• Planned	
	• Natural	
	• Accidental	
Foci		
	• Structure	
	• Process	
	• Behaviour	
	• Strategy	
	• Environment	
	• State	

Summary

In this chapter we have examined three basic building blocks deemed to be fundamental to understanding the nature of change: source, type, focus (Table 6.2). None of these in isolation are new concepts. However, they are vital to understand as a basic foundation for probing deeper into the nature and dynamics of change. In the next chapter these building blocks are further added to, with deeper forays into other subject domains being made.

7 Building blocks of change

Part 2: Embedded dynamics

> Consequential relations of nature are infinite in variety and he who is acquainted with the largest number has the broadest basis for the analogic suggestion of hypotheses.
>
> (Gilbert, 1896: 1)

Introduction

This chapter adds a further building block to our understanding of change developed so far. We travel outside established organisational thinking in search of change phenomena from the physical world. From the concepts encountered on this journey, several embedded dynamics of change are developed applicable to organisational life. These are presented as hidden engines of change, driving events and behaviour at micro levels of the organisation, and which often go unnoticed. Figure 7.1 adds embedded dynamics to the building blocks we have considered to this point. A number of writers have alluded to similar dynamics in their own work. So to set the scene we shall review their contributions briefly before moving on to explore some specific examples. For each embedded dynamic proposed a short technical description of the instructing physical change phenomenon is given as background. This is followed by a discussion of the system level and organisational insights that suggest themselves.

Hidden engines of change: embedded dynamics

Within any organisation at a given point in time there are a number of continual shifts and changes playing out at various levels. These are not planned changes with a defined beginning and end, but rather reflect the natural dynamics which take place internally. They constitute embedded dynamics of change and can be said to describe engines of change that form part of the very fabric and identity of an organisation. They are the main drivers of natural change in the sense that they are not consciously planned and controlled. However, they can also be caused by 'accident' as the result of some external disturbance or unexpected internal failure/success. Embedded dynamics of change exist at deep levels within an organisation, operating across more than one hierarchical level. They have the

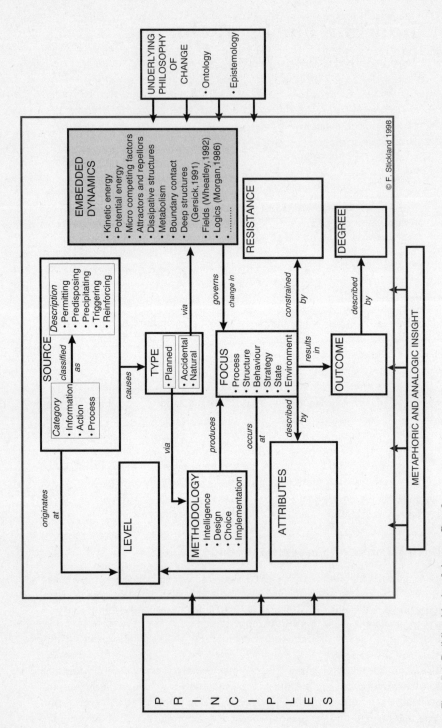

Figure 7.1 Building blocks of change: Part 2

© F. Stickland 1998

potential to significantly influence the effectiveness of any planned change being implemented.

Three organisation theorists mentioned in earlier chapters have proposed similar concepts to the notion of embedded dynamics being advocated here. The first is Gersick (1991) who has developed the concept of *deep structure* in her exploration of the differences between evolutionary and revolutionary change within organisations. Acknowledging deep structures she argues, is essential to understanding the phenomenon of change. She defines them as: 'a network of fundamental, interdependent "choices," of the basic configuration into which a system's units are organized, and the activities that maintain both this configuration and the system's resource exchange with the environment' (Gersick, 1991: 15).

As we saw in Chapter 2, Gersick examines six different knowledge domains and argues that such structures, once well established, determine what changes are permissible within the organisation. These tend to be incremental and evolutionary in nature. For revolutionary change to occur, the deep structure must be altered and broken down, 'leaving the system temporarily disorganised' (Gersick, 1991: 10). In time, new deep structures develop causing change behaviour to settle back into a more sedate, evolutionary pattern. Gersick's research suggests that deep structures represent fundamental drivers and controllers of change within organisations, which are largely implicit, unrecognised and often hidden. More significantly, they are the emergent, natural result of the complex interactions between the elements and relationships within the system.

The second organisation theorist is Gareth Morgan (1986) who advances the concept of *logics of change*. The three logics he suggests – based upon concepts from autopoiesis, cybernetics and dialectics – are primarily targeted at understanding change within social and organisational systems. He argues that they operate at a deep, micro level and underpin the reality of what we observe in everyday life. Like Gersick, he suggests that their origins are fundamentally natural – the emergent, synergistic result of internal tensions, contradictions, feedback loops and self-organising processes within the system.

Third, Wheatley (1992: 49) has taken the notion of *field* from the physical sciences: as in gravitational or magnetic field. This she abstracts metaphorically to a general level, defining fields as 'unseen structures, occupying space and becoming known to us through their effects'. She goes on to apply the field concept direct to organisations, arguing that:

> 'Organisational space can be filled with the invisible geometry of fields. Fields, being everywhere at once, can connect discrete and distant actions. Fields, because they can influence behaviour, can cohere and organise separate events'.

> (Wheatley, 1992: 55)

She gives several examples of such fields within organisations, including corporate vision, culture, common values and ideals. These, she believes, are capable of spreading out across an organisation, shaping and constraining changes that fall within their sphere of influence.

'Identifying the natural and unplanned change dynamics occurring across various foci is vital if an organisation is to self-monitor its operation and effectiveness in a given market.'

Thus the concepts of deep structures, logics and fields which are deeply enmeshed within the life and identity of an organisational system are all akin to the idea of embedded dynamics being proposed here. In keeping with the cross-discipline ideals outlined in Chapter 2, a number of embedded dynamics are suggested which are based on change phenomena in the natural sciences. To maintain a richness of description and show the origins of each, the change phenomena will be described briefly using the vocabulary of the original technical account. The principle at work will then be applied to an organisational setting.

The ties that bind: chemical bonding

Chemical bonds are those interactions or forces between atoms which hold them together to form molecules. The bondings are also capable of holding together ions, atoms and molecules as more complex structures. They can take the form of very weak dipole interactions (e.g. hydrogen bonds), stronger metallic bonds or extremely strong covalent and ionic bondings (Baum and Scaife, 1975). The latter two are of particular interest here and are explained in more detail below.

Covalent bonds

These bonds are formed by two atoms sharing the same pair(s) of electrons. The resulting attraction holds the atoms together. The hydrogen molecule is the simplest example of such bonding.

Ionic bonds

The creation of an ionic bond is generally considered to involve three steps:

*   By acquiring enough energy, an atom can discard one or more electrons to become a *cation* (i.e. a positively charged ion).
*   In a release of energy, an atom can gain one or more extra electrons to become an *anion* (i.e. a negatively charged ion).
*   The electrostatic attraction of the anion and cation results in the formation of an ionic bond.

It is important to note here that the electrostatic interactions in ionic bondings are not specific for any particular direction.

Chemical bonding as a concept can be used metaphorically to shed some light on the nature and magnitude of forces which hold system components together.

Change often involves breaking up existing structures and relationships, and predicting and manipulating the forces that hold them together. To do that effectively, gaining an understanding of what forces are operative at a micro level in a system, and how they are created, should be regarded as essential prior to attempting system change activities.

This will involve identifying what attracts system components to each other. It could be the inequality of some surplus in one and a lack in another – resources being exchanged for mutual benefit, thereby forming an association or relationship of an ionic nature. Bonding of this kind describes decentralised, more fluid types of system structure, where there are few internal rules and procedures dictating what relationships and interactions are permitted (non-directional attraction). System components are free to self-organise and establish links with others as seems most appropriate at the time. As a consequence, such systems will have a shifting and evolving structure, as resource ownership and the allocation of surpluses and deficits fluctuates over time. Examples include social and political affiliations within an organisation, or the growing entity known as the Internet or World Wide Web.

Alternatively, the glue holding two system components together may be based on the sharing of resources which neither possess independently. This covalent type of bonding would typically describe a more hierarchical and centralised type of organisation or system. In such a structure, designing and implementing effect change will involve isolating a communal resource which all system components share. Within an organisation, this could be a set of common values, collective experience or a centralised function like training. One possible strategy for achieving change in such systems may involve developing a substitute to replace the commonality completely, or merely to wean off the system components. This would weaken the unifying bond and make overall change implementation easier to achieve.

At its most fundamental level, this embedded dynamic is based on the phenomenon of chemical bonding, and describes change as competing forces of attraction and repulsion operating at a micro level. The attraction and repulsion between parts of an organisation constitutes a constant background noise of subtle, micro level change. At its core it assumes the existence of surpluses and deficits. These generate a natural competitive tension which can affect the strength of a system's structure, its stability at a macro level and its propensity to change if subject to some environmental jolt.

For example, consider the formation of cross-functional, multidisciplinary teams within traditional hierarchically based organisations. Line managers release resource from their own areas for assignment to such a one-off project team, if they deem the exercise to be of long-term benefit or politically expedient. If the project team falls behind schedule or fails to deliver, there is often pressure for the resource to be recalled. Organisations based upon matrix management structures attract and repel 'free-floating' individuals with specific skills and expertise – who often find themselves pulled between two or more projects. Because matrix structures lack the unity and cohesiveness of command which traditional structures possess (Mintzberg, 1979), resource flow tends to be more fluid between functions and departments. Support, advisory and head office administrative functions can often find themselves the subject of competing calls upon their resource.

Other examples of this embedded dynamic at work include personal relationship networks that grow and proliferate with an employee's length of service; levels of trust and co-operation between business units and departments which ebb and flow over time; and ownership and access to information such as performance data, customer feedback or peer review information. Each of these constitute the basis for a tie or bond within an organisation that will either bring together and reinforce or repel and fragment at the micro level.

Identifying that which binds, liberates and constrains interaction within an organisation should be high on the agenda for any practitioner seeking to initiate a planned change. Failure to do this will at best limit the degree to which the desired change occurs. At worst, the embedded dynamic of micro competing forces could significantly block and frustrate the change.

Boulders on the cliff edge: potential and kinetic energy

Kinetic energy

Simply put, kinetic energy is the energy a body acquires due to its motion through space and time. A boulder falling from a cliff acquires increasing kinetic energy as it falls, reaching a maximum just prior to impact. At an atomic or molecular level this notion is expressed as the Kinetic Theory of Matter, and explains the apparent random motion of particles in a vacuum, commonly known as Brownian motion.

It can be argued that dynamic systems possess energy resulting from their own internal processes, quite apart from any external inputs from the environment. This energy could be defined as an emergent property arising from the complex interactions and strong relationships between the elements of the system. In attempting to manage or predict change within such systems, some attempt must be made to assess the nature and extent of this energy. Planned system intervention could well turn such internal forces to good advantage, making change management and implementation more effective. Conversely, attempts to introduce changes which work against the system's internal forces or inherent 'kinetic energy' may well undermine the viability of the whole. Biological life itself is largely the result of complex biochemical forces and interactions taking place within an organism at a micro level. Disturbance of these can often be detrimental. On the other hand, trying to counter and overcome them in some systems may well be justified. Successfully introducing changes which achieve this will mean gaining beforehand a clear understanding of what kinetic energy barriers need to be overcome, and the effects of doing so.   .

Another useful concept suggested by the concept of kinetic energy is relative motion. The falling boulder possesses kinetic energy relative to the ground. If the ground were moving away from the boulder, the final impact and conversion of energy would be less. The relative motions or tendencies of different parts of an organisation with respect to each other are in constant flux. For example, relationships between departments and levels of trust between individuals are in constant movement. System components taken in their entirety possess a restless energy which is a function of their individual motions relative to each other. Whether it be electrons in an orbit shell, atoms in a lattice structure, commercial organisations in a market sector or share prices on a stock exchange, system elements can possess their own individual momentum with respect to each other that is continually shifting and changing. The effect within the system is to provide a constant background noise of micro level change. The net effect can be neutral for the system as a whole, if the fluctuations stay within broad parameters. On the other hand, the micro level shifts can be amplified and spontaneous self-organisation may occur if certain critical tolerance limits are exceeded. Traditionally, something akin to impact analysis is often undertaken to assess how and to what extent a particular change measure will affect the rest of an organisation. Considering relative motions during impact analysis can add a new dimension to the exercise.

Potential energy

This concept can generally be defined as the energy of charge in an electrical field, or the energy of mass in a gravitational field. Both definitions convey the idea of energy possessed by virtue of position. The former refers to an electrical charge or voltage. The latter is associated with the distance a body could move through space and time under the acceleration due to gravity.

To the physicist this would appear to be only a notional concept of energy. The boulder at the cliff top has a definable quantity of potential energy by virtue of its position. However, as soon as it begins to fall its potential energy decreases, tending to zero as it nears the ground. Strictly speaking, it is converted into kinetic energy, as Figure 7.2 illustrates.

Potential energy implies some tendency towards another position or state, with some associated energy loss. In terms of planned system change, just like kinetic energy it can be argued that the potential energy contained in a particular system state or mode of behaviour needs to be assessed prior to intervention. Similarly, before attempting to predict the nature and outcome of an unplanned change within a system, gaining an understanding of what forces lie latent in the prevailing system configuration is essential. Failure to do this could result in those forces being unleashed when the change action is started – like the boulder falling from the cliff top – as the potential energy is converted into kinetic energy. The end net result could be to inhibit the change measure being implemented or at worst cause significant damage to other elements and relationships within the system.

The embedded dynamic is similar to kinetic energy but this time the energy is latent and a function of relative position between system components. Examples

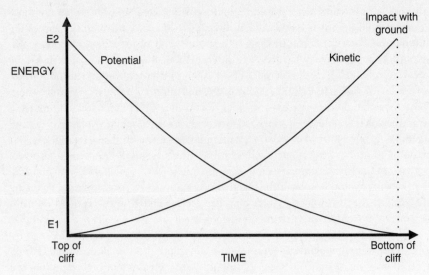

Figure 7.2 Energy associated with change in relative motion and position

of potential energy embedded change dynamics include hierarchy, rank, status and position within organisations and social groups. Often within group dynamics, individual behaviour is a function of who is present at the gathering and how influential they are perceived to be. This latent energy exerts a continual, subtle influence, changing behaviours from what they would otherwise be – all things being equal. It can be argued that what has been described as organisational politics (March, 1962; Pfeffer, 1981; Bower, 1983) is the result of this embedded dynamic of change.

These first three embedded dynamics represent a continual background source of deep level change against which larger transitions and transformation are played out – and sometimes spring from:

- micro level competing forces (chemical bonding);
- motion energy (kinetic);
- position energy (potential).

All three are to a greater or lesser extent a function of structural tension within an organisational system, and can provide the necessary variety (Ashby, 1956) at the micro level to allow creative and innovative behaviour to emerge.

Alcatraz without walls: chaotic repellors and attractors

The field of Dynamical Systems Theory (DST) is concerned with defining mathematically the rules which govern the dynamics of a system over time: 'it is the task of mathematical dynamical systems theory to investigate the patterns of how states change in the long run' (Hirsch, 1984). DST is concerned with both discrete and continuous dynamical systems, as Smale (1967), Guckenheimer and Holmes (1983), Aracil (1986) and Aulin (1987) have demonstrated. One of the fundamental concepts within DST is the notion that systems have *attractors* – that is, one or more states to which the behaviour and trajectory of a system will be drawn and ultimately settle in. These are referred to as structurally stable attractors if they are identifiable even in the presence of external perturbations and internal noise. Associated with attractors is the concept of initial conditions. If an attractor is active within a system, it will pull the system's initial conditions towards it over time. For example, things cool down and lose energy to their environment if left undisturbed. They are 'attracted' to a cold state. To a certain extent, the phenomena of natural ageing and death show an attractor at work, inexorably pulling an organism towards a certain end state. Similarly, swinging pendulums are drawn to a state of rest once isolated. As Swenson (1989) has noted, an attractor can be defined as:

> The time-independent (time-asymptotic) states, or limit sets, that attract initial conditions from regions around them – 'basins of attraction' – during a time dependent process (evolutionary behaviour) as t tends toward infinity. All real world macroscopic change is irreversible and hence governed by attractors, viz., the instability of entropy producing processes. . . . In this sense, all macroscopic change is (i) progressive (goes irreversibly towards an attractor), and (ii) goal driven (the attractor is the goal). The attractor drives the evolutionary behaviour by virtue of the instability of all states within the basin of attraction but off the attractor.
>
> (Swenson, 1989: 189)

More rigorous mathematical definitions of attractors are discussed in the literature (see Thom, 1975; Milnor, 1985; Zeeman, 1986) but the above is sufficient for the purposes of discussion here. As Swenson suggests, the ultimate attractor for all physical systems is thermodynamic equilibrium, where entropy is maximised and the system's identity disappears due to lack of functional structure. However, by far the more frequently occurring over shorter time scales are *emergent attractors*. These are attractors which govern emergent properties and behaviour of a system at the level of the whole, usually through some process of self-organisation.

The DST literature generally discusses three basic types of emergent attractor. The first is a simple *point attractor* which draws the system towards a stable state. For example: a marble in a bowl, whose motion will be drawn to and eventually come to rest at the bottom of the bowl; or homeostatic behaviour in biological systems. Other more complex point attractors have been discussed by Hanken (1983) and Nicolis and Prigogine (1989). Second, there is the limit cycle, closed curve or *periodic attractor* in which there are usually two points of attraction and the behaviour of the system oscillates between them. These have been identified within systems from a range of disciplines including economics (Sterman, 1988), chemistry (Tomita, 1986) and ecology (Toro and Aracil, 1988). The third type is known as a fractal, strange or *chaotic attractor* in which system behaviour appears to be completely random over time. Such systems are very sensitive to changes in initial starting conditions, and minor external or internal disturbances to those conditions in two identical systems can result in very divergent and complex behaviour. However, despite their apparent randomness, chaotic attractors identified to date that cause such non-deterministic behaviour are in fact stable structures which are highly ordered. Popular examples of fractal geometry demonstrate this – self-similar recurring structures in nature like fern leaves, clouds and crystals (see Mandelbrot, 1977; Peitgen and Richter, 1986; Garcia, 1991). In addition, most dynamical systems can possess more than one type of attractor simultaneously.

Zeeman (1988) has demonstrated the existence of *repellors*. That is, unstable states which by definition can never be achieved, as microscopic fluctuations prevent behaviour moving in that direction, driving the system towards an attractor. Conceptually, a repellor can be likened to the apex ridge on top of a roof which slopes off on both sides. Anything falling on the roof will immediately be 'repelled' down one side or the other. According to Zeeman, point and periodic repellors have been shown to exist, but so far no chaotic repellors have been identified.

With respect to understanding the phenomenon of change, attractors and repellors are capable of acting as engines, constantly pulling and pushing a system into different states and modes of behaviour. Imagine an Alcatraz prison with no walls. One would consider escape attempts to be the norm for any incarcerated on that windswept island. However, action is constrained by the several miles of icy cold water which isolate inmates from freedom. The water in effect acts as a powerful influence on behaviour, even though to the casual observer the opportunity for escape is blindingly obvious and there for the taking. So it is with attractors and repellors. They either encourage or inhibit specific behaviours and courses of action when, on the surface, there appears to be complete freedom of choice.

Drawing on the empirical work of Miller (1990) and Pascale (1991), Stacey (1993) has discussed the possible implications of point attractors towards stability and instability, for commercial organisations operating in a competitive environment. He argues that for an organisation to be successful in the long term, it must maintain a creative tension between these two point attractors, and exist within the border region that separates them – a region of *bounded instability*. Figure 7.3 illustrates these three positions and their characteristics. Stacey does not specifically discuss periodic attractors within an organisational context. Nonetheless his work demonstrates how concepts such as attractors can be abstracted from the natural and physical sciences, and their applicability explored within an organisational setting.

Wheatley (1992) has also examined the notion of attractor within an organisational context. She proposes the concept of *meaning* as a possible attractor – some corporate vision or statement which provides a coherent purpose and reference point capable of guiding and influencing individual action:

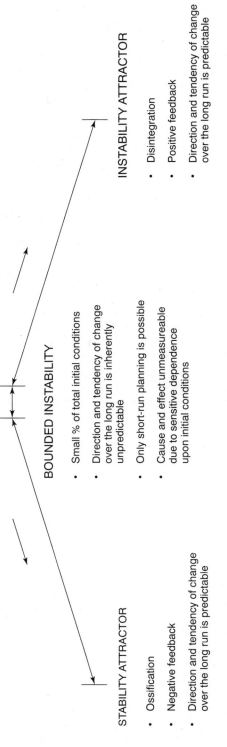

STABILITY ATTRACTOR

- Ossification
- Negative feedback
- Direction and tendency of change over the long run is predictable

BOUNDED INSTABILITY

- Small % of total initial conditions
- Direction and tendency of change over the long run is inherently unpredictable
- Only short-run planning is possible
- Cause and effect unmeasureable due to sensitive dependence upon initial conditions

INSTABILITY ATTRACTOR

- Disintegration
- Positive feedback
- Direction and tendency of change over the long run is predictable

Figure 7.3 Attractors of stability and instability (based on the work of Stacey, 1992, 1993)

> When a meaning attractor is in place in an organisation, employees can be
> trusted to move freely, drawn in many directions by their energy and
> creativity. . . . We know they will all be affected and shaped by the attractor,
> their behaviour never going out of bounds. We trust they will heed the call of
> the attractor and stay within its basin.
>
> (Wheatley, 1992: 136)

Wheatley's 'meaning attractor' can be interpreted as a means of constraining
change, restricting it within certain limits. She draws parallels between fractal
structures in nature, and self-similarity and consistency in human and organisational behaviour. Despite the unpredictable and chaotic appearance of many
organisational settings, she argues there are patterns, common behaviour traits
and recursive structures present which limit and shape macro level behaviour.[1]

There are a number of other examples where the notion of attractor can be
applied within organisations. *Career progression* is one of them – employees being
drawn inexorably towards the next rung on the corporate ladder, the next box on
the organisation chart. Whatever the higher position has to offer, be it additional
status, power, intellectual challenge or opportunity, organisations that have
clearly established career paths will provide an attractor for their staff which
influences their behaviour if they succumb to its influence. Not all employees, of
course, do succumb. Some do not find the prospect of more corporate politics and
increased responsibility attractive. Others are simply happy with their lot and glad
to leave work at a reasonable hour every day.

It could be argued that a closely related attractor to career path is that of
reward structure. The nature of the attraction is somewhat different here, being
financial as opposed to status or intellectual advancement. Again, this attractor
is only a strong one if the company's reward policy and salary structure is widely
known among staff, and the human resource function is seen to be adhering
to it.

Another possible candidate for an attractor embedded dynamic is *culture* –
either organisational or national. Hofstede (1991) defines culture as collective
preference for one state of affairs over another.[2] Collective preference which
draws behaviours and practices internally will tend to influence the way in which
business gets done. For example, a risk averse, cost conscious, lumbering bureaucracy type culture constitutes a strong attractor or behavioural predisposition
which is very durable – and therefore difficult to move the organisation away
from without specific targeted change initiatives. National cultures represent an
interesting example of where the attractor of collective preference exists at the
societal level. For example, the high tolerance of uncertainty and ease with which
Swedes operate in unstructured, ambiguous situations are national traits which
find their way into the organisation. The Japanese, on the other hand, are
continually seeking to remove uncertainty from their working environment
through, for example, the use of information technology or highly structured
organisation and formal protocols. Obviously, such behavioural attractors at a
national level are vital to consider when planning cross-border working, mergers,

joint ventures and acquisitions. The reality is that, sadly, they are rarely considered or dealt with effectively.[3]

Strong leadership can also provide the opportunity for another attractor to operate within the organisation – corporate vision or strategy. This builds on Margaret Wheatley's meaning attractor discussed earlier. A well-developed and clearly communicated vision can provide a focus around which staff behaviours can coalesce – forming a powerful embedded dynamic within the organisation. In seeking to attract 'hearts and minds' around a core vision and see this translated into improved business performance over time, other components of the organisation must also be aligned. For example, staff will not fall into the 'attractor' of a new corporate vision espousing flexibility with customers, rapid decision-making and greater employee ownership if the systems, processes and procedures which underpin operational life are slow, management dependent and internally focused.

Focal points of attraction and repulsion which draw individual and organisational behaviour towards or away from certain states constitute deeply embedded dynamics of change. Within large multinational organisations, middle layers of management can act as an attractor towards stability and eventual stagnation. In their efforts to maintain the status quo, they can inhibit innovation, stifle creativity and dampen down second order change initiatives to first order wherever possible. Conflicting pulls for attention such as personal development and career advancement, versus loyalty and commitment to the company, parallel the phenomenon of an attractor – depending upon whether behaviour oscillates regularly between the two (periodic), or whether it is a complex pattern of behaviour which attempts to satisfy the attraction of both by existing at the boundary (chaotic). The conflicting pulls towards encouraging innovation and creativity on the one hand, and adopting a risk averse, defensive attitude to ensure the maintenance of a stable operating environment on the other, are common tensions which clearly need to be kept in balance.

Conversely, organisations may be pushed away from point repellors such as risk-taking behaviour, or a particular management style. This could be because of some event in the organisation's history like the dismissal of the finance director because of fraud, or a major downsizing exercise which left those remaining with permanent behavioural scars and fear of putting one's head above the parapet. Events such as these sear themselves into corporate memory and culture. Thereafter, staff behaviour and management style is deeply affected, for example, the way in which decisions are made, how work is allocated, or the manner in which performance is assessed. Taking the initiative, stepping outside standard procedures in order to meet a customer requirement, or providing upward feedback to the manager all become 'repelled' behaviours which are inherently undesirable following such events. Eventually they become so embedded within the way the organisation does business that they begin to shape its culture. Before launching into culture change programmes or defining a new set of corporate values to move towards, it is critical to identify such repellors and the events that created them.

The concept of a repellor may also be a useful notion through which to analyse behavioural taboos within organisations, such as completing the financial year significantly under budget, or freely relinquishing resources to other parts of the business. Such repellors cause certain behaviours and practices to dominate the organisation's culture. In organisations with a strong culture of blame attachment and penalty enforcement for mistakes, a repellor behaviour could constitute 'accepting problem ownership', 'taking the initiative' or 'demonstrating innovative and creative conduct'.

'Attractors and repellors are capable of acting as engines, constantly pulling and pushing a system into different states and modes of behaviour.'

Other theorists have begun to investigate the implications of DST for understanding change within social systems and organisations (see, for example, Gaustello, 1995 and Kiel and Elliott, 1995). However, this is a relatively new line of research and much still remains to be done, particularly in establishing the full significance and potential of attractors and repellors for human activity systems.

Transition fuel: metabolism

As the following quote demonstrates, the process of metabolism is one of the most fundamental driving forces behind change in an organism:

The processes of life require transformations of energy to drive chemical reactions. Metabolism, the totality of interactions and changes of molecules and ions within a living organism, is controlled so that the organism is able to maintain its complex organisation by a balance between destruction and synthesis [and] change its organisation, as in development.

(Hardin and Bajema, 1978: 37)

At the general systems level the phenomenon of metabolism suggests several parallels. Fundamentally, it is a process of energy conversion which keeps the organism alive over time. There are two main processes of change taking place in metabolism. First, that which maintains an internal dynamic equilibrium. At a subsystem level, changes are taking place to convert and transform the raw materials required just to keep the whole system in its current state. These change processes are essential to system viability and although they are mostly unseen they maintain the system's ultimate emergent property: its identity within a given environment.

Second, metabolism provides the impetus for change processes that cause the system to change state, that is, to reorganise its internal structure, modify its behaviour and cause it to move into a new plane of existence with its identity intact. This second aspect of metabolism is crucial if the system is to remain in harmony with its environment. As in the biological realm, if an organism is subject to environmental extremes beyond its ability to compensate, it dies. So with systems generally – they can only adapt in the short run within certain tolerance bands which are a function of their internal structure and 'metabolic rate'. Planned interventions which do not ensure that the system's metabolic infrastructure is able to fuel and maintain the new structures or processes being introduced are doomed to failure. It is important to make the distinction here between one-off resource inputs tailored to assist a particular change event and the essential ongoing ability to convert external resources into a form suitable for internal consumption. For example, a baby relies on its mother's milk immediately after birth which has been shown to contain a host of essential minerals, vitamins, antibodies and nutrients specifically designed to increase its growth and resilience against disease (Harvey, 1988). Later in life the child must extract these necessary inputs from other foods and convert them via the normal process of metabolism. In the same way, an organisation may receive an injection of training and special assistance from a consultancy to help with a particular transformation – but if its long-term identity and viability are to be maintained, it must have developed the ability to convert resources into revenue itself, through its own internal business processes. Neglect or overstretching of this internal resource conversion infrastructure in the context of an increasingly hostile environment or rapid internal structural growth could be disastrous.

This micro level embedded dynamic is responsible for the transformation of raw materials from the environment into usable internal resource. It is essential in order to ensure:

- system viability and identity can be maintained within a given environment;
- the system has sufficient resources and energy to undergo change and adapt, in order to remain viable in a changing environment.

This is a natural, purposeful and continuous embedded change dynamic and numerous organisational examples could be considered. The processing of staff queries and requests by centralised head office functions such as human resources or finance is a critical conversion activity in organisational life. Training and education for new employees to ensure they are capable of adding value and contributing to the productivity and profitability of the organisation is another key ongoing metabolic process. The conversion of raw data about competitor prices and products into a digestible intelligence report, from which an appropriate marketing strategy can be derived demonstrates the necessary conversion process of environmental data into usable internal management information. These are all vital metabolic transformations at the micro level occurring continuously throughout the organisation. Without them, business would soon grind to a halt. Neglecting them during large-scale change projects could leave pockets of the organisation without the ability to convert what they need to operate effectively. Analogous with the loss of a kidney or part of the intestine, the organisation stumbles on, but is severely hampered and well below full strength.

When change is not change: dissipative structures

Other research in the field of DST has investigated in some detail certain chemical reactions and processes classed as *dissipative* (Nicolis and Prigogine, 1977; Prigogine, 1980). Chemical systems composed of atoms and molecules can be located in a given point in space and time, at a given density. It is well known that such systems normally obey the Second Law of Thermodynamics and tend towards molecular disorder as they seek thermodynamic equilibrium. However, under certain conditions such systems can exhibit remarkably coherent and organised behaviour. Specifically, these conditions include:

- Transferring energy with the environment at a level sufficient to offset the progress of internal entropy
- Possessing internal feedback loops connecting all constituent parts
- Have far-from-equilibrium or chaotic processes at work within the system.

(Jantsch, 1980a; Allen, 1981)

If these conditions are present, at a certain critical point the system can undergo a remarkable change: 'characterised by the coherent behaviour of an incredible number of molecules . . . [and] new organised states of matter, whose importance has now been confirmed for numerous chemical and biological reactions' (Allen, 1981: 27).

These systems have been called *dissipative structures*, based on their ability to exchange energy with their environment and in so doing to change their internal structure from one of increasing entropy to one of order through a process of self-organisation and coherent behaviour. As Prigogine and Stengers (1984: xv) have noted 'order and organisation can actually arise "spontaneously" out of disorder and chaos through a process of self-organisation'. Often, the order and structure will appear at a visible macro level and will persist as long as the energy transfer with the environment lasts (Briggs and Peat, 1989). A good example is the Great Red Spot visible on Jupiter. This is a persistent feature visible on the planet's equatorial belt through a medium-sized telescope – a vast atmospheric storm which has raged for centuries amidst a sea of continually changing eddies and currents. Exchanging energy with the turbulent environment around it, the storm has managed to maintain its shape and structure over time.

Conceptually, the phenomenon of dissipative structures has much to offer. It is closely allied to the notion of self-organisation and suggests that, given sufficient energy interfaces with a chaotic environment, a system can establish a dynamically stable identity and structure of its own which is a function of the inter-dependence between its component parts. Several authors have explored parallels between dissipative structures and organisations. Zimmerman (1992) likens it to the concept of self-renewing organisations (Hedberg *et al.*, 1976; Pascale, 1991), arguing that organisations must develop the capability to be self-reflective if they are to co-evolve with their environment. Here we see considerable agreement in principle with the Critical Systems movement (see Flood and Jackson, 1991c) which also advocates self-reflection within organisations. Zimmerman (1992) goes on to argue that if organisations are to learn and adapt within a turbulent environment they must, among other things, create redundancies and parallel pathways in their internal interactions, and attempt to increase both the number and intensity of external interactions with their environment. She also suggests that organisations which undergo significant transformations in structure and output, and yet retain a continuity of focus and identity, have processes at work within them which are akin to dissipative structures.

Stacey (1993) discusses the phenomenon of dissipative structure as being midway between the pull towards stability on the one hand and chaotic instability on the other. With respect to organisational systems, he likens a dissipative structure to:

> Consensus on and commitment to the implementation of an innovation, that is a new strategic direction or significant change in some aspect of the business. It requires continual inputs of attention, time and resource to sustain. . . . Such states are consequently short lived, periodic rather than continuous.
>
> (Stacey, 1993: 231)

Wheatley (1992) compares dissipative structures to organisations which maintain well-defined internal structural stability, and yet remain open to the environment over time. She suggests as an example a company which is organised around core competencies:

> It can respond quickly to new opportunities because it is not locked into the rigid boundaries of preestablished end products or businesses. Such an organisation is both sensitive to its environment, and resilient from it . . . The presence of a strong competency identity makes the company less vulnerable to environmental fluctuations . . . [yet] wide open to new opportunities and ventures that welcome their particular skills.
>
> (Wheatley, 1992: 93)

The phenomenon of dissipative structures provides the conceptual basis for a powerful embedded dynamic of change within organisations. It demonstrates that micro level change can be in perpetual creative tension with apparent macro level stability as the two trade off each other, given sufficient energy exchange with the environment. For example, consider the subtle interplay between changing customer needs and expectations and a company's internal processes which attempt to meet them. This is a careful balance which has to be continuously managed. With excessive internal structure the organisation becomes too rigid to respond to market needs when they shift. On the other hand, with over-engineered processes and too little structure the organisation is unable to marshal its resources to focus adequately on delivering effectively for the customer.

Another example is the way in which product image as perceived by customers and shareholders has to be maintained at some appropriate level. Resources and effort have to be expended to achieve the desired influence over external image, which is in a perpetual state of flux. Effective market exploitation requires a balance between good product image and external perception on the one hand, and appropriate internal resource allocation and organisational feedback mechanisms on the other. The initial random and somewhat chaotic *pull* of customer and industry perception versus the planned and carefully orchestrated *push* of product design, internal organisation structure and marketing effort meet all the conditions necessary for a dissipative structure to emerge. The presence of positive feedback in marketplace buying behaviour can also hasten the establishment of a customer–product relationship.[4] Thus, creating a market from a multitude of unstructured expectations, unarticulated needs and potential buyers is one possible manifestation of a dissipative structure at an organisational level.

At another level of analysis, interaction with and learning from an organisation's heroes represents a further example of this embedded dynamic at work. Great individuals of the past who exist in corporate folklore, or who still walk the corridors of power as figureheads, can represent models of inspiration and leadership or outstanding personal achievement. Their presence provides a certain stability and reference point for a constantly changing sea of employees moving up and down the corporate ladder. Learning from them or about them and allowing that knowledge to alter individual values, aspirations and behaviour over time constitutes a subtle and yet influential dynamic of change embedded within the heart of a business.

This embedded dynamic of dissipative structures produces counter-intuitive, self-organising behaviour from a previously unstructured and disordered state, under the influence of some external source or environmental energy transfer. Deeply enmeshed within an organisation, it draws in energy – such as best practice, customer loyalty or staff learning – and gives off energy to its immediate environment, including product/service offerings, role models and sales and marketing effort.

Boundary contact: environmental coupling

The change phenomenon behind this embedded dynamic is closely associated with the phenomenon of metabolism discussed earlier. The metabolic processes necessary for living are generally proportional to a cell's volume. A cell's metabolism relies upon exchanges with the environment, i.e. ingestion of food and removal of waste products. Environmental exchanges are directly proportional to a cell's surface area. Hence, the surface to volume ratio of a cell is critical to its survival and is generally maintained within definite bounds. This ensures the metabolic rate remains fairly constant. Should a cell grow in size without a change in shape, it would find it progressively more difficult to maintain sufficient exchanges with the environment to cope with increasing metabolic needs. As a general rule, cells overcome this problem by dividing periodically.

Some cells have high surface area:volume ratios because of their specialist functions, for example, alveoli cells which ensure high oxygen and carbon dioxide transfer within the lungs. Intestinal villi have a similar property, to facilitate the digestion process. It is a well-documented observation that unicellular organisms have a large surface area membrane in relation to their volume. In general, small organisms are better able to satisfy their metabolic needs by diffusion than large organisms.

Environmental exchanges are also directly affected by the motion of the environment relative to the organism. Food and predators are typically environmental elements which an organism interacts with during its life. Encountering or avoiding them successfully requires the setting up of some motion between itself and the environment. There are typically three types:

1   The motion of the organism through the environment. This a very common way of ensuring environmental contact, e.g. fish, birds.
2   The organism being fixed to a geographic locality of environmental movement, e.g. coral (moving underwater currents), spider (web trap) or mussels (tidal flows).
3   The attachment of the organism to a fixed position, and propelling the environment through its body in a perpetual filtering motion, e.g. sponge and oysters.

The clear principle implicit here is that a system has exchanges with the environment which need management. This is not a new idea, but the volume:surface area ratio metaphor does suggest several intriguing implications. First, a system interacts with or 'touches' the environment at certain specific points on its boundary. Depending upon the type of exchange being examined, the interactions could take place:

*   *At every point along the boundary* – organisational parallel: bankruptcy/ liquidation; full integration merger.
*   *At specific points dictated by forces in the environment* – organisational parallel: outside investigations into suspected fraudulent activity; drop in demand for product/service; block share buying by an acquisitive predator.
*   *At specific points dictated by elements within the system* – organisational parallel: release of a new product; statements made by the public relations department; entry into a new market via product diversification.

Opportunities and influences for change are a function of the degree of contact which a system has with its environment. This in turn is partly related to the system's 'surface area', but perhaps of more significance are the actual number of interaction points along its boundary at a given point in time. This is an important distinction because the existence of a boundary with the environment is not necessarily synonymous with contact with that environment at a given location on the boundary.

This metaphor goes beyond what is normally termed 'boundary management' as it raises issues fundamental to the nature of change. Philosophically, there has to be a boundary with something. What that 'something' is largely defines the boundary itself and the type of interactions taking place across it. The perspective and understanding of those involved will also affect boundary and interaction definitions, as several theorists have noted (Checkland, 1981; Jones, 1982; Flood, 1987). As we saw in Chapter 4, an organisational boundary can be defined in terms of relationships and environmental interactions, not just in structural terms (see Smith, 1982). William Berquist talks of organisational *edges*.

As far as corporate change is concerned, the important consideration is to what extent a business will be forced to undergo change should the boundary be breached. How likely is it that an interaction will occur? Does the business have control over when or if the interaction will occur, and influence over where on its boundary it will happen? Answers to these questions are essential if an organisation is to navigate into the future effectively, as it moves through an infinite 'possibility space', learning and adapting as it does so. Knowledge about what kind of environment lies the other side of critical points on the boundary at a specific point in time is therefore essential. Long-term planning is useless in today's fast-moving business environment. Attempting to predict what the future holds except in very broad generic terms is a futile exercise. Take an average bank. A stock market crash, aggressive acquirer or rogue trader are all events that could hit it tomorrow – demanding a change response.

Some systems choose to have their boundaries in particular places so as to minimise or maximise contact with certain elements in the environment and the subsequent change it may bring. For example:

- flower stalls outside train stations (maximise);
- crabs bury themselves in the sea bed for protection (minimise);
- streamlined aircraft body panels (minimise) or wing span for lift (maximise).

Other systems plan 'temporary exposure' of some of their parts to selected parts of the environment, e.g. the press office of a political party or a submarine periscope. More indirect boundary touching involves mere observation of the environment, and making internal behaviour or structure changes as a result of the perceptions, impressions and interpretations of the changing world outside. An appreciation of the dynamics of environmental interaction and how the boundary is to be defined are crucial for senior managers in order to understand the potential forces and change sources they are trying to navigate a path through.

As an organisation moves through the infinite possibility space that constitutes its environment, this change dynamic at the boundary is continually at work. Any given interaction or contact of a particular part of the organisation with a specific 'possibility' or part of the environment can potentially have change consequences for part or all of an organisation. It can be likened to ongoing friction which produces minor first order change at the micro level for most of the time, similar to the background noise of change generated by our first three embedded dynamics. Occasionally it may result in major change.[5]

What is being proposed then is an embedded dynamic of minor, friction-like changes, caused by day-to-day operation in a given market, that are a function of the composition of the boundary, how staff, systems and procedures perform at that boundary, and the 'real time' knowledge an organisation has about what lies on the other side.

Summary

In this chapter we have discussed a fourth building block to change, that of embedded dynamics, as shown in Table 7.1.

Table 7.1 Embedded dynamics of change – key concepts

Underlying dynamic	Physical metaphor	Section heading
Micro competing forces	Chemical bonding	*The ties that bind*
Natural internal energy	Potential and kinetic energy	*Boulders on the cliff edge*
Inbuilt tendencies towards certain states and behaviours	Attractors and repellors from Dynamical Systems Theory	*Alcatraz without walls*
Life-sustaining energy conversion processes	Metabolism	*Transition fuel*
Self-creating internal order from external flux	Dissipative structures	*When change is not change*
Encounters across the boundary with the outside world	Environmental coupling	*Boundary contact*

Identifying the natural and unplanned change dynamics occurring across various foci is vital if an organisation is to self-monitor its operation and effectiveness in a given market. The embedded dynamics of change proposed in this chapter go some way to demonstrating how important ongoing background, unplanned change can be in organisational life. These often unseen dynamics and feedback networks at the heart of the organisation can hold the key to effective performance. If, by taking some advice from the natural world, we have uncovered a few of them here, there must surely be more. Those highlighted are not exhaustive or exclusive by any means, but merely guides to where intrepid organisational thinkers who are willing to step beyond the confines of their own discipline will no doubt find more.

8 Building blocks of change
Part 3: From levels to labelling

> That physical, biological, and cultural changes occur is well known. But how change is conceived is not so well known.
>
> (Bahm, 1979: 131)

Introduction

This chapter introduces another four building blocks, as Figure 8.1 illustrates. First, we look at the notion of levels and the various ways in which change across different levels can be described. Then a number of basic attributes of change are offered: common characteristics which can be helpful when attempting to diagnose or describe a specific change situation. This is followed by a discussion of how change is labelled in order to convey the degree to which it has occurred. Measuring and describing the extent of a given change can be a subjective and highly controversial undertaking. Finally, the chapter closes by proposing four principles of change which can often be seen at work within systems of all kinds – including organisations. These principles are not suggested as all-encompassing maxims for change practitioners to live by. Rather they are offered as basic considerations which, if not acknowledged, will significantly reduce our ability to understand and manage change – whether it be planned or natural.

Levels and layers: looking for change

This building block is concerned with the level of resolution or depth associated with a given change. The concept of levels of change was a recurring theme among the change perspectives surveyed in Chapter 5. The notion of a sequence of lower and higher levels has been influential in western thinking since Plato, as Whyte (1970) has noted. Grene (1967) has explored the question of whether 'a one-level ontology [is] adequate to account for the major areas of human experience'. She comes to the conclusion that it is not and discusses how a many level ontology can be constructed. Beer (1979, 1981, 1985) has developed arguably the most focused model of the organisation which incorporates the

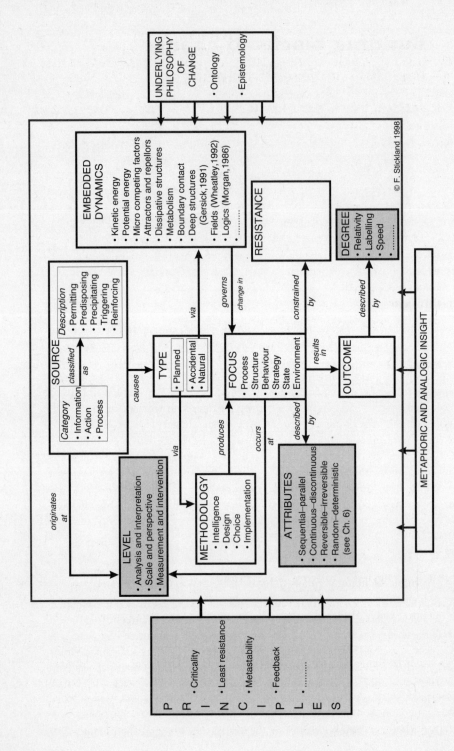

Figure 8.1 Building blocks of change: Part 3

concept of recursive levels.[1] This enables several analytical slices to be taken through the organisation, and basic structural command and control mechanisms to be identified at each one. Bunge (1959, 1960a, b, 1963) has proposed nine different types of level and these are illustrated in Figure 8.2. He argues that the concept of emergence over time between levels could occur from low to high levels and from high to low levels. Hierarchy theory has also been greatly concerned with the concept of levels (see Pattee, 1973; Miller, 1978; Allen and Starr, 1982; Wilby, 1994) as it attempts to describe the relationship between a given observed phenomenon and the observer – across disciplines.

The notion of levels has been discussed and articulated in detail by many writers. With regard to understanding change specifically, it offers several thoughts that are helpful. Traditionally, change has been viewed at the macro level within social systems and seen as predictable, linear and gradual (Daniels, 1990). However, with the rise of systems thinking and complexity science there has been a growing awareness that short-term micro level fluctuations and events are of equal if not greater significance in understanding change dynamics. A number of change phenomena from the physical world will be considered later which demonstrate this.

'With such a ubiquitous phenomenon as change, diversity of opinion, perspective and contribution have to be valued if we are ever to understand it more deeply.'

With respect to the notion of change, the term 'level' has several different meanings, specifically: analysis and interpretation; scale and perspective; measurement and intervention. Each of these will now be explored.

Analysis and interpretation

First, change can be analysed and interpreted at differing levels, as Berg (1979: 52) has observed:

'A simple dichotomy entails differentiating between surface interpretations (which deal with easily apparent activities and events) and interpretations in depth (which deal with hidden, unconscious, or latent structures and processes).'

In terms of Bunge's classification, category three – degree of analytical depth – is most appropriate here. Clearly one's philosophical position is of immense significance (individualist or objectivist) in determining the actual level at which the change phenomenon is interpreted. For example, the individualist may interpret change events at the level of the cognitively obvious, limited only by the

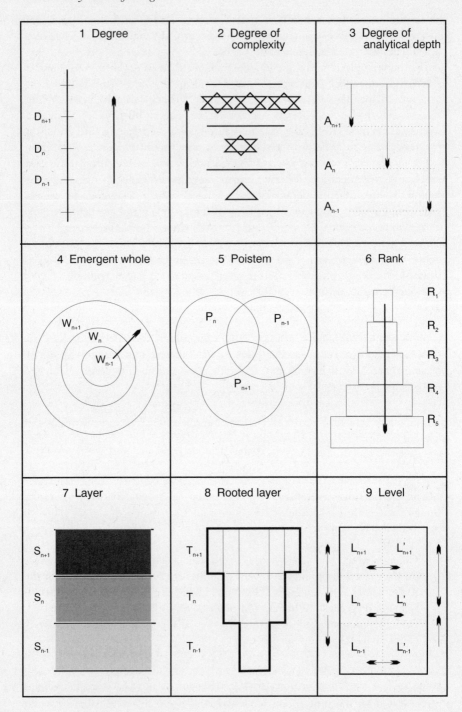

Figure 8.2 Various perspectives on the notion of level (adapted from Bunge, 1960a, b)

labels and descriptions available to him. The objectivist, on the other hand, may well acknowledge the existence of deeper change dynamics which he cannot directly perceive and analyse.

In attempting to describe the change dynamics in and between levels, Wilber (1983) has discussed two types of level associated change: translations and transformations. These provide a clear analytical framework within which level related change can be interpreted. *Translations* concern horizontal movements within hierarchical levels, which perform an important integrating and stabilising function, 'filling in or fleshing out the surface structures of a given level' (Wilber, 1983: 48). In terms of Bunge's classification, translations would concern category seven and the lateral interactions within category nine. In an organisational setting, this might be the political jockeying for position among similar grades of staff or heads of department immediately prior to some corporate restructuring. *Transformations*, on the other hand, concern vertical movement between levels and changes in deep structures which constitute 'the *rules* of the game, the *patterns* that define the *internal relations* of the various pieces to each other' (Wilber, 1983: 46; original emphasis).[2] Taken together, translations and transformations would correspond to the interactions within Bunge's category nine.

Ensuring that the interpretation of a change at a given level is appropriate (individualist) or 'correct' (objectivist) is complicated by the fact that the observer is often an integral part of the system he is attempting to understand. This is a particular problem within social systems. Involvement at the micro level can obscure macro level dynamics and vice versa. As organisation theorists Quinn and Anderson (1984: 16) have observed:

> The inability to see the overall phenomenon as an unfolding macro process is closely paralleled by the inability to see the underlying patterns of inter-connected, dynamic, cyclical actions which initiate and control the problem.

The identification of structural levels is another way in which change dynamics can be analysed and interpreted. Structure is one aspect not explicitly captured in Bunge's categories. Attempting to understand the change dynamics between structural levels is important as Briggs and Peat note:

> Changes which take place on the micro scale instantaneously effect changes on the macro scale and the reverse. Neither really 'causes' the other in the usual sense. Micro evolution doesn't build up in steps to create a macro evolution, nor do great shifts in macro structures cause the micro world to respond. Each level is connected to the other by complex feedback mechanisms. They cause each other simultaneously.
>
> (Briggs and Peat, 1984: 26)

While Briggs and Peat were referring explicitly to change dynamics within physical systems, the above quote is also arguably applicable to social systems and interacting human behaviours.

Downs (1967) has gone a stage further in attempting to identify and define specific structural levels at which change occurs. He postulates that social systems – in particular bureaucracies – possess four distinct structural layers, each possessing different propensities to change:

> The shallowest consists of the specific actions taken by the bureaucracy, the second of the decision making rules it uses, the third of the institutional structure it uses to make those rules and the deepest of all its general purposes.
>
> (Downs, 1967: 167)

Here we see change becoming more radical to the organisation the deeper one descends, with a change to strategy or purpose at level four potentially having the most profound effect.

Scale and perspective

The second theme which the notion of levels contributes to a better understanding of change is that of scale. The importance and necessity of being aware of the position and time frame of the observer cannot be overestimated:

> The distinction between 'micro' and 'macro' is one of scale and perspective. An individual, for example, may be a macro structure for a bacterium, but a micro structure for society.
>
> (Ford and Backoff, 1987: 110)

Systems science refers to this as *levels of resolution* (Flood and Carson, 1988) and it is closely associated with the concepts of system hierarchy and emergence (category four in the Bunge classification). As mentioned in Chapter 5, the speed with which time passes within the system being examined, relative to the observer, is one aspect that must be taken into account when dealing with change. Principles of relativity abstracted from the work of Einstein (1921, 1952) apply equally to any observer–system relationship. The other aspect is the plurality and diversity of information that is uncovered when the scaling is adjusted, and the level of resolution is increased or decreased. As Wilby has noted:

> Choice of scale is determined by the observer and that choice defines the hierarchical structure revealed, processes within the system, and inter-relationships seen within the system's structure. Any change in the resolution used to examine the system alters the definition and the information gained from the study. It also effects a bias on further description of the system in that alternative perspectives, and possibly radically different system descriptions, can be obtained by altering the scale and resolution of the study.
>
> (Wilby, 1994: 660)

Measurement and intervention

This leads on to the third aspect of levels: measurement. Failure to give due consideration to scale and perspective when studying change can result in measurement difficulties. Let us return to the climatology example we started with in Chapter 2. Climatologists face a significant measurement problem as they:

> tend to think in global terms since that is the scale at which weather generating processes operate. Limitations of data and technology result in their models making predictions at a regional scale at best. . . . Most measurements of the responses of organisms to their environment are made on an organism scale or smaller, because of the technical difficulty and expense of working at a larger scale.
>
> (Scholes, 1990: 351)

As a result, theorising about change phenomena takes place at one level, but actual measurement and analysis to validate any theories generated occurs at another level – one which is easy and expedient to access. This results in a gap between theoretical progress and practical endeavour. Scholes (1990) argues that this can be overcome in principle by measuring change phenomena at the level or scale at which they occur, wherever possible. Failure to do this can lead to key change dynamics and processes being missed. As one commentator has noted, essential to effective change measurement is:

> amassing detail on the correct scale to perceive the phenomenon under examination. Look at the world in detail too fine grained, and its common sense rules vanish into quantum interference; look at gases in too fine detail and the thermodynamic concept of entropy vanishes, taking much of what is meant by time with it. The whole notion of what is simple and what is complex depends upon getting your point of view correctly course grained.
>
> (*Economist*, 1994: 107)

Some traditional disciplines measure behaviour and change dynamics at the micro level in a rationalist manner, through the lens of the macro level. For example, economics has traditionally employed macro aggregates and econometric representative agents to describe and account for micro economic activity. Economists Hayek (1988) and Pearce (1994) have identified two weaknesses with this approach to measurement. First, having defined the macro level measures of change activity, there is a tendency to relate and connect them together. However, this would seem inappropriate, as Pearce has noted:

> Why, in a complex system, should there be any stable relationship between aggregates that are the product of many changing relationships between

individual agents? Clearly, any complex system will have emergent and aggregate properties and many of the emergent properties will in turn feed back to the behaviour of individual elements of the system.

(Pearce, 1994: 105)

Second, in identifying macro aggregates within complex systems, statistical methods are often used which are not subtle enough to capture the intricate dynamics at the micro level. This can be due to the inherent difficulties of measuring change variables at the micro level. But whatever the reason, the resulting macro measures are likely to be epistemologically unrepresentative of all the change dynamics occurring at lower levels. After all, the 'sum of the parts is greater than the whole', but the introduction of statistical measurement with its susceptibility for cumulative averages and aggregates can often obscure the logic of this well-known adage.

There is a tendency to think of levels within the organisation just in terms of the organisation chart and management hierarchy. Nevertheless, there are numerous ways in which change manifests itself within and across different types of level. For example, the notion of level applies to:

- Target employee groupings such as individual, group/team, department/ function or whole organisation.
- Employee expectations about the future: reward, security, job role.
- Processes (in a BPR sense):

  - strategic high level
  - core business level
  - activity level
  - task level.

- Staff competence: experience and training.
- Understanding of the corporate mission and strategy.
- Staff loyalty and commitment.

All of these can be thought of at different levels and would probably look different at each one. Failure to acknowledge their existence during change management can lead to effort and resources being dissipated without the desired change being sought or, worse still, other unanticipated changes taking place elsewhere within the organisation. Assuming that the change target is homogeneous wherever it exists is a natural but somewhat questionable assumption which may well be made without thinking too much about it.

At what level we choose to view something within the organisation therefore has important consequences for our subsequent analysis. Scale, measurement and interpretation are three useful guides for thinking about levels when analysing or managing multi-layered change dynamics.

Attributes of change

As a building block, attributes of change can be added to endlessly, depending on focus and interest. Three basic attributes are offered here: sequential versus parallel change; continuous versus discontinuous change; and reversible versus irreversible change.

Sequential versus parallel

Does a given change phenomenon follow a progressive, linear cause and effect pattern, or is it composed of multiple and interdependent change events occurring simultaneously across the organisation? The notion of interdependence within and between systems has been highlighted by a number of disciplines, ranging from international relations (Keohane and Nye, 1989); chemistry (Maturana and Varela, 1987); economics (Arthur, 1994; Pearce, 1994) to social history (Bahm, 1979). Indeed, Bahm describes the significance of this change attribute well:

> Conceiving causation of particular events and processes as not only multi-levelled, but possibly omnilevelled, the complexities of seemingly simple causation becomes obvious. . . . Understanding the omnipresence of the whole–part causation seems essential to the economics of interdependence. As multi-level organisations become more intricately complex, each change, deficiency, disease, or destruction in any part tends to become more serious as it endangers other parts and wholes.
>
> (Bahm, 1979: 136)

Wimsatt (1980) even goes so far as to suggest that the notion of levels and hierarchy within systems thinking has been an impediment to recognising and understanding multilevel interdependent change across systems. This change attribute seeks to highlight whether a change is part of a linear chain of events within a given domain and time frame, or whether it is enmeshed within parallel and interconnected streams of change activity.

If we think back to the Burke–Litwin model outlined in Chapter 4 (Figure 4.1), attempting change in more than one box at once is almost certainly going to lead to simultaneous parallel change within the organisation.

Continuous versus discontinuous

This characteristic endeavours to describe the extent to which change phenomena within a system are related in time and space. Does the change occur in a smooth, constant and uninterrupted flow of events, or is it characterised by discrete, sudden and separated change events, lacking in continuity? Clearly, the time scale and level of resolution are important here. What might appear to be an isolated, discontinuous change event or series of events over a short time scale may be fundamentally related to other similar changes occurring outside the observer's time horizon or at another level of resolution, forming part of a continuous change process. Indeed, Lenz and Engledow (1986) suggest that an organisation's environment is continuously in a state of transition, and that internal observers only perceive change as discontinuities because of the cognitive constraints to which they are subject: 'what executives reference as new competitive realities are probably new meanings assigned to continuous adjustments' (Lenz and Engledow, 1986: 343). Similarly, continuous change events may share a common source but could differ in type, causing the observer to view them as unrelated and discrete incidents.

Reversible versus irreversible

Is a given change permanent and unalterable, or can it be reversed and the system put back to its original state? This change attribute has been widely debated over the past century, particularly within the physical and natural sciences. Classical Newtonian physics believed that change was inherently reversible. Indeed, Einstein argued that the concept of irreversibility 'is an illusion, a subjective impression, coming from exceptional initial conditions. . . . There is no irreversibility in the basic laws of physics' (Einstein and Besso, 1972: 203). However, as Prigogine (1981) has argued, time-orientated changes such as those found in chemistry and biology are largely irreversible. If a change is to be reversed, knowledge of the initial conditions that lead to the change must be obtained. But as conceptual advances in quantum theory have shown, this is not possible in practice:

> Theoretical reversibility arises from the use of idealisations in classical or quantum mechanics that go beyond the possibilities of measurement performed with finite precision. The irreversibility that we observe is a feature of theories that take proper account of the nature and limitations of observation.
>
> (Prigogine, 1980: 215)

The concept of entropy – a measure of disorder (or more formally a measure of the unavailability of system energy to do work) – is closely associated with this change attribute. According to the Second Law of Thermodynamics, the entropy of a closed system will increase with time. As a consequence, entropy will in part determine the direction of natural change in a closed system. Wheatley (1992: 76) has described entropy as 'an inverse measure of a system's capacity for change'. Most changes require energy to move the system from one state to another and therefore low entropy is usually necessary if change is to be achieved – particularly when little external intervention and environmental exchange is possible.

At a macro level within social and organisational systems, certain changes are somewhat reversible but not without first causing other changes elsewhere. For example, a planned change of corporate structure could be implemented and then reversed back to the old original structure several months later. On paper, at a macro level reversibility would have been achieved. However, it could well cause behaviour and process changes at micro levels within the organisation, and could even affect the overall state of the organisation: staff become unsettled; productivity and employee morale fall; corporate credibility suffers. These are all changes from the original initial conditions and so theoretically, although the structure change may be reversed back to what it was, the overall result must be deemed fundamentally different from the initial organisational reality.

So for short-term, macro-level analysis, approximate reversibility becomes possible within organisations, but over the long term and considering all levels, change must be regarded as irreversible.

Degrees of change: the labelling dilemma

The degree, severity or extent of a given change phenomenon is an area in which many labels have been freely and liberally employed. This is the focus of our next building block. The efforts of theorists in many disciplines to document degrees of change have resulted in a bewildering array of names, classifications and labels. One common theme to have emerged, however, from these classifications is the distinction between first and second order change (Levy, 1986; Krovi, 1993) as discussed in Chapter 4. This is essentially a measure of how radical the change is in terms of altering the identity of the system.

Another way to distinguish between first and second order change is through the notions of system improvement and design. Van Gigch (1974: 2) has defined system improvement as 'transformation or change which brings a system closer to standard or to normal operating conditions [and] carries the connotation that the design of the system is set, and that norms for its operation have been established'. Defined in this manner, improvement equates to first order change. It should be noted that the term implies no value judgement about whether the change is beneficial or harmful. System design, on the other hand, describes a more fundamental change with significant implications for system identity: 'Design is a creative process that questions the assumptions on which old forms have been built. It demands a completely new outlook and approach' (Van Gigch, 1974: 2). This is clearly more akin to second order change.

There are two other aspects to the 'degree of change' debate that need to be considered. The first relates to the apparent speed of the change relative to the observer. This captures the clichéd distinction between slow, incremental change and more rapid change. First order transitions are often associated with slow change and second order transitions with more rapid change. However, the apparent rapidity of the passage of time must not be allowed to confuse events and obscure fundamental dynamics of change. Events compressed into a short time period may in fact only constitute first order change, but for the observer at the time they can appear far more radical – due to the inability to follow cause and effect. Similarly, second order change can occur over long periods of time and as a result go unnoticed by the observer, who may only be conscious of changes within his own much shorter time frame which, taken in isolation, display all the characteristics of incremental first order change. As we have seen, time must be regarded as a key metric when studying the dynamics of systems.

The second aspect which has caused difficulty in defining a common terminology for assessing degrees of change is the position of the observer relative to the system – in both time and space. For example, consider what are often interpreted as quiet, stable periods of human history such as the so-called Dark Ages (AD 500–1000), and the formation of the American colonies (1730–1850):

> On closer inspection, these periods turn out to have been periods of great fundamental growth and of the enrichment of the ensemble of learning resources and possibilities, which then in turn led to the emergence of novel and temporary more relevant patterns. . . . The subsequent age thus may impress observers with its apparent conservatism and stability, while at the same time embodying continued and important processes of change.
>
> (Deutsch, 1966: 171)

Different reference points and historical standpoints give different perspectives and images of change. Perceiving whether a change is first or second order and what descriptive label to give it will then to some extent be a function of the observer's position in time and space, relative to the change in question.

Hence, at the heart of this difficulty in defining degrees of change are fundamental issues of measurement concerning the role and position of the observer. This takes us back to the objectivist–individualist debate discussed in Chapter 5. As Dimond and Ellis (1989) have noted, measurement is based on the conceptual activity of comparison:

> Measuring the concept of change can only take place in a physical reality by being able to deal with the observable, through the sense impressions of the individual, that is applying properties of objects and events in such a way as to make them measurable and, hence, taken to have the ability to describe those characteristics of the system under investigation.
>
> (Dimond and Ellis, 1989: 49)

However, the subjective nature of human sense impressions can result in a plurality of perceptions, providing a range of descriptive labels for the same change phenomenon – each individual assessing the change according to their own internal criteria and experience of similar phenomena elsewhere. Labels to describe what are perceived to be greater and greater degrees of change abound: incremental; progressive; fundamental; radical; revolutionary etc. The search for more dramatic, all-encompassing adjectives develops into a semantic game, which becomes ever more difficult to sustain as they are gradually exhausted. For example, some recent research undertaken to explore the economic, social and political changes taking place in eastern Europe since the end of the Cold War (Kamall, 1994) found existing change models and labels incapable of capturing the enormity of the transitions that had occurred and were still occurring. Kamall considered creating new labels such as 'hyper-change' and 'meta-change' but concluded that this would only exacerbate the current confusion and fail to address the real need: a change framework which would describe the fundamental nature and dynamics of change, clearly delineating at a systemic level the various properties and attributes change phenomena can possess.

The presence or absence of some universal, unchanging reference point is key to this building block of change. If a *relativist* stance is taken, then no common reference point for comparison exists and therefore a generic 'degree of change' measure across different types of organisation and change phenomena is not possible. Reality can only be understood from the perspective of those immediately involved. Describing change relies on a rich source of descriptive metaphor and analogy, to assist the change labelling process. The *rationalist*, on the other hand, needs a fixed set of concepts and givens against which to make assessments and compare different degrees of change. It is hoped some of the building blocks outlined in this chapter will partly fulfil the needs of the rationalist, and those described in the following chapters will provide some change imagery to help the relativist.

Three aspects of change degree have been considered here then: namely perception issues concerning the speed of the change, relativity issues concerning the position of the observer with respect to a given change phenomenon and the problem of change labelling.

Four change principles

Practitioners skip at your peril

The natural sciences offer the organisational thinker a multitude of parallels about change from which some generic principles can be drawn. Here we shall just look at four which the author has found particularly helpful during change management assignments. These attempt to capture recurring themes and common principles shaping change activity from a range of subject domains. As can be seen from Figure 8.1, they do not apply exclusively to the change foci outlined in Chapter 6, but can be seen at work within all the building blocks being proposed.

What goes around comes around: feedback

Relationships between two or more components of a system which contain a causal loop will engender a feedback process. Numerous natural and physical phenomena are governed by feedback mechanisms, from the simple to the complex: thermostatic heating controllers to weather systems. Many writers have recognised the existence and importance of feedback processes, particularly in the fields of management cybernetics and system dynamics[3] where causal loops are explicitly modelled in an attempt to assess the impact of a change in one component upon the rest of the system. Soft operations research has recently begun to model organisational feedback processes and business work flows, with the advent of personal-computer based business modelling software (see Ould, 1995; Pearman, 1995). Both positive and negative feedback processes are fundamental to many change phenomena. Positive feedback loops will amplify any input they receive causing a move away from the equilibrium reference state, whereas negative feedback loops will use the output to reduce the input, thereby causing a move towards stability. Senge (1990) calls the latter balancing feedback and describes how it is essential for goal-oriented behaviour, as it acts to narrow the gap between the desired state and the actual state. As a driver and sustainer of change, the notion of feedback is central to understanding change dynamics.

Figure 8.3 demonstrates how feedback can be modelled. This type of modelling not only increases our understanding of how a given organisational scenario actually changes and behaves over time, but also provides a basis for planning and implementing change once the feedback dynamics are fully understood. Being aware of feedback as an ever-present principle during change management is essential if we are to improve the effectiveness of the intervention. Too often we slip into the habit of seeing change as a purely linear A to B transition with a limited number of variables when planning and designing change programmes. Feedback could take us to Z and back before we reach our destination, with a myriad of unconsidered interconnected variables influencing our journey.

'Theorising about change phenomena takes place at one level, but actual measurement and analysis to validate any theories generated occur at another level – one which is easy and expedient to access.'

Old habits die hard: metastability

The principle of metastability will be illustrated here by turning to the domain of physical phase transitions. In its broadest sense, a phase transition can be described as the process of transformation from one state of matter or 'phase' to another, typically where there is a distinct qualitative difference between the two phases (Bruce and Cowley, 1981), for example, the freezing of water to form ice or the condensing of vapour to form liquid. It is an area rich with theories and concepts attempting to describe the dynamics of change. There are two main categories of phase transitions: first and second order. Figure 8.4 describes the difference between these two categories.

We are interested here in first order phase transitions, which typically start from a state where a substance remains in a locally stable condition beyond the point when it should normally start to undergo change. This is known as existing in a state of *metastability*. Examples include super cooling: water droplets can remain naturally unfrozen in the atmosphere at temperatures far below 0° C, until disturbed. Likewise, the temperature of a vapour can be lowered well beyond the

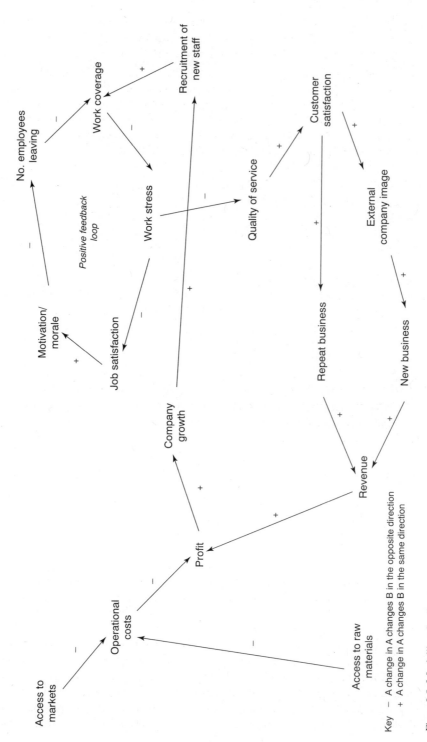

Key – A change in A changes B in the opposite direction
     + A change in A changes B in the same direction

Figure 8.3 Modelling feedback

FIRST ORDER PHASE TRANSITIONS

These are typically transitions between two phases which are both ordered, but in distinctly different ways. The transition from one type of ordering to the other tends to be discontinuous. Characteristic first order transitions usually start from a position where the substance remains in a locally stable state beyond the point when the next phase transition should have started, for example, water remaining in liquid form below freezing point, or being heated above boiling point without turning into steam.

SECOND ORDER PHASE TRANSITIONS

As opposed to first order, second order transitions generally occur between disordered and ordered states, in a smooth, continuous way, for example, the transition between paramagnetism and ferromagnetism occurs at the critical Curie temperature. Heat up a ferromagnet and as it nears the Curie temperature the normal internal interactions which cause the magnetic dipoles to line up in parallel begin to break down. As a result, the degree of spontaneous magnetism gradually moves smoothly and continuously to zero.

Figure 8.4 First and second order phase transitions

point where condensation into a liquid should occur. Similarly, under the right conditions, a liquid can be super heated beyond its boiling point without undergoing a phase transition to a vapour.[4] Such metastable states are highly sensitive to external random noise and contamination, which in the right quantities can cause the metastability to break down, triggering the normal phase transition. Predicting when or how the phase transition will occur is acutely difficult. However, what is clear is that the external noise must be of sufficient magnitude if it is to 'knock' the system out of its local metastable equilibrium and into a more thermodynamically stable state. For the transition to take place, the system must move through temporary states of higher energy than the metastable state. It must overcome what is known as a 'free energy barrier'. If the free energy barrier is too high, the probability of the transition occurring will be low.

The notion of metastability is particularly relevant to organisations. At a conceptual level, it has been reviewed in detail by Jantsch (1980b) – including the interaction between microscopic and macroscopic factors in determining the nature and duration of a metastable state. As a principle, metastability may explain why many organisational change measures do not achieve their objective following implementation. Introducing changes which set some part of the organisation at an 'artificial' level are doomed to failure in the long run, unless considerable resources are expended to maintain it there. Once the implementation team leave and the realities of day-to-day business reassert themselves, the new procedures and methods of working can seem untenable, causing behaviour to 'deteriorate' back to the old regime. This reversion can happen either suddenly, following some triggering event (first order), or gradually over time (second order). Designing effective changes which will survive, and achieve their objectives, requires careful consideration and analysis of the environment in which they will operate. This is an area sometimes neglected by organisational change practitioners – focusing on results without giving sufficient attention to long-term resilience and viability of the changes being implemented.

In essence, a metastable state will deteriorate over time, when the artificial conditions which keep it stable are disturbed, and it is forced to seek a lower equilibrium level by exploiting and diminishing local imbalances that have been created. Consider the implementation of a new computer system which replaces many manual and time-consuming procedures. Soon after installation, staff may gradually begin to revert back to the old clerical procedures. Why? If insufficient training and support are provided prior to the transition and the new computer system is not thoroughly tested, when the switchover occurs the whole arrangement can soon become difficult to sustain. It may remain metastable in the immediate short run, but staff disenchantment and frustration, software bugs and inappropriate functionality, plus the commercial pressure to get the job done, all conspire to force the new regime to break down, allowing the old, stable operational practices to reassert themselves.

Thus the principle of metastability can be key to understanding why some implemented changes do not meet their objectives in the long run. In chaos theory terms, stable states can act as an attractor, given the right environmental disturbances, and can pull locally established behaviours and practices away from metastable states towards a more dominant corporate standard – or vice versa. We return to phase transitions in the next chapter as this fascinating change phenomenon has much to teach both the change theorist and practitioner.

From a spark to a flame: criticality

Many change phenomena in the natural world have a life cycle of activity centered around a critical point or value. The build-up to the change would involve *permitting*, *predisposing* or *precipitating* sources, up to the point where a key triggering event takes place. This has been observed by others as a common feature of change phenomena:

> In every domain, when anything exceeds a certain measurement, it suddenly changes its aspect, condition or nature. . . . Critical points have been reached, rungs on the ladder, involving a change of state – jumps of all sort *in the course* of development.
>
> (de Chardin, 1961: 78)

In his discussion of synergetics, Hanken (1981, 1983) explores the role of critical values in the process of change. He views them as the product of competing internal dynamics, created by specific combinations of parameters:

> Because of internal fluctuations, the system tests different configurations or
> 'modes'. Competition between different kinds of such modes sets in, and
> eventually one or a few kinds of modes win over.
>
> (Hanken, 1981: 17)

Talking about systems generally, Allen (1981) uses the term *critical parameter* to
describe essentially the same thing. Upon reaching a certain value for such a
parameter, a fundamental instability can be formed: 'This threshold marks the
point at which the least fluctuation can cause the system to leave its uniform
stationary state. When this occurs, a fluctuation is amplified and drives the system
to some new state' (Allen, 1981: 27).

Within organisational systems, this same principle has been seen at work: 'it
seems that an initial key event or decision [i.e. *source* category] causes an
imbalance that either requires or facilitates a series of subsequent environmental,
organisational, or strategy-making changes' (Miller and Friesen, 1980a: 271). The
critical point acts as a defining constraint which determines the boundaries
and operational limits of the system, providing it with a unique identity. Those
boundaries cannot be crossed without the system changing in some manner. The
behaviour of autocatalytic sets[5] and the notion of 'critical mass' in nuclear fission
illustrate that reaching the boundary and crossing it is a function of both the
number of internal elements and the level of feedback and interaction between
them. These define some *threshold of complexity*. If the threshold is not reached,
the system may be consigned to *pejoristic* internal changes and possible stagnation.
On the other hand, reaching and crossing the threshold can result in variety,
innovation and *melioristic* type change.

An obvious example concerns the human psychology involved in achieving
some transition, found in most organisations: 'in any complex change process,
there is a critical mass of individuals or groups whose active commitment is
necessary to provide the energy for the change to occur' (Beckhard and Harris,
1987: 92). Similarly, simmering political and social unrest can be triggered
into sudden public disorder at some critical point – usually caused by an event or
decision taken at a local, micro level. Examples include the Bradford riots in
the UK during 1994, said at the time to have been caused by the death of a
young person 'joy riding'; the Los Angeles riots sparked by the beating and
arrest of a black citizen by white policemen. These critical points very quickly
move the system from a state of uneasy equilibrium to one of instability and
disequilibrium.

'Too often we slip into the habit of seeing change as a purely linear A to
B transition with a limited number of variables when planning and
designing change programmes. Feedback could take us to Z and back
before we reach our destination, with a myriad of unconsidered
interconnected variables influencing our journey.'

As a principle of change, trying to discover the possible range within which key organisational variables such as job satisfaction, home–work life balance or training levels will 'go critical' and trigger a major internal upheaval can help management navigate smoothly through change and transition into the future.

Taking the easy route: least resistance

The atoms and molecules of a crystal form themselves into definite, ordered patterns, arranged into regular and symmetrical lattice positions. The precise ordering at the atomic scale is mirrored at the macro level, with the overall geometric shape of the crystal corresponding to the internal symmetry of these patterns. The edges and faces of the crystal are described in terms of axes of symmetry, planes of symmetry and a centre of symmetry (Partington, 1944).

What are the implications of all this? Crystals break into pieces with plane faces meeting at sharp, precise edges. When broken they show cleavage or split along definite preferred directions. This is known as *crystalline fracture*. It differs from conchoidal fracture which refers to the way in which amorphous solids like glass break into very irregular pieces. Amorphous solids lack precise, symmetrical ordering in their atomic lattice structure and tend to possess no definite, regular external shape as a result.

An insightful change principle is suggested here, namely that change occurs where possible along the line of least resistance. Nature generally prefers the easiest path, whether it be lightning strikes, river flow or heat loss. Crystalline fracture suggests that systems which are highly structured and based on a definite ordering of their component parts will be more susceptible to change in certain directions. A knowledge of the underlying structural features at a micro level can lead to a greater understanding of how and why systems tend to undergo change in particular areas and ways in response to some external stimulus.

Considered metaphorically, this phenomenon also suggests that 'amorphous' systems with little formal structure or internal framework are susceptible to change in many directions. It could be argued that such systems are more flexible to change (albeit unpredictable), unlike 'crystalline' systems whose internal symmetry and structure largely dictate what changes are permissible. Both Anderson (1972) and Jantsch (1980b) have noted that the spontaneous breaking of symmetries present in a system can generate variety and lead to increased complexity. However, preserving key lines of symmetry can also provide a predictable and controllable means of change along certain strategically useful directions, and therefore should not be eliminated or dismissed arbitrarily.

Abstracted to an organisational level, this principle suggests that change will be most likely to take place along paths where there is little to impede it, subject to an organisation's structure and operational rigidity. Structural boundaries and clear lines of symmetry will define where change is most likely to occur with ease. Change phenomena which demonstrate this principle at work are often associated with sequential cause and effect chain events. This has important implications for planned change activity. Knowledge of the underlying informal structures and networks within a business is essential if effective change measures are to be designed. Failure to identify parts of the organisation where resistance to change will be weak may result in achieving a greater degree of change than desired. On the other hand, radical change may be possible with far less resource and energy if key lines of weakness are exploited during change management.

For example, change in political systems can sometimes be best accomplished by basing the change measure around some existing structural feature, like an issue of common concern or a cultural norm. UK government expenditure reductions in the area of defence in the early 1990s, and the subsequent reorganisation of military organisations, were linked to the end of the Cold War and decreasing political tensions in East–West relations. Within commercial organisations, making some connection between a desired internal change that will be difficult to achieve (such as management rationalisation, culture change or business unit sell-offs) with some existing internal issue which is dominating corporate decision-making (such as environmental awareness, health and safety concerns or compliance with industry/government regulations) can make implementation that much easier. Issue linkage can be an effective way of capitalising on lines of least resistance within social and organisational systems.

Summary

This chapter has added four additional components to the building blocks we have covered so far, as shown in Table 8.1.

Table 8.1 Summary of Chapter 8 building block concepts

BUILDING BLOCK	DESCRIPTION	
Levels	• Analysis and interpretation • Scale and perspective • Measurement and intervention	
Attributes	• Sequential versus parallel • Continuous versus discontinuous • Reversible versus irreversible • Random versus deterministic (Ch. 6)	
Degree	• Speed of change • Relative position of the observer • Change labelling and description	
Principles	*Principle*	*Physical metaphor*
What goes around comes around	Feedback	Various
Old habits die hard	Metastability	Phase transitions
From a spark to a flame	Criticality	Various
Taking the easy route	Least resistance	Crystalline fracture

Each of these building blocks are merely offered as pegs to stimulate thinking. Doubtless there will those who will want to expand some of them or suggest additional lines of thought – particularly within the 'principles' and 'attributes' components. This is welcomed and encouraged. With such a ubiquitous phenomenon as change, diversity of opinion, perspective and contribution have to be valued if we are ever to understand it more deeply. In the next chapter attention turns to the question of resistance to change, where once again the physical sciences have much to teach us.

9   Building blocks of change

Part 4: Resistance and endings
explored

Theoretical simplifications, or generalizations, may serve to identify key features, common properties, or important relationships among various phenomena. But more important, a concept which encompasses a broad range of phenomena may also serve as the anchor for a theoretical framework which, in turn, may catalyze specific hypotheses, predictions or tests.

(Corning, 1995a: 665)

Introduction

In this chapter, our attention turns to that ongoing problem for change managers – resistance. Again drawing from change phenomena in the natural and physical sciences, a number of generic categories of resistance are described. A better understanding of what causes resistance and the various ways in which it manifests itself will go some way towards helping practitioners to deal with it more effectively. The chapter concludes with a discussion of outcomes and endings, and offers four broad categories for thinking about how organisation changes and transitions end – if indeed they ever do. Figure 9.1 highlights all the building blocks covered in this chapter. As before, each section begins with a brief explanation of the physical change phenomenon behind the idea being proposed, followed by a discussion of the analogic change parallels it offers.

Exploring resistance to change

That change is often resisted within social systems is well documented. History is replete with examples of resistance to change such as the introduction of street lighting, railways, electricity, cars, umbrellas and typewriters (Thomas, 1937; Barber, 1952). Greater exposure to change has certainly not decreased our resistance or made us less wary of it. As Alvin Toffler observed back in 1970, 'Among many there is an uneasy mood – a suspicion that change is out of control.' If anything, change is more prevalent now than ever before and yet our reluctance to embrace it has not diminished.

Building upon the research of Beckard and Harris (1987), there would appear to be four broad responses to change within organisations:

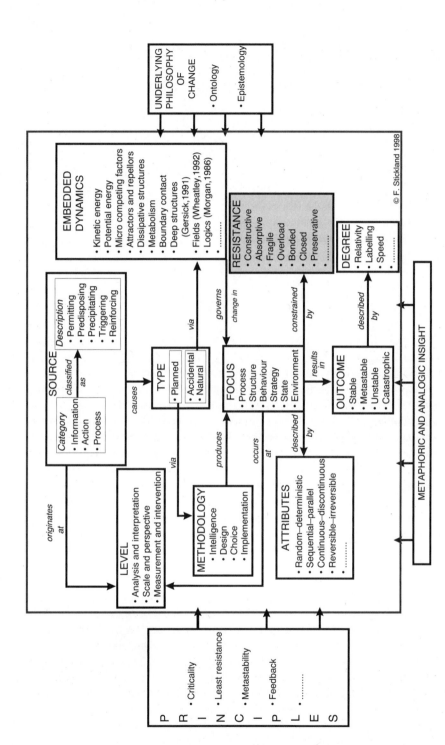

Figure 9.1 Building blocks of change: Part 4

- prevent it from occurring (*intransigence*);
- let it happen (*indifference*);
- help it happen (*co-operation*);
- make it happen (*engagement*).

Clearly, from a change management perspective these attitudes represent four points on a scale from little or no resistance (engagement), to deliberate, active blocking of change (intransigence). Resistance is a rich and complex concept, and deserves much greater attention than it often gets during change management exercises. Here, some general categories of resistance will be described, drawn once again from change phenomena found in the natural world.

Change in chains: nuclear fission

Constructive resistance

The process of initiating, sustaining and controlling a nuclear chain reaction has to represent one of the ultimate examples of change management. Harnessing the power of a nuclear material such as uranium requires the initiation of a chain reaction within the critical mass of the fuel's nuclei. In addition to the desired energy released, the fission process produces fast neutrons as byproducts of the reaction. In a nuclear reactor these are often slowed down by a graphite lattice framework, so they can be absorbed by other fissionable nuclei. In addition, rods of neutron-absorbing boron steel can be lowered into the whole structure to moderate further the reaction and control the amount of fast neutrons. Without such essential moderation the reaction would soon run out of control with devastating consequences. Figure 9.2 attempts to portray this process.

This describes a classic example of a change process under very strict control, achieving a desired outcome. Several general change ideas are obvious here. First, to initiate change, some 'critical mass' is required. There must be some basic level of interaction between elements. These could be exchanges with the environment or internal maintenance type relationships. Some input, relationship, emergent property or element must be present in sufficient quantity or strength to enable the change process to start. Within an organisation this could equate, for example, to a common vision of the future, levels of staff training, motivation or quality of product.

What is often viewed as resistance can sometimes be due to nothing more than a lack of critical mass. Attempting to change the way in which staff interact with customers and respond to their needs through extensive role playing, hiring enthusiastic customer service supervisors and introducing colourful uniforms for staff may not have the desired effect. Why? Because the level of knowledge and familiarity which frontline staff have about the product could be too low. Or the quality of the product itself may be insufficient to inspire confidence in the people who have to sell it. Critical mass, commitment, learning, energy, enthusiasm – call it what you will – is missing. This can be perceived as active resistance, but it is in

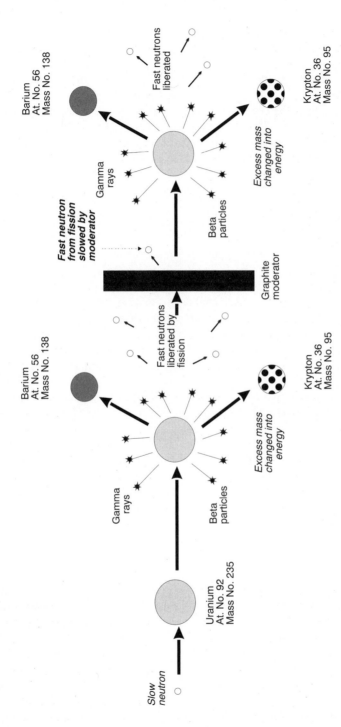

Figure 9.2 Chain reaction resulting from fissionable U-235 nuclei, with moderated neutrons

fact very passive, almost unconscious in nature. Diagnosing where 'lack of critical mass' resistance is at work and targeting the deficiency specifically can prevent much effort being wasted on other more elaborate incentive and behaviour change schemes.

But perhaps more interesting is another insight into resistance which nuclear reaction gives us. Within the core of a nuclear reactor, it is the resistance to change which produces the desired product – heat that is channelled to produce steam. A natural chain reaction is initiated but contained within strict limits. It is this moderation or blockage which defines the nature, magnitude and direction of the change. Here resistance is actively sought as it is essentially constructive – capable of achieving an *outcome* which can be planned for and anticipated. Without such resistance and rigorous containment, the change would run out of control, causing immense destruction and delivering nothing of value.

In organisational terms this can equate to staff chafing at the existing systems, policies and procedures which define the confines of their work environment. This offers the potential to generate creative tension and apparent contradiction, which in the short run can lead to resistance, particularly at the design phase of change methodologies. Producing practical change options and creative solutions to organisational problems is a challenge that most companies face. Political agendas, fear of losing power and the triumph of individual over corporate interests all conspire to resist radical change suggestions during the design phase. How often do we see transformational change programmes trumpeted from the board room end up as minor improvement projects that tinker cosmetically with the business?

However, properly channelled and encouraged within a controlled environment, such design phase resistance can be harnessed to generate innovative change ideas and commitment to eventual change implementation. The key is to keep staff informed of developments and ensure that they have an opportunity to react to the design options. The heat and frustration of the initial resentment towards change can then be moderated and employed successfully. Approaches such as Interactive Management (Warfield, 1982; Warfield and Cardenas, 1993) and creative problem-solving (Land, 1982; McCaskey, 1982; Gronhaug and Kaufmann, 1988) are good examples of ways in which resistance to change can be dealt with constructively and positively. Other examples of this type of resistance include trade union involvement that constricts an organisation's room for manoeuvre or attempts to set wages and working practices that are in its members' interest. The friction generated can force both parties to agree on more constructive solutions which are in the interests of all – but only after senior management's change intentions have been 'moderated' and contained by the union to reflect wider opinion.

Taking up the slack: phase transitions

This is an area of condensed matter physics which has been under intensive investigation in recent years. As we saw in the previous chapter, a phase transition describes the process of transformation from one state of matter or 'phase' to another – such as boiling water into steam (first order) or loss of magnetism (second order) (see Figure 8.4). With phase transitions, the forces and interactions occurring at an atomic level have a significant role to play in affecting the actual temperature and magnitude of the final transition. Macroscopic factors, such as what kinds of symmetry and dimensionality define the ordered phase, determine the critical behaviour close to the transition temperature. The extent to which very large collections of particles interact and influence each other increases significantly as the critical temperature is reached.

Many interesting trigger questions can be drawn from phase transition theory which are useful for change managers to pose during planned interventions. For example, consider the following:

- Does either the original state or proposed destination state of the organisation possess some kind of structural order?
- If so, how will that order or lack of it affect organisational behaviour during the transition, and the magnitude and direction of the change?
- What attributes of the organisation are likely to be key determinants of the eventual change?
- At what level of resolution are those attributes: the level of the macroscopic whole or individual elements?
- Are they structural or process type attributes?
- What 'energy barriers' must the organisation overcome if it is to move from one locally stable state to another?
- What are the critical values of external forces necessary to bring about the change? Are they fixed, or dependent upon the sensitivity of the organisation to disturbance?

Asking questions such as these prior to commencing a change programme can lead to a deeper understanding of the nature of the change itself, even if the answers are not easily forthcoming. What key internal or external factors initiate it? What direction it will take? What internal processes and attributes characterise it – at both macro and micro levels of analysis?

Absorptive resistance

One special kind of phase transition is isothermal change. This refers to the ability of a substance to be subject to some kind of change but to remain at a constant temperature, usually during phase transition. A good example of an isothermal change process is demonstrated by the concept of latent heat. This can be defined as the heat absorbed or evolved during a change of state or simply the heat required to cause a change of state.[1] Continued heating of a substance close to phase transition will produce little or no change in temperature (see Figure 9.3). Then at some critical point the temperature will begin to rise and the effects of the phase transition become more discernible. Latent heat reveals an important

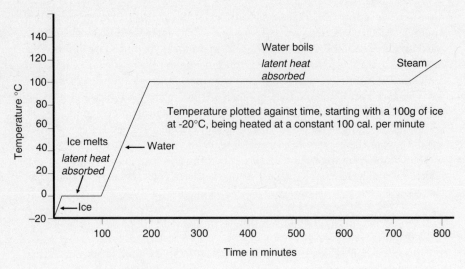

Figure 9.3 Latent heat absorption during ice–water–steam changes

principle of change. In applying some environmental input designed to cause an internal change, the ability of a system to absorb that input *without* undergoing the desired change must be considered. Therefore, before attempting to manipulate or change some attribute, element or relationship, the 'latent heat capacity' of the system needs to be assessed and an understanding gained of the way in which energy is absorbed or reflected.

Latent heat and the concept of isothermal change suggest metaphorically that certain organisational situations, processes or structures have the ability to absorb energy up to a point, before undergoing change. As with physical phase transitions, the direction and magnitude of the eventual change may be undesirable, and the timing unpredictable. During change interventions, this metaphor could help practitioners in their thinking about those components of the organisation which are likely to resist change, and how to plan resource allocation in order to overcome that resistance effectively. A distinction is made here between resistance to change due to absorption capacity, and resistance due to *inertia*. The latter is a direct function of mass (or lack of, see Constructive Resistance), whereas the former is a direct function of a system's ability to absorb energy.

Therefore, this type of resistance describes the ability of a system to remain unchanged in the short run, despite being subject to specific change pressures. It describes an ability to absorb the energy of change agents directed at it and, at the macro level at least, to show no signs of change. In essence, absorptive resistance is equivalent to 'taking up the slack', acting as a buffer and insulating a system from change until certain tolerance levels are reached and critical thresholds are exceeded. Increasing the amount of resources devoted to tackling a particular problem (e.g. staff retention) will in the short run be unlikely to yield significant improvements. But if the pressure for change is maintained long enough, or increased, something must give and behaviour will change. However, it may not be in the desired direction and the problem could merely undergo a transformation and manifest itself in another guise at some other level of the organisation.

Change on the boundary: self-organised criticality

Fragile resistance

The study of complex physical systems with many interacting elements, and their behaviour and evolution over time has been the focus of much attention in recent years.[2] In particular, theories are currently being developed to describe cascading change and the intricacies of the change process during the two-way transition between ordered and chaotic states. The work of Bak *et al.* (1988) on self-organised criticality is of particular interest. Simply put, the theory proposes that 'many composite systems naturally evolve to a critical state in which a minor event starts a chain reaction that can affect any number of elements in the system' (Bak and Chen, 1991: 26).

As a description of change this theory is of special interest, because it challenges the notion that a large, complex system undergoes change usually when an environmental influence dislodges it from some internally maintained equilibrium. Rather it suggests that such systems only exist in temporary stable states, in perpetual 'criticality', where small perturbations can give rise to both large and small system changes. The theory also presents the paradox of dynamic continual change at the micro level coexisting with stability and continuity at the level of the whole. Obviously these descriptions of change are not applicable to all types of system but, as Bak and his colleagues indicate, they may well lead to important discoveries about the nature of change in many fields concerned with large composite systems, including economics, biology, ecology and geology.

Resistance to change in some organisational situations can be very short lived and susceptible to complete breakdown by minor disturbances. Fragile resistance is particularly applicable to large homogeneous groups of employees or organisations with many interacting business units. Take, for example, factory floor staff, nurses or computer programmers. If there is a common professional identity or shared sense of adversity, such groups can move very fast in mood, opinion and collective response. Whether it is an industry pay dispute, health and safety concern or unfair dismissal issue, if a large employee group decides they are unhappy, management can soon find it has an escalating problem on its hands. Customer groupings can behave in the same manner by boycotting products or setting buying trends within a matter of weeks for fashionable products. The trigger can often be something relatively minor – a chance corridor conversation, a leaked letter or a bad customer incident that gets widely communicated. Resistance to the trend in such situations is often a token gesture by those in opposition. There is little or no absorptive ability within large composite human activity systems. People are too close together with too much in common for any significant resistance to establish itself. Sometimes the resistance is just sufficient to keep the system on the boundary between stability and change, and in so doing defining the operational limits and identity of the system. This constitutes fragile resistance and represents a weak defence before giving way to a transition resulting in a temporarily more stable state that is easier to maintain. Take an industrial dispute scenario. Striking employees often reject the initial pay offer before caving in to the next one because they are unable to maintain any coherent, sustained collective stance against corporate pressures to return to work. Once the trickle back to work starts, a hole in the dam appears and it is often only a matter of time before the rest of the herd follows. Positive feedback processes and what Arthur (1994) has called *increasing returns* can be instrumental in hastening the collapse of such fragile resistance. As with the Stock Market crash in October 1997, even the braking mechanisms and buffers built into the trading system since the previous major crash had little effect once the selling trend was underway. In a stock market situation a large numbers of buyers and sellers all suddenly act as one homogeneous group and work together to cause the slide. In such large composite systems of people, any defence can only be precarious and constitute fragile resistance against disturbances, with the system structure being particularly vulnerable.

Protocol breakdown: adiabatic change

Overload resistance

Adiabatic change is a thermal change process that takes place in a substance, without the addition or removal of heat from its environment. An example of an adiabatic process is the temperature change of air sealed in a compression cylinder. The alternating compression and rarefaction of the trapped air occurs so fast that it is unable to conduct the local heatings and coolings away from the locations at which they are generated. As a result, the temperature change created in a stratum of air becomes locked in. Normally, as a gas expands it cools down and when compressed it heats up. However, in this situation Boyle's Law is unable to assert itself and the normal internal heat transfer process by convection does not have time get established before the next volume change.[3]

This change process parallels situations where an organisation is being subjected to some environmental influence which is changing in magnitude very rapidly. As a result, the normal internal mechanisms and processes for coping with and responding to it are not able to function adequately – if at all. Standard operating procedures are not effective and localised 'overheating' may occur, potentially causing long-term damage to both staff morale and business efficiency.

For example, an organisation may experience a dramatic and unexpected rise in demand for its product. In the normal course of events, gradually rising demand could be matched by the introduction of extra production capacity to meet it. However, in the face of a sudden, enormous increase in demand, the firm cannot resort to 'standard procedure' and the workforce may be put under extreme pressure to increase output with existing resources. The stresses created throughout the organisation in attempting to deal with this external contingency may result in unforeseen internal changes. The culture may start to shift as employees become dissatisfied with unacceptable working hours, intolerant management eager to maximise revenue and a pressurised working environment. Internal processes and procedures may be circumvented, as it becomes clear that they are not capable of dealing with the demand. Shortcuts and 'work arounds' are developed and institutionalised. Minor day-to-day operational problems are left unresolved and the organisation slips unaware into the early stages of entropic decline.

> Radical planned change rapidly introduced within an organisation by a new CEO or management team of an acquiring company can deliver disappointing results. Management actions which seek to effect some change within the business by activating or accelerating internal feedback mechanisms and adaptive responses can fail because they overload the prevailing operational infrastructure.

Most organisations unconsciously rely on the establishment of norms, staff expectations and implicit psychological contracts between employee and employer in order to get business done. Given enough time for adjustment and realignment, these can shift and flex in response to some minor incremental changes. But major change can violate these to the point that the normal corrective adjustment processes are not given time to operate. Normal emotional cycles of transition are infringed upon and the desired change just does not materialise. The absence of change can be perceived as deliberate resistance, but in fact may be no more malicious than a complete breakdown of the organisation's natural abilities to cope and adapt accordingly.

One other result of overload resistance is to immunise the staff within the organisation against the desired transition, by using an inappropriate change *source* which is too intensive and causes more harm than good – thus rendering the business incapable of change along that line in the future.

Dissolving the glue: shared electrons

Bonded resistance

As we saw in the previous chapter, chemical bonding relies on the sharing of electrons to bind elements together. As with chemical elements, organisational components are joined together by relationships of varying intensity. A common link for many businesses is the sharing of resources between functions and process flows, tying them together. Consider the unifying influence of performance management systems, appraisal processes or common customer groups which all provide the potential for different departments to unite together in behaviour and outlook. Planned change interventions which do not acknowledge such pre-existent unifying factors are destined to be ineffective in the long run. Measurement regimes drive behaviour – you get what you measure. Organisation-wide measurement regimes such as a corporate balanced scorecard (Kaplan and Norton, 1996) will help bond an organisation together around the key variables being assessed. On the one hand, this is good as it can provide a shared view and vision for the business that is essential for growth and healthy performance. On the other hand, it can also inhibit change initiatives which seek unconsciously to challenge at a local level the behaviours and practices being rewarded and reinforced across the business at a corporate level. An imbalance and tension can be set up, with staff resisting the local change because they are wedded via a psychological contract, technological solution or internal service level agreement to another part of the business. Bonded resistance of this kind can be quickly overcome if the bond is first identified and then 'dissolved' or weakened in some way. This can be done by providing a substitute to replace the commonality, thereby increasing the propensity towards change. Alternatively, the introduction of a 'catalyst' designed to diminish the strength of the offending bond may be just as effective. For example, the use of 360° feedback to demonstrate to staff how the adoption of a particular practice or interpretation of a service level agreement is not wholly in the organisation's best interests. Such feedback can have the effect of altering the orientation of the resisting staff and loosening the bond somewhat, thereby preparing them for the impending change. Other examples of bonded resistance within organisations include reliance on old technology, union support, management style and working procedures and regulations. Attempting to change mental models and mindsets can help break down some of the dependencies and make the desired change easier to achieve. Alternatively, the existing mindset could be used as a basis for introducing and selling the planned changes by presenting them in a way which is familiar and comfortable, using the language of the current paradigm. In short, change practitioners should seek to highlight where the sharing of resources and organisational ties is likely to impede their change initiative. The bond can either be leveraged and used, or dissolved as a means of achieving the intended change.

Persuasions to change: noble gases to alkali metals

Closed resistance

Group VIII of the Periodic Table is a set of chemical elements commonly known as the *noble gases*: helium, neon, argon, krypton, xenon and radon. They are chemically very inactive. Normal attempts to make them react with other elements to create compounds involving even the most severe reducing and oxidising agents have proved unsuccessful.[4] If you can remember your high school chemistry, there are several reasons for the chemical inertness of Group VIII elements:

- Full outer electron shell configurations mean that there are no free electrons in the bonding orbital (outer shell) to pair with those of another element (ns^2np^6 with the exception of helium – $1s^2$).
- The atoms exist in a stable energy state. Evidence for this is generally seen to be characteristic breaks in the electron configurations for Group VIII elements.
- High ionisation potentials and small atomic radii cause an atom's electrons to be strongly bound. Small atomic size reduces the chance of electron loss, upon which most chemical behaviour and reactivity is largely reliant.

The combination of these factors means that noble gas electron arrangements are very stable, and mostly unaffected by environmental influences. Each atom lives for the most part in isolation, interacting very little with its neighbour (Moeller, 1959).

Group I elements, on the other hand, commonly known as *alkali metals*, can be considered to represent the other end of the chemical 'reactivity' spectrum: lithium, sodium, potassium, rubidium, cesium, francium. They lie at the opposite side of the Periodic Table and their characteristics reflect this positioning:

- They all possess a single valence electron in the outer shell [$np^6(n+1)s^1$ with the exception of lithium – $1s^22s^1$].
- They have a low ionisation potential. This means an atom can easily lose its single electron in the outer bonding orbital.
- They possess a large atomic size and a body-centred cubic lattice structure, with only a single potential bonding atom. This allows electrons to pass between atoms easily, enabling good conductivity, but makes the element soft and gives it a low melting point.

These factors together make for a very reactive set of chemical elements.

Group I and Group VIII elements have fundamentally different persuasions to change. One is extremely stable, almost resistant, the other very open and susceptible. An analysis of the reasons behind these two extreme tendencies, and an abstraction of the lessons gleaned, offers some novel insights. As in economics, a model representing each end of the spectrum of possibilities (e.g. perfect competition and monopoly) provides a basis for examining and understanding the grey area of reality in between.

A full outer electron shell denotes stability. Viewing a single atom as a system, it can be seen that environmental forces for change can be countered and resisted by ensuring no surplus or deficit develops which could be taken advantage of by some external agent. In addition, the maintenance of strong internal relationships prevents parts of the system from becoming isolated and unsupported. In the case of Group VIII, elements are so stable that almost all interactions are between like atoms, and not with those of another element. This would tend to parallel more closed systems, where environmental exchanges are infrequent.

Large atomic nuclei with available electrons in the outer shell parallel those complex systems which undergo change simply because they appear to have resources surplus to requirements. Or perhaps they have grown too large, becoming unable to maintain effective internal control and co-ordination over all their component parts. It is interesting to note that a collection of like Group I atoms develop an emergent property – conductivity – under the influence of an externally applied voltage. Therefore, because of specific internal characteristics and structural resource configurations, certain environmental influences can induce internal changes within the system by exploiting instabilities that exist at the micro level.

For example, within organisations such induced change can be seen in the dynamics of sell-offs and acquisitions. A highly successful business unit or trading entity within a holding group that continually seeks more autonomy from its controlling parent can become very difficult to maintain control over.

> Consider the case of the German-based Hypobank which set up a mortgage business in the UK called MSL during the 1980s. MSL became very successful, but also increasingly more and more difficult for its German executives to control remotely. The organisational culture and management style of MSL were significantly different to those of its parent and could not be kept easily under the sway of the corporate centre. Being such an attractive proposition as a stand-alone, self-contained business, MSL was eventually acquired by another organisation some years later. Metaphorically, one could argue that it became an available electron in the outer shell.

Inherently stable Group VIII elements in the Periodic Table provide us with the notion of closed resistance. We see this within organisations where some business units may be so self-contained and able to exert such tremendous influence over their constituent parts, that change sources from the outside have little or no impact. Such operations may possess highly co-ordinated command and control structures and attempt to limit environmental exchange to an absolute minimum. Internal free energy levels will be relatively low, with strong bonding between elements. Family-run businesses are perhaps the best example of this type of resistance to change, demonstrating a reluctance to move with the times, preferring the traditions of their predecessors, whether it be whisky distilling, furniture manufacturing or car sales (see Beckford, 1992). Within a given industry, the vast majority eventually stagnate and go out of business. However, some will survive because their 'old and traditional' approach to producing the product – whatever it might be – acquires a desirable novelty value. This provides them with a strong competitive advantage and enables them to stay in business by occupying a small niche in the market.

Other evidences of closed resistance include parochial, inward-looking organisations that are more concerned with the purity and sanctity of company procedures and processes than adjusting to the needs of a changing market. Public sector organisations have a tendency to operate like this, forcing those who interact to do so not for mutual convenience, but for their convenience. Watching the deregulation trend in the UK of public sector utility companies moving into the private sector is reminiscent of our Group VIII elements having to take on Group I characteristics. Even several years on, the old inert command structures and decision-making process can still hold sway over their ability to change.

Maintaining identity: autopoiesis

Preservative resistance

Autopoiesis refers to purposeful self-renewal within biological systems, which in the process of transition allows internal structure and identity to be maintained (Maturana and Varela, 1972). At a cellular level, the interactions within and across a cell membrane are often cited as autopoietic in nature:

> On the one hand we see a network of dynamic transformations that produces its own components and that is essential for a boundary; on the other hand, we see a boundary that is essential for the operation of the network which produced it as a unity.

> (Maturana and Varela, 1987: 46)

Associated with autopoiesis is the concept of *structural coupling*, where environmental perturbations trigger structural changes within an autopoietic unity. For example, forests and climate can be described as structurally coupled, each causing changes in the other. Structurally coupled autopoietic systems have two important characteristics:

- The interaction is mutual, leading to a complex interdependent relationship.
- The actual changes which are triggered in a system by environmental disturbances from its coupled partner are determined by the system's own internal structure.

The environmental disturbance can either cause the system to self-organise back to its original stable state via homeostasis, or the perturbation can cause the system to search for 'new developmental pathways through successive instabilities' (Sahal, 1979: 130). Within biological systems, the latter process has been termed *homeorhesis* by Waddington (1968) and represents more than just adaptation and evolution over time. Consistent with autopoiesis, internal integrity and identity are maintained during a perturbation, but the time scale during which renewal takes place can be relatively short. For example, the plant *Sagittaria Sagitufolia* grows leaves and flowers when on land but is capable of transforming itself into an aquatic form when flooded with water within a few days, and reverting back to land form when the water subsides (Maturana and Varela, 1987). The short time scale and reversible nature of the change clearly indicates that this is not adaptation in the traditional sense. Rather, the potential for these major changes is already a property of the plant's structure and identity – the environmental disturbance merely triggers it.

Structural coupling and the notion of autopoiesis suggest two fundamental aspects of change. First, changes initiated within an organisation by an environmental disturbance can be governed by the internal function and structure of the business itself. This provides an alternative change dynamic to that historically advanced by some theorists: that internal change is wholly shaped and determined by some external disturbance. The second insight which these natural science phenomena offer us is that change and renewal at a micro level can co-exist with constancy and stability at the macro level – indeed, that the micro level change can be essential to preserving systemic identity and structure over time. Once again we see an example of the pull towards two separate attractors within a system, but here they are operative at distinctly different hierarchical levels and are complementary.

The phenomenon of autopoiesis is receiving greater attention in recent years among theorists concerned with studying general trends in nature and society, covering areas such as global ecology, social psychology and cognitive evolution.[5] However, there have been attempts to use the phenomenon of autopoiesis specifically to explore the nature of change. In the mid-1970s, Zeleny and Pierre (1976) attempted to develop an analytical framework based upon autopoiesis that supports the notion of discontinuous system change leading to higher levels of development. Their work provided an additional change dynamic to reinforce the Punctuated Equilibrium school of thinking discussed in earlier chapters.

Of interest to us here, however, is the insight that autopoiesis provides into a particular type of resistance, which we shall call *preservative resistance*. According to Newton's third law of motion, to every action there is an equal and opposite reaction. Preservative resistance draws on the idea of survival and identity defence that is at the heart of autopoiesis. When a change influence is brought to bear upon a system, it can react back reciprocally in an attempt to maintain its internal structure and homeostatic stability. Within organisations this can be manifest in the form of willful opposition to a change, in an attempt to block anything new. Often, the response from the change agent is to push back harder still and enforce the change through some compulsory mandate – creating offence and ill-feeling among those involved. Hoffman (1981), Bednarz (1988) and Goldstein (1988) have explored ideas similar to the notion of Newtonian 'push back' resistance being proposed here – specifically within organisations and social systems where autopoietic principles of self-preservation are at work.

As a means of overcoming and reframing such resistance, Goldstein (1988) has gone further, suggesting that the questions and mindset of those attempting to achieve change should be altered:

From: 'Where do we need to add force to get this group changing?'
To: 'How is the resistance to change a manifestation of the will to survive of this work group?'

From: 'How is this resistance an impediment to our intentions?'
To: 'How can this resistance be reframed to express its affirmative core?'

From: 'How can we overcome the resistance?'
To: 'What does the resistance tell us about the homeostatic "settings" of this system?'

(Goldstein, 1988: 25)

This requires asking 'Second Loop Learning' questions (Argyris and Schon, 1978) which seek to explore the nature of the resistance and work with it, as opposed to against it. The entrenched positions that develop during union negotiations over pay, or the fierce dialogue and posturing that can occur in the Board room when corporate and personal empires are at stake, are good examples of preservative resistance in action. Identity must be maintained and the prevailing structures, processes and capabilities within the organisational unit under threat shape the nature of the defensive response.

> 'How often do we see transformational change programmes trumpeted from the Board room end up as minor improvement projects that tinker cosmetically with the business?'

This concludes our look at resistance. The natural and physical sciences have a great deal to teach anybody seeking a better understanding of resistance to change. The seven categories offered in this section are certainly not comprehensive, but merely an attempt to highlight some of the dynamics at work when resistance to change manifests itself.

Turkeys do not vote for Christmas, as we all know. Sadly, there has been a tendency within our organisations to treat people like turkeys, keeping them in the dark right up until the last minute and then springing change on them. Why? Maybe because we do not understand resistance well enough and are afraid to deal with it as a potential issue early on. Fears of having change blocked can often evaporate with the morning sun if we are willing to consider it upfront, and ask sensible questions about where resistance is likely to come from and what is driving it. It can be surprising how much of the opposition can then be specifically targeted and constructively dealt with – gaining support in the process from those whose working lives will be affected by the change. The different types of resistance which we have looked at here go some way to demonstrating that the concept is far richer than we are often prepared to believe. It need not always equate to stubbornness, defiance and obstructive opposition. Viewed in those terms, it will be dealt with in those terms – with potentially damaging consequences. Stepping back and trying to understand why the resistance is there allows some space to give the 'turkeys' a chance to vote and voice the reason behind their reluctance to change. By understanding resistance better we are by definition learning more about change itself, and therefore enhancing our ability to manage it more effectively.

Outcomes and endings

Our building blocks for change would not be complete without covering the end of the change journey. Here we are concerned with the condition or status of the change focus, subsequent to the change. The inherent difficulty is to identify at what point in time and space a given change activity finishes. If the building blocks outlined so far have been used to help chart a course through a particular organisational change, it is hoped that some of the boundaries, hidden dynamics and operational parameters of the change will have been defined to the extent that a distinct cut-off point can be specified. To conclude this chapter, let us consider what the end of the journey might look like.

From stability to reversibility

The first and most obvious conclusion of a given change is that it leads to stability. That is to say, no further change of the same *source, type* or *focus* is deemed likely in the medium term, all things being equal. The focus of the change will have reached a point of robust equilibrium – either *static* or *dynamic*. As we have seen, static equilibrium may result in organisational decline if the business becomes closed to further sources of change (internal or external). Stable change outcomes may be the result of a point attractor embedded dynamic or merely the cessation of source input activity. In terms of the organisational change foci that we considered in Chapter 6, stable change outcomes as defined here are less likely to be achieved in *environment, state* and *behaviour* targeted change. With change in these foci, there are too many variables and opinions to still once the end of the Gantt chart is reached. Like slowing a supertanker or attempting to bring a marble to rest on a flat plate, stability can take longer and involve more concentrated effort than we often realise. One important question, of course, is whether stability is actually desirable in certain organisational settings. We shall consider this further in the last chapter, when the ultimate test is applied: was the change successful and for whom?

A second possible outcome for any organisational change is that of *metastability*. This describes a condition of stability, but only in the short term while certain specific, local conditions prevail such as the presence of a manager on second-ment, the involvement of a management consultancy, a period of low product demand or high staff morale. As we saw with the principle of metastability, in some systems any equilibrium reached can be fragile and sensitive to minor disturbances, which could cause change activity to recommence. Metastable change outcomes are usually an intermediate stage, part of a series of change activities. The next stage – should the metastability be disturbed – is usually known or at least broadly predictable. Metastable outcomes cannot be sustained indefinitely without the expenditure of considerable resource and energy, and will normally deteriorate down to a more stable state.

Our third category of change outcome is *instability*. Here, the result of a given organisational change leaves it with an inherent instability and propensity to change unpredictably in the future. This differs from the metastable outcomes above in that there is no stability, even in the very immediate term. Subsequent changes could be of any *source*, *type* or *focus* and occur at any *level*. There could be a strange attractor at work within the business, not permitting it to settle in or move towards a state of equilibrium (dynamic or otherwise). Often perpetual instability is caused by an unstable environment – such as high inflation or political uncertainty. Emerging business markets in the Far East or Latin America illustrate this well. Those companies which are able to thrive and survive in ambiguous, inherently unstable market environments do so by being willing to live with perpetual instability internally – particularly strategy, structure and process foci. Like those rare organisms scientists occasionally discover which have the ability to live in the most inhospitable places on earth, so many fledgling organisations have learnt how to change, grow and adapt in seemingly unconducive environments – challenging our established assumption that instability and chaos are inherently undesirable.

We are told that organisms found in the depths of the sea or living on volcanic vents have much to teach us about surviving and thriving against all the odds. A Brazilian market trader or an entrepreneur from Shanghai are also people we should be more eager to learn from about how they navigate through ceaseless and sometimes traumatic change that leads to yet more instability.

A fourth possible change outcome which we are very occasionally forced to consider is *catastrophic* change. This outcome category describes foci changes that result in the immediate and sudden collapse of an organisation. Following some process, structure or behaviour change, for example, the business may be left in an unviable state such that its identity and key revenue-generating processes can no longer be maintained. The behaviour of an options trader within Barings Bank allegedly resulted in an evolutionary change in the corporate financial state of the bank over a period of several years – the outcome of which could be described as catastrophic. The bank lost its identity and ability to trade immediately the change in the corporate balance sheet came to light. This particular example illustrates the importance of measurement in understanding the nature of change phenomena. While the losses remained unmeasured due to ineffective back office, administrative and regulatory procedures, the change in corporate financial state was not perceived and therefore not acknowledged as real, i.e. in individualist terms. Philosophically, it could be argued that the bank became an unviable entity many months before it was actually declared bankrupt.

During periods of economic recession, catastrophic change is more prevalent. Natural life cycle type changes that occur within any business could bring it to an end – declining market niche, loss of a charismatic founding visionary, or the entry of larger competitors with less to lose and more patience to wait for a financial return. Alternatively, it may be the result of a planned change initiative such as business acquisition and asset stripping deliberately to divest organisational entities which do not fit with a given conglomerate portfolio. Some catastrophic outcomes are the result of business restructuring changes to diversify and enter additional markets, or undergoing a radical strategic repositioning. Such entrepreneurial ventures can fail due to higher than expected entry costs, longer than anticipated investment returns or just simply overestimating customer demand and projected revenue streams.

Summary

In this chapter we have considered a few of the lessons that the physical sciences have to tell us about resistance to change, and what we are likely to find at the end of the change journey. Table 9.1 summarises the main concepts that have been introduced.

Table 9.1 Summary of Chapter 9 building block concepts

Concept	Physical example	Section heading
Constructive resistance	Nuclear fission	*Change in chains*
Absorptive resistance	Phase transitions	*Taking up the slack*
Fragile resistance	Self-organised criticality	*Change on the boundary*
Overload resistance	Adiabatic change	*Protocol breakdown*
Bonded resistance	Atomic bonding	*Dissolving the glue*
Closed resistance	Noble gases and alkali metals	*Persuasions to change*
Preservative resistance	Autopoiesis	*Maintaining identity*
Change outcomes	• Stability • Metastability • Instability • Catastrophe	

This concludes our foray outside the confines of the traditional management literature. It is hoped that the building blocks in their entirety may go some way towards helping us better understand this all-consuming, ever-present phenomenon which is assailing our organisations and demanding a response. The next chapter endeavours to put into context the building blocks we have covered, and offers some thoughts on how the reader can develop them further.

10 Making it work and making a difference

The challenge facing modern managers is to become accomplished in the art of using metaphor to find new ways of seeing, understanding and shaping their actions.

(Morgan, 1993: 10)

Introduction

Our journey is almost over. We have trawled through a number of disciplines in search of inspiration to meet the challenge facing today's fast-moving organisational environment, where change has become increasingly complex and for many a way of life. As stated at the outset, the purpose was not to be prescriptive and offer some comprehensive, all-embracing theory of change. Rather, it is hoped that having read this far these pages will have provided a flickering candle with which to explore a vast Aladdin's cave, rich with concepts, metaphors, descriptions and insights into the dynamics of change. Only a tiny selection has been examined briefly here, but a world awaits for the curious manager, academic or consultant who is eager to learn from other knowledge domains, in their quest to gain a deeper understanding of change. In part, this book has attempted to provide the reader with a basis for meeting the challenge that Gareth Morgan puts before us in the opening quote above.

This closing chapter considers two ways in which readers can explore further on their own. In addition two essential questions are posed for both practitioners and academics: what constitutes successful change, and when does a change metaphor become reality? These are intriguing and yet important questions which certainly warrant discussion. The chapter finishes with some suggestions for further research: areas of the cave worthy of more detailed inspection as subject domains which potentially have a lot to offer the change thinker.

A framework for thinking

The building blocks for change that have been described in this book are offered only as a beginning. They are not intended to provide a prescriptive model for describing and managing change, but merely an initial framework for thinking about an increasingly important phenomenon. If some of the concepts they contain have sparked an idea, a 'what if' question, or connected with a business problem you are currently faced with, then they have achieved their purpose. Predicting the future of organisations is becoming an increasingly futile task. There are too many variables to consider, all interacting in a complex web of interdependence. We are moving from a world in which we determine our destination and staging points in traditional corporate planning style to a world in which we must learn to navigate a path into the future between myriad possibilities, never setting our strategic sights too far ahead. There are few givens, few absolutes any more, around which we can base our change journey. Perhaps there never were and we convinced ourselves that they existed. Either way, the old deterministic cow paths for thinking and dealing with change must now give way to alternatives. What is urgently required is a sound understanding of how change works, what drives it and shapes it within our organisations. Fundamentally, it is the engine which propels an organisation from the cloying affections of the past, through the challenges of the present and into the future. As a framework for thinking, it is hoped that the building blocks provide some clues as to how that engine works and what critical parts it contains. While no model can ever fully capture reality and explain events, models do help to structure thinking and guide enquiry. As Warner Burke has observed:

> 'Provided we do not allow ourselves to be trapped by a particular model, and as a consequence "not see" certain, critical information about an organisation, using a model for diagnosis is highly beneficial. A sufficiently comprehensive model can help us to organise data in useful categories and see more easily and quickly domains in the organisation that need attention.'
>
> (Burke, 1992: 138)

Each new change scenario that we encounter is unique and will contain some nuance or twist which needs to be fully understood. Thinking about each scenario in terms of the general building blocks outlined in Chapters 6, 7, 8 and 9 will help put shape and colour to how we perceive and interpret it. Probing for hidden dynamics not immediately obvious, looking for root cause by exploring sources and triggers, or simply understanding the basic feedback processes at work between the key variables can all add up to a more comprehensive understanding of the situation.

Nonetheless, the particular change metaphors and analogies on which these building blocks are founded are limited. There is nothing like being able to dig one's own well for intellectual inspiration and creative insight when faced with a complex change situation. Whether you are a researcher looking to unravel events and learn something from a case study situation, or a manager planning a large-scale, multilevel change programme which threatens to rewrite your diary for the next eight months, nothing beats the personal insight and hard-won flash of inspiration. The next section offers a way of generating your own change metaphors and analogies to complement those offered in the building blocks earlier.

A guide for enquiry

In taking further the approach and ideas presented in this book, there are some simple stages in thinking which can soon generate fresh and novel insights into change for yourself. A certain intellectual curiosity is necessary to begin with, but as with anything in life, the hardest step is just getting started. In this case, all we have to do is open our mental eyelids and survey what we see.

Step 1: Opening your eyes to the world around

The natural and physical world offers a multitude of examples of change phenomena over a range of time scales: 'Things go slowly for a time and nothing seems to change – until suddenly the eggshell cracks, the branch blossoms, the tadpole's tail shrinks away, the leaf falls, the bird moults, the hibernation begins' (Bridges, 1980: 5). The diversity of such change phenomena is vast. This first step merely requires you to identify suitable candidates from a range of disciplines which you think are sufficiently intriguing to warrant further investigation. In choosing your selection of change phenomena, several criteria should be borne in mind where possible.

- The phenomenon should be well documented and widely described in the relevant scientific literature.
- Ideally, there should be established theories which attempt to explain the phenomenon.
- The phenomenon should not be too obscure or wrapped in complex and highly technical language; those which are capable of being readily grasped by the non-specialist are ideal.

The objective should be to select phenomena which are rich enough in description and conceptually deep enough to allow metaphoric and analogic abstraction and reasoning later on. In this respect, comprehension by the non-specialist is of great importance. Trawl far and wide. As can be seen from the change phenomena presented in earlier chapters, in some cases one need progress no further than a high school chemistry book for initial inspiration. However, this is best followed up with a more in-depth look at how and why the change phenomenon occurs if the underlying dynamics are to be better understood. A good dictionary of science can also be a great help in 'surfing' through established science concepts to kick-start the imagination. Being open, for example, to hearing how the physicist or geologist describes and models change can be the starting point to broadening one's thinking about how change can be conceived and managed. Developing an intellectual curiosity for change as it manifests itself in other walks of life is an essential first step. There is a common misconception that we have to be specialists in a given subject in order to enjoy the fruits that it has yielded over the years. Certainly there is often a complex language and history to most disciplines in the natural and physical sciences. However, the last twenty years have seen an explosion in the volume of information available to the average person, through both electronic and paper media. There are many excellent and very readable scientific texts accessible to the layman and those without a formal background in the subject. They can provide a window on subject domains previously closed to the uninitiated – albeit a somewhat misty window.

Step 2: Thinking beyond the next management fad

The next stage is to analyse the theories and concepts employed by the relevant scientific community to describe and explain the change phenomenon (see Figure 10.8). This raises a somewhat controversial issue. A long-standing point of discussion within the philosophy of science literature is whether or not observation and description of a given phenomenon can be made independently of pre-existing theory (see Hanson, 1969; Carnes, 1982). The view taken here is that the specialist probably cannot describe a phenomenon within his or her field without seeing it through the lens of prevailing theory. The non-specialist, however, perhaps ignorant of the appropriate theoretical language and technical parlance, may be able to perceive and describe the phenomenon in some other way. This alternative account could well offer novel and conceptually useful metaphors and analogies not captured by the more formal theory-laden description of the specialist. Thus, contributions from those not familiar with the existing theoretical explanations for the phenomenon in question can be of great value in helping to avoid overlooking any subtle conceptual insights. In this way, both the formal explanations and theories of the original discipline and the descriptions of the non-specialist can be explored.

Either way, the objective of this step is to immerse oneself in the imagery, vocabulary and mindset of change descriptions on offer. Obviously, there is no way of achieving the same degree of familiarity with the explanatory theories as the specialist – particularly if complex mathematical models are involved. Nonetheless, a basic understanding of the key concepts can often be quickly obtained. It should not be forgotten that this is an exercise in high level, qualitative knowledge gathering, not quantitative analysis.

Step 3: Using your organisational creative juices

By this final step, your investigation of the change phenomenon should have produced a number of isomorphic concepts, as well as some rich metaphors and analogies. As we saw in Chapter 2, metaphorical thinking is becoming well

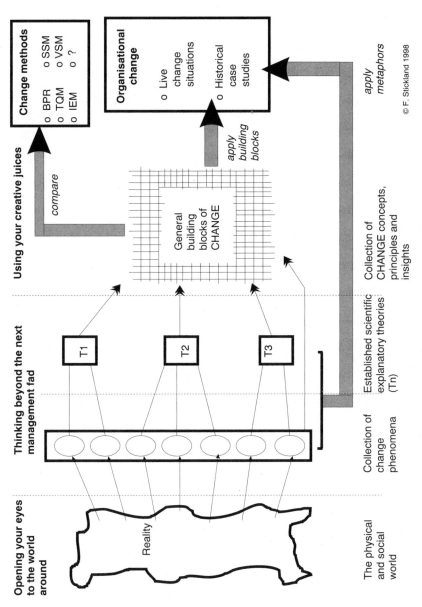

Figure 10.1 Investigating change – applying insights to the organisation

established as an explicit tool with which to study various facets of system behaviour, particularly within organisation theory. Having identified a number of change phenomena of interest, and explored the concepts, language and models that have been developed to describe them, you are then in a strong position to begin drawing tentative parallels with organisations. We all live by analogy and metaphor. Americans love their sporting analogies to describe business situations, from 'going the whole nine yards' to 'hitting a home run'. They are so embedded in how people think that they become an integral part of language and description. Why? Because they bring a visual and almost tangible descriptive value to the thinking process beyond conventional business vocabulary.

Armed with several intriguing change concepts full of metaphoric and analogic potential, your capacity to think creatively about a specific organisational change situation increases significantly. This final step involves making comparisons between the metaphor's concepts and the organisation – or indeed any other type of system. Beer (1966, 1984) has outlined a formal method of applying concepts from one subject domain to another. This is an excellent way of exploring change metaphors and analogies in an organisational setting. Figure 10.2 attempts to demonstrate a variation on Beer's original method, illustrating how to discover whether a particular metaphor can offer significant insight into a given change situation.

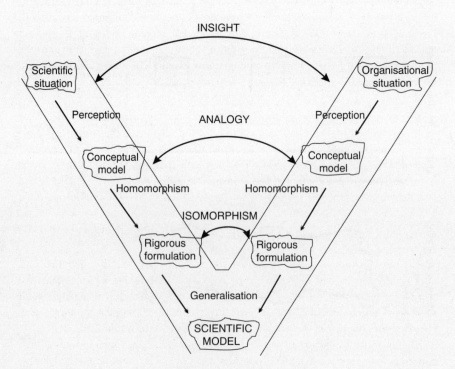

Figure 10.2 Learning from a metaphor (adapted from Beer, 1984)

The key stages are as follows:

1 *Find initial insight*: generate a general comparison between some change phenomenon within the natural/physical sciences and a given organisational scenario. This is usually in the form of a metaphor: A is like B due to loose similarities 1, 2, 3, etc.
2 *Explore the analogy*: explore the similarities in more detail by stating them explicitly. It can be useful to create a conceptual model for both the change phenomenon and the organisational scenario to clarify thinking.
3 *Undertake mapping*: identify specific one-to-one relationships between the two models or situations. The purpose of such *homomorphic* mapping is to eliminate inappropriate aspects of the comparison which do not correspond or are not applicable.
4 *Assess implications*: draw out any implications of the analysis for the organisational scenario, for change planning, diagnosis or management.

For specific examples of how Beer's method has been applied in practice, see Clemson (1984) and Tsoukas (1991). The original approach suggested that a formal scientific model should be built which captures the generic insights from the two situations. However, for our purposes here a qualitative approach is more appropriate, in order to gain a deeper conceptual understanding of the nature and dynamics of organisational change. A good example of how an initial insight from biology led to a new way of describing the organisation can be found in Goullart and Kelly (1995), *Transforming the Organisation*. They take a metaphor from genetics of the *genome* or genetic imprint and propose twelve corporate chromosomes, viewing the organisation as a *biological corporation*:

> Together, these chromosomes represent the integrated 'software' that governs biocorporate life. . . . The role of the CEO and the leadership team is to act as *the genetic architects of the corporation*. As such, they are not concerned with the minutiae of corporate life, but with splicing the right genes, of the right chromosomes, at the right time, and in the right place to enable the twelve bio-corporate systems to interact with each other in the best possible way.
>
> (Goullart and Kelly, 1995: 8; original emphasis)

Their book draws out the implications and parallels of the genome and chromosome metaphor to the full, applying it to a whole range of areas from the role of the leadership, the organisation structure and strategy formulation through to reward mechanisms. Without explicitly using Beer's approach, their work clearly shows the power of working through the four steps outlined above.

Having looked at ways in which the cross-discipline approach espoused here can be actually used, it is time to consider a couple of key questions which so far have not been addressed.

A question of metaphor

An important issue that we have not examined so far relates to the transference of ideas and concepts from one subject domain to another – in particular, from the natural and physical sciences to the organisation. Social systems such as societies or organisations are composed of intelligent, sentient individuals capable of purposeful decision-making in an attempt to influence their future. Physical systems, on the other hand, arguably possess no such conscious or cognitive ability, being made up of electrons, atoms and molecules. This distinction raises an interesting point of debate. Can the concepts and phenomena abstracted from a 'physical' source domain be said actually to exist in a 'social' target domain, or are they merely being used in some metaphorical sense to draw out parallels and make comparisons between the two disciplines? Most of the scholars discussed in this book who have explicitly taken concepts from one discipline and applied them in another, have not directly addressed this question. The reader is often left to make his or her own judgement on whether their use is real or metaphorical. Indeed, at a recent workshop on chaos theory applications within the social sciences none of the speakers explicitly stated their position on this issue. Afterwards, the author conducted a survey on the point from those who had presented research papers. The response was split between those who viewed the identification of chaotic attractors and fractal structures within their target social system as real, and those for whom it was merely a metaphoric comparison. One individual declared after some thought, that he honestly did not know and had never considered the point. If the above survey is considered representative, it demonstrates that there is considerable ambiguity among researchers on the matter.

Two writers have made their position clear. Zimmerman (1992) uses the phenomenon of a dissipative structure in physical science to describe self-organising social structures such as organisations. She warns against taking metaphors literally:

> A caution is necessary about the risk of mapping from the physical to the organisational or to the cognitive levels of analysis. The objective of this comparison is not to show definitively that self-renewing organisations *are* dissipative structures. Instead the metaphor of dissipative structures may shed light on some dimensions or ways of understanding organisations to enhance the management of co-evolution. The use of metaphor is merely the first stage in the process.
>
> (Zimmerman, 1992: 12; emphasis added)

On the other hand, Wheatley (1992) takes a different view. While acknowledging the use of metaphor for description, she argues that some natural science phenomena can actually be identified within organisations. As an example, she uses the phenomenon of a field to conceptualise customer service within a chain of retail stores:

At one level, thinking about organisational fields is metaphoric, an interesting concept to play with. But the longer I have thought about it, the more I am willing to believe that there are literal fields within organisations. I can imagine an invisible customer service field filling the spaces of . . . stores . . . helping to structure employee's activities, and generating service behaviours whenever the energy of an employee intersected with that field.

(Wheatley, 1992: 53)

Whichever view one holds has serious implications for measurement and organisational change activities. Therefore, this issue needs to be articulated and better understood if effective methods and approaches are to be developed which can harness the enormous potential of cross-discipline transference of ideas. Within this book, concepts and phenomena of change have only been employed metaphorically to aid description, stimulate discussion and encourage a deeper conceptual understanding of change as a phenomenon. For example, the embedded dynamics of kinetic energy, potential energy and micro competing forces, discussed in Chapter 7, are merely an attempt to demonstrate that an important component of change in any system is the background noise of micro level friction and chance encounters between system elements – whether they be molecules or human individuals. Clearly, there is not an exact one-to-one mapping between Brownian motion and social interaction. Nonetheless, there are enough significant analogic parallels to make the comparison conceptually beneficial, and to generate some rich descriptive imagery.

The perceived utility and importance of metaphorical thinking is heightened by such cross-discipline research. In the quest for a greater understanding of discipline specific phenomena, as soon as one steps outside of one's own subject domain in search of other ideas and concepts, one is confronted with metaphor and analogy. Any approach which does advocate the exploration of several disciplines must address the question of metaphor, and explain how it is to be dealt with. By definition the two are inextricably linked.

'There is nothing like being able to dig one's own well for intellectual inspiration and creative insight when faced with a complex change situation. Whether you are a researcher looking to unravel events and learn something from a case study, or a manager planning a large-scale, multilevel change programme which threatens to rewrite your diary for the next eight months, nothing beats the personal insight and hard-won flash of inspiration.'

Defining successful change

What we have been concerned with in this book is to highlight some of the fundamental components of change and uncover a few of the hidden dynamics that shape it. Being able to place a value judgement on the final outcome and ascribing a good or bad label has not been of interest. Rather, the priority has been to try and understand the mechanics of change itself, in the belief that this puts the change practitioner in a better position accurately to diagnose the organisation when change is not working effectively. However, it is acknowledged that with any transition there can be winners and losers. Too often within our changing organisations we forget to ask the 'success for whom' question. For whom is the change deemed successful? And perhaps more importantly, who is it that defines what success should look like for a given change – the consultant, the management team, the academic or the staff affected? Adding customers and shareholders to the list of contenders blurs the issue even more. Too often in change interventions we see the consultant dictating what the criteria for effectiveness should be and how 'success' is best defined. Cameron and Whetten (1981) convincingly demonstrated this with their empirical study of how 'effectiveness' is perceived within organisations. The views, assumptions and criteria for success and effectiveness of those working within the organisation may well be different from those designing and managing the change intervention itself. Other internal departments and functions may even have differing success criteria. Therefore, any change intervention aimed at improving organisational effectiveness – in whatever area – must attempt to understand the meaning and importance which organisational members attach to what constitutes successful change.

The work of Checkland (1972) on Soft Systems and Mason and Mitroff (1981) on Strategic Assumption Surfacing and Testing are two examples of how the richness of 'success perception' can be captured, to inform the design of an intervention before it begins. Stopping to ask the 'success for whom' question can help clarify how best to label and position the eventual change. It can also assist in identifying more precisely what change foci will be affected.

Suggestions for further research

Having surveyed a number of areas within the traditional three sciences, it is appropriate at this point to refer the interested reader to some other fascinating areas where organisational change metaphors abound. Only a limited number of change phenomena and perspectives have been covered here. Clearly, a much wider examination of change covering more subject domains could enhance our understanding still further. The emerging discipline of Complexity Science – with its emphasis on modelling and understanding processes of change and evolution within dynamic complex systems – is likely to be a good hunting ground for further perspectives, phenomena and general principles of change. Specialist fields such as cellular automata (Dewdney, 1985; Wolfram, 1986), neural networks and adaptation (Forrest, 1991), genetic algorithms (Goldberg, 1989) and artificial life (Langton, 1989; Langton *et al.*, 1992) are all likely to contain change ideas worth exploring and building into the change building blocks developed to date. As has already been emphasised, in their current form the building blocks represent only an initial attempt to capture some of the main themes and principles of change within the organisation, drawing from the theories and concepts of relatively few subject domains. It is hoped that others will see the merits of the approach and seek to broaden our understanding of change by looking even further afield.

> 'What is urgently required is a sound understanding of how change works, what drives it and shapes it within our organisations. Fundamentally, it is the engine which propels an organisation from the cloying affections of the past, through the challenges of the present and into the future.'

Second, there are other ways in which the building blocks could be applied within organisational change thinking. As Figure 10.1 illustrates, one way is by using them to investigate existing change methodologies and philosophies, such as Business Process Re-engineering, Soft Systems Methodology or Total Quality Management. A comparison could be made between the general underlying dynamics and principles of change embodied within the building blocks, and the assumptions and perspectives on change implicit within each methodology. For example, does a given change methodology have a rich enough understanding of *resistance*? Does it acknowledge the existence of multilevel, multispeed change? Does it assume change is achieved via simple linear cause–effect relationships that can be modelled? Does BPR give sufficient consideration to change and dynamic interaction between different process levels during process analysis and redesign (see Stickland, 1996). Research of this type to assess to what extent the building blocks reflect the traditions and assumptions inherent in our change methods – and vice versa – would be another useful way of exploring further the practical implications of a deeper knowledge of change. Nonetheless, regardless of the way in which the building blocks are employed, it is hoped that they will be honed and refined by others in the future.

To conclude, it is the author's belief that lying hidden among the multitude of specialist disciplines of the natural and physical sciences is a wealth of rich and insightful change concepts, suitable for abstraction at a general level and application as metaphors and structural analogies into other fields of study – particularly organisational behaviour and management theory. As we have seen, a number of theorists have focused on imagery and concepts from what has become known as the 'new sciences' – embracing disciplines such as quantum mechanics and chaos theory and drawing parallels with organisational behaviour. Certainly these more recent scientific developments have much to contribute to organisational thinking and we have considered here what some of them have to offer the student of change. However, let us not forget the more mundane and well-established scientific concepts. As previous chapters have demonstrated, they also have a great deal to offer to organisational thinkers and managers and should not be neglected by those looking for new imagery and insight with which to face the future.

In time, it is hoped that the initial framework of building blocks that has been suggested can be expanded and modified by others to provide a broad conceptual foundation which captures more accurately some of the common principles, perspectives and dynamics of change; not some all-encompassing, grand theory or rigorous prescriptive methodology, but a means of guiding enquiry and promoting creative and original thinking about an important universal phenomenon. Such a foundation is urgently required, both as a basis for developing new and non-prescriptive strategies for change management, and to assess the theoretical footing and validity of the many approaches to organisational change already in popular use.

Notes

1 Managing change: the problem redefined

1 Of approximately 1,400 journals monitored by the Bath Information Data Services (BIDS – Social Science Database) in 1995, the author found over 550 were devoted to change of one sort or another.
2 See Badertscher (1982) and Callan (1993).
3 The term *transition* will be used interchangeably with *change* throughout the book. While it is acknowledged that transition alludes more to the actual passage from one state to another, the two words are virtually synonymous in popular meaning. Many will also associate the term more with personal and individual adjustment, due to the excellent work of William Bridges (1980). The issue of labelling change will be discussed in more detail in Chapter 8.

2 Moving beyond the conventional: systems thinkers unite

1 Perhaps the most comprehensive history of systems thinking up to the early 1970s can be found in Lilienfield (1978). Developments since then are best described by journal publications such as *Systems Research* (John Wiley), *Systems Practice* (Plenum Press) and the annual proceedings of the International Society for the Systems Sciences, which was born under the auspices of the American Association for the Advancement of Science.
2 Two terms are often used here: *homology* and *isomorphy*. An homology is a general comparison which highlights similarities in structure and form between two things, but not function. An isomorphism describes a specific one-to-one mapping of some attribute or property from one thing onto another. It is a direct comparison as opposed to some vague generalisation that two things bear similarity.
3 The advent of the biological metaphor (see Bogdanov, 1913; Bertalanffy, 1949) and Gestalt psychology and field theory (see Whitaker, 1965; Katz and Kahn, 1966) began to challenge this machine-like view of the organisation. See Ackoff (1981) for a more detailed examination of this transition from the machine age to the systems age in organisational thinking.
4 See, for example, Berlinski (1976), Lilienfield (1978) and Naughton (1979) for a critique of General Systems Theory.
5 Other examples of such work include Klir (1969, 1985), Mesarovic and Takahara (1975, 1988), Nicolis and Prigogine (1977).
6 Other examples of work at the more qualitative end of GST include Lasker (1983), Robbins and Oliva (1984), Barrow (1991), Buckner (1995), McNeil (1995).
7 The Primer Group is one such organisation taking GST thinking from the textbook into education and application. See www.isss.org/primer/primer.htm for more information.

8   Examples abound of direct use of metaphor in the organisational literature. Beer (1981) and Tsoukas (1991) demonstrate this well. Other specific examples include: information systems (Walsham, 1991; Merali and Martin, 1994); creative management (Van Gundy 1988; Senge, 1990; Henry, 1991); General Systems Theory (Rapoport, 1988) and Critical Systems Thinking (Flood and Jackson, 1991a, b).

9   See, for example, Hanwell (1980) and Battan (1984) for a readable and more detailed description of atmospheric motion as a change phenomenon.

10 Lorenz (1963), Thom (1975), Smale (1980), West (1985), Bak and Chen (1991) are examples of other scientists who have encountered this distinction over the years.

3 Organisational change thinking: a look back

1   See, for example, Gilbreth and Gilbreth (1914), Fayol (1916), Davis (1928); Gulick and Urwick (1937), Mooney and Reiley (1931) for further reading on the scientific–rational view.

2   See, for example, Mayo (1933), Myers (1934), Barnard (1938) and more indirectly the research by Maslow (1943) on human motivation. Consolidating the human relations approach later were theorists such as Bennis (1959), McGregor (1960) and Likert (1967). All were proponents of a human relations approach.

3   Prominent advocates of the contingency approach included Simon (1947), Burns and Stalker (1961), Woodward (1965), Katz and Kahn (1966), Lawrence and Lorsch (1967), Thompson (1967).

4   See Ashby (1960), Beer (1981, 1985), Robb (1985), Espejo and Schwaninger (1993).

5   More detailed historical accounts can be found in Zaltman and Duncan (1977), Goodman (1982), Porras and Robertson (1987).

4 Tentative beginnings: some pioneers reviewed

1   Allison describes the Cuban Missile Crisis through various conceptual lenses, focusing on different units of analysis – leading to different interpretations of and justifications for the events that took place.

2   See, for example, Parsons (1960), Miller and Rice (1967), Buckley (1968), Clegg and Dunkerly (1980) and Koontz *et al.* (1984) – who all describe a macro, systemic view of the organisation.

3   See Weick (1969) and Janis and Mann (1977) for a discussion of this issue.

4   See, for example, Zmud and Armenakis (1978) and Terborg *et al.* (1980) for further development of the alpha, beta, gamma change taxonomy.

5 Forsaking pride and prejudice: multiple perspectives on change

1   Burrell and Morgan (1979) have explored some of the fundamental assumptions that underpin theoretical and methodological research in the social sciences. Specifically, they discuss the differing stances adopted by social theorists in the areas of ontology, epistemology, human nature and methodology. Chalmers (1982) has identified a similar set of assumptions for the natural and physical sciences. Some of the concepts that they examine are a useful starting point for looking at the various assumptions upon which our understanding of the notion of change is based. The way in which change is perceived and interpreted as a phenomenon is greatly influenced by these assumptions. To simplify the explanation, the labels and terms used by Chalmers are adopted in this chapter.

2   A distinction can be made here between change as a concept and change as a phenomenon. This is essentially an ontological distinction between the phenomenon

of change as it 'occurs' and the concepts and theories of change which are used to describe our perception and experience of it.

3   Burrell and Morgan (1979) explore this distinction in some detail and describe the differences in the *deterministic* and *voluntaristic* philosophical positions that underpin it.
4   Several authors have explored this issue in detail: see Taylor (1921), Bock (1956), Moore (1963).
5   See Capra (1975), Stapp (1982, 1985), Villars (1983), Leggett (1986) for a more detailed examination of this area.

6 Building blocks of change: Part 1   The basics

1   These two schools of thought are described as *determinist* and *voluntarist* by Burrell and Morgan (1979) and underpin this debate about change sources and origins.
2   For examples of simple modelling approaches suitable for analysing change sources see Coyle (1977), Wilson (1979), Sterman (1994). More advanced approaches can be found in Puccia and Levins (1985).
3   See, for example, Mills and Standingford (1963) for an excellent overview of organisation and methods.
4   The notion of organisational life cycles has been widely discussed in the literature. The interested reader is referred to the population ecology work of Hannan and Freeman (1977) and Rundall and McClain (1982).
5   See Porter (1990), Treacy and Wiersema (1993), Drucker (1994), Hamel and Prahalad (1994) for four views of strategy which offer a good starting point for thinking about strategic change and repositioning.
6   In soft systems methodology terms (Checkland, 1972) they represent the domain of the transformation process, the 'T' of CATWOE: in other words, that which is being changed or transformed.

7 Building blocks of change: Part 2   Embedded dynamics

1   Morgan (1991) has described the management of change as a process of attempting to move the organisation from one attractor to another. This is another way of using the metaphor to help understand change at more of a macro level. Thinking of an attractor as an embedded dynamic, on the other hand, focuses attention down to more behavioural and operational levels, where their existence shapes and drives change at the micro level.
2   Other definitions of culture contain similar themes, including *shared assumptions* and a common *set of norms and values*.
3   See the experiences of a large pharmaceutical merger – the collision of two very different national culture attractors, *Wall Street Journal*, 5 February 1997.
4   See Brian Arthur's (1994) explanation of the role of positive feedback in giving VHS the dominance over Beta in the VCR battle for critical market share.
5   As earth travels through space, it encounters numerous minor meteorites from deep space which burn up harmlessly in the atmosphere. Sometimes earth will encounter far larger objects which can cause significant changes within the planet's climatic and ecological systems. In organisational terms, these major disturbances may represent events such as privatisation, industry deregulation, hostile takeover bids or the advent of some new ground-breaking technology – these are all boundary contacts that have to be responded to reactively, or viewed as contingencies which must be anticipated and prepared for. Some of these more macro variables are modelled by Porter's (1980) five forces.

8 Building blocks of change: Part 3   From levels to labelling

1 Stafford Beer has developed the Viable System Model of an organisation, in which the notion of recursion is critical. Recursion can be defined as *structural invariance* at different levels of a system.
2 In biological terms, these two types of level change are akin to *morphostasis* and *morphogenesis* respectively (see Wilden, 1980; Smith, 1984; Ford and Backoff, 1987).
3 See Ashby (1956), Beer (1985), Espejo and Schwaninger (1993) within the management cybernetics literature and Wolstenholm (1990) and Sterman (1994) for examples of feedback processes within the system dynamics field.
4 For further detail see Waldram (1985).
5 Autocatalytic sets consist of reactants where one or more of the eventual reaction products is itself a catalyst for the reaction pathway. See Kauffman (1991, 1992) who has attempted to apply concepts of autocatalysis to organisational settings.

9 Building blocks of change: Part 4   Resistance and endings explored

1 See Williams *et al.* (1968).
2 See Stein (1989), Jen (1990), Waldrop (1992).
3 See, for example, Railston (1953) who describes this process well.
4 Krypton, neon and radon do react with fluorine and oxygen, but only under special conditions.
5 See Combs (1992), Goertzel (1993), Laszlo (1994).

Bibliography

Abraham, R.H. (1981) 'The function of mathematics in the evolution of the noosphere', in E. Jantsch (ed.) *The Evolutionary Vision*, Westview Press: Colorado, pp.153–168.

—— (1988) 'Dynamics and self organisation', in F.E. Yates (ed.) *Self Organising Systems and the Emergence of Order*, Plenum Press: New York, pp. 3–22.

Ackoff, R.L. (1974) 'The systems revolution', *Long Range Planning*, vol. 7: 2–20.

—— (1979a) 'The future of operational research is past', *Journal of the Operational Research Society*, vol. 30:

—— (1979b) 'Restructuring the future of operational research', *Journal of Operational Research Society*, vol. 30: 189–200.

—— (1981) *Creating the Corporate Future*, John Wiley: New York.

Alberts, B. (1989) *Molecular Biology of the Cell*, 2nd edn, Garland Publishing: New York.

Allen, P.M. (1981) 'The evolutionary paradigm of dissipative structures', in E. Jantsch (ed.) *The Evolutionary Vision*, Westview Press: Colorado, pp. 25–72.

Allen, P.M., Herman, R. and Prigogine, I. (1977) 'The evolution of complexity and the laws of nature', in E. Lazlo and J. Bierman (eds) *Goals in a Global Community*, Pergamon Press: New York.

Allen, T.F. and Starr, T.B. (1982) *Hierarchy: Perspective for Ecological Complexity*, University of Chicago Press: Chicago.

Allison, G.T. (1971) *Essence of Decision*, Little, Brown: New York.

Andersen, D.F. (1988) 'Chaos in system dynamics models', *System Dynamics Review*, vol. 4 (1–2): 3–13.

Anderson, P.W. (1972) 'More is different: broken symmetry and the nature of the hierarchical structure of science', *Science*, vol. 177: 393–396.

Angrist, S.W. and Helper, L.G. (1967) *Order and Chaos*, Penguin: London.

Applebaum, R.P. (1970) *Theories of Social Change*, Markham Publications: London.

Aracil, J. (1986) 'Bifurcations and structural stability in the dynamical systems modelling process', *Systems Research*, vol. 3 (4): 243–252.

Argyle, M. (1974) *The Social Psychology of Work*, Penguin: London.

Argyris, C. (1962) *Interpersonal Competence and Organisational Effectiveness*, Tavistock Institute: London.

Argyris, C. and Schon, D. (1978) *Organisational Learning: A Theory of Action Perspective*, Addison-Wesley: Reading, MA.

Aron, R. (1961) *Introduction to the Philosophy of History*, Beacon Press: Boston, MA.

Arthur, W.B. (1994) 'Positive feedbacks in the economy', *McKinsey Quarterly*, vol. 1: 81–95.

Ashby, W.R. (1956) *An Introduction to Cybernetics*, Chapman and Hall: London.

—— (1960) *Design for a Brain*, 2nd edn, Chapman and Hall: London.

Ashton, D. (1948) *The Industrial Revolution 1760–1830*, Oxford University Press: Oxford.

Asimov, I. (1981) *Change*, Coronet Books: London.

Aulin, A. (1987) 'The method of causal recursion in mathematical dynamics', *International Journal of General Systems*, vol. 13: 229–255.

Ayer, A.J. (1936) *Language, Truth and Logic*, Gollancz: London.

Badertscher, D.G. (1982) 'An examination of the dynamics of change in information technology as viewed from law libraries and information centres', *Law Library Journal*, vol. 75 (2): 198–211.

Bahm, A.J. (1979) *The Philosophers World Model*, Greenwood Press: London.

Bai-Lin, H. (ed.) (1984) *Chaos*, World Scientific: Singapore.

Bak, P. and Chen, K. (1991) 'Self-organised criticality', *Scientific America*, January: 46–53.

Bak, P., Chen, K. and Wiesenfeld, K. (1988) 'Self-organised criticality', *Physical Review A*, vol. 38 (1): 364–374.

Barber, B. (1952) *Science and the Social Order*, Free Press: Glencoe, IL.

Barnard, C.I. (1938) *The Function of the Executive*, Harvard University Press: Cambridge, MA.

Barnett, S. (1996) 'Style and strategy: new metaphor, new insights', *European Management Journal*, vol. 14: 347–355.

Barrow, J.D. (1991) *Theories of Everything*, Oxford University Press: Oxford.

Bartlett, C.A. and Goshal, S. (1989) *Managing Across Borders: The Transnational Solution*, Harvard Business School Press: Boston, MA.

Bartunek, J. and Louis, M. (1988) 'The interplay of organisation development and organisational transformation', *Research in Organisational Change and Development*, vol. 2: 97–134.

Bateson, G. and Bateson, M.C. (1988) 'The structure in the fabric', in G. Bateson and M.C. Bateson *Angels Fear: Toward an Epistemology of the Sacred*, Macmillan Publishing: London, pp. 151–167.

Battan, L.J. (1984) *Fundamentals of Meteorology*, 2nd edn, Prentice-Hall: Englewood Cliffs, NJ.

Baum, J.A. and Singh, J.V. (1994) *Evolutionary Dynamics of Organisations*, Oxford University Press: Oxford.

Baum, S.J. and Scaife, C.W. (1975) *Chemistry: A Life Science Approach*, Macmillan Publishing: New York.

Baumgartner, T. and Burns, T.R. (1976) 'Open systems and multilevel processes: implications for social research', *Journal of General Systems*, vol. 3: 25–42.

Beach, S.D. (1980) *Personnel*, Macmillan: London.

Beckford, J.L. (1992) 'Passing on a family business, or a family business passing on', *Systems Practice*, vol. 5 (5): 543–560.

—— (1993) PhD thesis, Hull University, England.

Beckhard, R. and Harris, R.T. (1977) *Organisational Transitions*, Addison-Wesley: Reading, MA.

—— (1987) *Organisational Transitions: Managing Complex Change*, 2nd edn, Addison-Wesley: Wokingham.

Bednarz, J. (1988) 'Autopoiesis: The organisational closure of social systems', *Systems Research*, vol. 5 (1): 57–64.

Beer, S. (1966) *Decision and Control*, John Wiley: Chichester.

—— (1970) 'Managing complexity', in *The Management of Information and Knowledge*, UGPO: Washington DC, pp. 41–61.

—— (1979) *The Heart of the Enterprise*, John Wiley: Chichester.

—— (1981) *Brain of the Firm*, John Wiley: Chichester.

—— (1984) 'The viable system model: development, methodology and pathology', *Journal of Operational Research Society*, vol. 35 (1): 9.

—— (1985) *Diagnosing the System for Organisations*, John Wiley: Chichester.

Begun, J.W. (1994) 'Chaos and complexity: frontiers of organization science, *Journal of Management Enquiry*, vol. 3: 329–335.

Beishon, J. (1980) *Systems Organisation: The Management of Complexity*, Open University Press: Milton Keynes.

Beishon, J. and Peters, G. (eds) (1981) *Systems Behaviour*, Open University Systems Group, Harper and Row: London.

Bell, W.G. (1994) *The Great Plague of London*, Bracken Books: London.

Bemelmans, T.M. (1984) *Beyond Productivity: Information Systems Development for Organisational Effectiveness*, North-Holland: Amsterdam.

Bennis, W.G. (1959) 'Leadership theory and administrative behaviour', *Administrative Science Quarterly*, vol. 4: 259–301.

—— (1963) 'A new role for behavioural sciences effecting organisational change', *Administrative Sciences Quarterly*, vol. 8: 1963–1966.

—— (1966a) *Changing Organizations*, McGraw-Hill: New York.

—— (1966b) *Operational Research and the Social Sciences*, Tavistock Institute: London.

—— (1970) 'A funny thing happened to me on the way to the future', *American Psychologist*, vol. 25 (7): 595–608.

Bennis, W.G., Benne, K.D. and Chin, R. (eds) (1970) *The Planning of Change*, 2nd edn, Holt Rinehart and Winston: London.

Benson, J.K. (1977) 'Organisations: a dialectical view', *Administrative Science Quarterly*, vol. 22: 1–21.

Berg, P.O. (1979) *Emotional Structures in Organisations*, University of Lund Student Literature, Sweden.

Berlinski, D. (1976) *On Systems Analysis*, MIT Press: Cambridge, MA.

Bertalanffy, L. von (1949) 'Zu einer allgemeinen systemlehre', *Biologia Generalis*, vol. 3: 23–29, 19: 114–129.

—— (1950) 'The theory of open systems in physics and biology', *Science*, vol. III: 23–29.

—— (1962) 'General systems theory – a critical review', *General Systems*, vol. vii: 1–20.

—— (1968) *General Systems Theory*, George Braziller: New York.

Bettis, R.A. and Donaldson, L. (1990) 'Market discipline and the discipline of management', *Academy of Management Review*, vol. 15 (3): 367–368.

Bhaskar, R. (1975) *A Realistic Theory of Science*, Leeds Books: Leeds, pp. 152–163.

Biggart, N.W. (1977) 'The creative–destructive process of organisational change', *Administrative Science Quarterly*, vol. 22: 410–426.

Black, M. (1962) *Models and Metaphors*, Cornell University Press: Ithaca, NY.

Blake, R.R. and Moulton, J.S. (1983) *Consultation*, Addison-Wesley: Reading, MA.

Blau, P.M. (1961) 'The dynamics of bureaucracy', in A. Etzioni (ed.) *Complex Organisations*, Holt, Rinehart and Winston: New York.

Bock, K.E. (1956) *The Acceptance of Histories*, University of California Press: Berkeley.

Bogdanov, A.A. (1913) *Vseobshaya Organizatsionnaya Nauka: Tekologia*, vol. 1, translated into English by P. Dudley, Hull University, M.L. Semenov: St. Petersburg, Russia.

Boguslaw, R. (1965) *The New Utopians*, Prentice-Hall: Englewood Cliffs, NJ.

Bohm, D. (1957) *Causality and Chance in Modern Physics*, Routledge and Kegan Paul: London.

—— (1978) 'The implicate order: a new order for physics', *Process Studies*, vol. 8: 73–102.

—— (1980) *Wholeness and the Implicate Order*, Routledge and Kegan Paul: London.

Bohm, D. and Peat, F.D. (1987) 'Revolutions, theories and creativity in science', in *Science, Order and Creativity*, Routledge: London, pp. 15–62.

Bohr, N. (1928) quoted in *Nature Supplement*, vol. 121: 78.

—— (1928) 'The Como lecture', reprinted in *Nature*, vol. 121: 580.

—— (1948) *Dialectica*, vol. 2, p. 312.

Boland, R.J. and Greenberg, R.H. (1988) 'Metaphorical structuring and organisational ambiguity', in L.R. Pondy, R.J. Boland and H. Thomas (eds) *Managing Ambiguity and Change*, John Wiley: Chichester, pp. 17–36.

Bondi, H. (1965) *Relativity and Common Sense – A New Approach to Einstein*, Heinemann: London.

Borowitz, S. and Beiser, A. (1966) *Essentials of Physics*, Addison-Wesley: Reading, MA.

Boulding, E. (1981) 'Evolutionary visions, sociology and the human life span', in E. Jantsch (ed.) *The Evolutionary Vision*, Westview Press: Colorado, pp.169–194.

Boulding, K. (1956a) 'General Systems Theory – The Skeleton of Science', *Management Science*, vol. 2: 197–208.

—— (1956b) 'Towards a general theory of growth', *General Systems*, vol. 1: 66–75.

Bower, J. (1983) 'Managing for efficiency, managing for equity', *Harvard Business Review*, August: 83–90.

Boyd, R. (1979) 'Metaphor and theory change: what is a metaphor for?, in A. Ortony (ed.) *Metaphor and Thought*, Cambridge University Press: Cambridge.

Brager, G. and Holloway, S. (1992) 'Assessing prospects for organisational change: the uses of force field analysis', *Administration in Social Work*, vol. 16 (3–4): 15–28.

Bridges, W. (1980) *Making Sense of Life's Changes*, Addison-Wesley: Reading, MA.

—— (1993) *Job Shift*, Addison-Wesley: Reading, MA.

Bridgman, P.W. (1961) *The Nature of Thermodynamics*, Harper Torchbook: New York.

Briggs, J. and Peat, F.D. (1984) *Looking Glass Universe: The Emerging Science of Wholeness*, Cornerstone Library: New York.

—— (1989) *Turbulent Mirror*, Harper and Row: New York.

Brown, R. (1988) *Group Processes: Dynamics Within and Between Groups*, Blackwell: Oxford.

Bruce, A.D. and Cowley, R.A. (1981) *Structural Phase Transitions*, Taylor and Francis: London.

Buck, R.C. (1956) 'On the logic of general behaviour systems theory', in H. Feigel and M. Scriven (eds) *Minnesota Studies in the Philosophy of Science*, vol. 1, University of Minnesota: Minnesota.

Buckley, W. (1968) 'Society as a complex adaptive system', in W. Buckley (ed.) *Modern Systems Research for the Behavioural Scientist*, Aldine Publishing Company: Chicago.

Buckner, R. (1995) 'General systems theory numerical evaluation', in *Proceedings of the 39th Annual Meeting of the International Society for the Systems Sciences*, Free University: Amsterdam, pp. 608–619.

Bunge, M. (1959) 'Do the levels of science reflect the levels of being?', in C.C. Thomas *Metascientific Queries*, Springfield: IL.

—— (1960a) 'Levels: a semantic preliminary', *The Review of Metaphysics*, vol. 8: 396–406.

—— (1960b) 'On the connections among levels', *Proceedings XII International Congress of Philosophy*, vol. VI: 36–48 Metaphysics and the Philosophy of Nature, Sansoni: Florence.

—— (1963) *The Myth of Simplicity: Problems of Scientific Philosophy*, Prentice-Hall: New York, Chapter 3.

—— (1979) *Treatise of Basic Philosophy*, vol. 5, Reidel: Dordecht, Holland, pp. 210–214.

Burke, E. quoted in *The Penguin Dictionary of Quotations* (1986), Omega Books: London.

Burke, W.W. (1992) *Organisational Development*, Addison-Wesley: New York.

Burke, W.W. and Litwin, G.H. (1989) 'A causal model of organisational change and performance', in J.W. Pfeiffer (ed.) *Developing Human Resources: 1989 Annual*, University Associates: San Diaego: pp. 277–288.

—— (1992) 'A Causal Model of Organisational Performance and Change', *Journal of Management*, vol. 18 (3): 532–545.

Burnes, B. (1992) *Managing Change*, Pitman Publishing: London.

Burns, T. and Stalker, G. (1961) *The Management of Innovation*, Tavistock Press: London.

—— (1966) 'Mechanistic and Organic Systems of Management', in T. Burns and G. Stalker *The Management of Innovation*, Tavistock Press: London.

Burnyeat, M. (1990) *The Theaetetus of Plato*, trans. M.J. Levett, Hackett Press: Indianapolis.

Burrell, G. and Morgan, G. (1979) *Sociological Paradigms and Organisational Analysis*, Heinemann: London.

Buss, A.R. (1974) 'Multivariate model of quantitative structural and quantistructural onto-genetic change', *Developmental Psychology*, vol. 10: 190–203.

Butler, V.G. (1985) *Organisation and Management*, Prentice-Hall: London.

Callan, V.J. (1993) 'Individual and organisational strategies for coping with organizational change', *Work and Stress*, vol. 7 (1): 63–75.

Cameron, K.S. and Whetten, D.A. (1981) 'Perceptions of effectiveness over organisational life cycles', *Administrative Science Quarterly*, vol. 26: 525–544.

Campbell, N.R. (1957) *The Philosophy of Theory and Experiment*, Dover Press: New York.

Cannon, W.B. (1963) *The Wisdom of the Body*, W.W. Norton: New York.

Capra, F. (1975) *The Tao of Physics*, Wildwood House: London.

Carnes, J.R. (1982) *Axiomatics and Dogmatics*, Christian Journals: London.

Cassirer, E. (1946) *Language and Myth*, Dover: New York.

—— (1955) *The Philosophy of Symbolic Forms*, vols 1–3, Yale University Press: New Haven, CO.

Chalmers, A.F. (1982) *What is this Thing Called Science?*, Open University Press: Milton Keynes.

Checkland, P.B. (1972) 'Towards a systems based methodology for real world problem solving', *Journal of Systems Engineering*, vol. 3: 87–116.

—— (1981) *Systems Thinking, Systems Practice*, John Wiley: Chichester.

—— (1985) 'From Optimizing to Learning: A Development of Systems Thinking for the 1990's', *Journal of the Operational Research Society*, vol. 36:

—— (1988) 'Researching systems methodology', keynote address delivered at the 10th Anniversary Conference of the UK Systems Society, Hull.

Child, J. (1972) 'Organisation structure, environment and performance: the role of strategic choice', *Sociology*, vol. 6: 1–22.

Churchman, C.W. (1970) 'Operations research as a profession', *Management Science*, vol. 17.

—— (1979) *The Systems Approach*, Dell: New York.

Clarke, P.A. and Ford, J.P. (1970) 'Methodological and theoretical problems in the investigation of planned organistional change', *Sociological Reveiw*, March: 29–52.

Clarke, P. and Starkey, K. (1988) *Organisational Transitions*, Pinter: London.

Claude, S.G. (1968) *The History of Management Thought*, Prentice-Hall: Englewood Cliffs, NJ.

Clegg, S. and Dunkerly (1980) *Organisation, Class and Control*, Routledge and Kegan Paul: London.

Clemson, B. (1984) *Cybernetics: A New Management Tool*, Abacus Press: Tunbridge Wells.

Cohen, R. (ed.) (1992) *Studies in Historical Change*, University Press of Virginia: Virginia.

Coleman, J.C., Butcher, J.N. and Carson, R.C. (1984) *Abnormal Psychology and Modern Life*, 7th edn, Scott-Foresman: Glenview, IL.

Coleman, J.S. (1968) 'The mathematical study of change', in H.M. Blalock and A.B. Blalock (eds) *Methodology in Social Research*, McGraw-Hill: New York.

Collins, L.M. and Horn, J.L. (eds) (1991) *Best Methods for the Analysis of Change*, American Psychology Association: New York.

Combs, A. (ed.) (1992) *Cooperation: Beyond the Age of Competition*, Gordon and Breach: Berkshire.

Conner, P.E. and Lake, L.K. (1988) *Managing Organisational Change*, Praeger Publishers: New York.

Corning, P.A. (1983) *The Synergism Hypothesis: A Theory of Progressive Evolution*, McGraw-Hill: New York.

—— (1995a) 'Synergy: a unifying concept?' *Proceedings of the 39th Annual Meeting of the International Society for the Systems Sciences*, Free University: Amsterdam, pp. 663–685.

—— (1995b) 'Synergy and self-organisation in the evolution of complex systems', *Systems Research*, vol. 12 (2): 89–121.

Cowan, G. (1992) quoted in M.M. Waldrop *Complexity: The Emerging Science at the Edge of Chaos*, Penguin: London, p. 356.

Coyle, R.G. (1977) *Management Systems Dynamics*, John Wiley: Chichester.

Crombie, I.M. (1963) *An Examination of Plato's Doctrines*,: New York.

Cronbach, L.J. and Furbey, L. (1970) 'How should we measure 'change' – or should we?' *Psychological Review*, vol. 74 (1): 68–80.

Crosby, P.B. (1979) *Quality is Free*, McGraw-Hill: New York.

Cummings, T.G. and Huse, E.F. (1989) *Organisation Development and Change*, West Press: St. Paul, MN.

Cvitanovic, P. (ed.) (1984) *Universality in Chaos*, Adam-Hilger: Bristol.

Cyert, R.M. and March, J.G. (1963) *A Behavioural Theory of the Firm*, Prentice Hall: Englewood Cliffs, NJ.

Daellenbach, H.G., George, J.A. and McNickle, D.C. (1983) *An Introduction to Operations Research Techniques*, Allyn and Bacon: Boston, MA.

Dahrendorf, R. (1959a) 'Social theory, social research and a theory of action', *American Journal of Sociology*, vol. 16: 1309–1335.

—— (1959b) *Class and Conflict in Industrial Society*, Stanford University Press: Stanford.

Daniels, S. (1990) 'Case load dynamics and the nature of change', *Law and Society Review*, vol. 24 (2): 299–320.

Davenport, T. (1993) *Process Innovation*, Harvard Business School: Boston, MA.

Davies, L.J. and Ledington, P. (1988) 'Creativity and metaphor in soft systems methodology', *Journal of Applied Systems Analysis*, vol. 15: 31–35.

Davies, P.C. (1980) *Other Worlds*, Abacus: London.

—— (1988) *The New Physics*, Cambridge University Press: Cambridge.

Davies, P.C. and Gribbin, J. (1991) *The Matter Myth*, Penguin: London.

Davis, R.C. (1928) *The Principles of Factory Organisation and Management*, Harper and Row: New York.

De Bono, E. (1971) *Lateral Thinking for Management*, American Management Association: New York.

De Chardin, T. (1961) *The Phenomenon of Man*, Harper: New York, p. 78.

De Greene, B. (ed.) (1970) *Systems Psychology*, McGraw-Hill: New York.

Deming, W.E. (1982) *Quality, Productivity and Competitive Position*, MIT Press: Cambridge, MA.

D'Espagnat, B. (1976) *Conceptual Foundations of Quantum Mechanics*, 2nd edn, Benjamin: Reading, MA.

—— (1989) *Reality and the Physicist*, Cambridge University Press: Cambridge.

Deutsch, K.W. (1966) *The Nerves of Government*, Free Press: New York.

Dewdney, A.K. (1985) 'Computer recreations', *Scientific America*, May, vol. 252 (5): 10–16.

Dewey, J. (1935) *Liberalism and Social Action*, Putnam: New York, p. 83.

Dimond, A.J. and Ellis, K. (1989) 'Technological change and the human aspect', in R.L. Flood, M.C. Jackson and P. Keys (eds) *Systems Prospects – The Next Ten Years of Systems Research*, Plenum Press: New York, pp. 47–50.

Downs, A. (1967) *Inside Bureaucracy*, Little, Brown: Boston, MA.

Drucker, P.F. (1986) *Innovation and Entrepreneurship*, Pan: London.

Dubin, R. (1958) *The World of Work*, Prentice-Hall: New York.

Economist (1994) *Simplicity and Complexity*, 9 July: p. 107.

Eigen, M. and Schuster, P. (1979) *The Hypercycle: A Principle of Natural Self-Organisation*, Springer: Kiedelberg, Berlin.

Einstein, A. (1921) 'Lecture on the theory of relativity', in A. Einstein (1954) *Ideas and Opinions*, Alvin Redman: London, pp. 246–249.

—— (1950) quoted in K.R. Popper (1982) *The Open Universe*, Hutchinson: London.

—— (1952) *Relativity – The Special and General Theory*, trans. R.W. Lawson, Methuen: London.

—— (1963) quoted in A. Forsee (1963) *Albert Einstein: Theoretical Physicist*, Macmillan: New York, p. 81.

Einstein, A. and Besso, M. (1972) *Correspondence 1903–1955*, Herman: Paris.

Eldredge, N. and Gould, S.J. (1972) 'Punctuated equilibria: an alternative to phyletic gradualism', in T.J. Schopf (ed.) *Models in Paleobiology*, Freeman and Cooper: San Francisco, pp. 82–115.

Emerson, R.W., quoted in W. Bridges (1980) *Making Sense of Life's Changes*, Addison-Wesley: Reading, MA.

Emery, F.E. and Trist, E.L. (1965) 'The causal texture of organisational environments', *Human Relations*, vol. 18: 21–32.

Engles, F. (1959) 'Socialism: utopian and scientific', in L.S. Feuer (ed.) *Marx and Engels: Basic Writings on Politics and Philosophy*, Anchor Books: Garden City, pp. 68–111.

Espejo, R. (1987) 'Cybernetic method to study organisations', in *Problems of Constancy and Change, Proceedings of the 31st Conference International Society for General Systems Research*, Budapest, vol. 1: 323–336.

Espejo, R. and Schwaninger, P. (eds) (1993) *Organisational Fitness: Corporate Effectiveness through Management Cybernetics*, Campus Verlag: Frankfurt.

Fain, H. (1970) *Between Philosophy and History*, Princeton University Press: Princeton, NJ.

Farre, G.L. (1968) 'On the linguistic foundations of the problem of scientific discovery', *Journal of Philosophy*, vol. 65: 779–794.

Fayol, H. (1916) *Administration Industrielle et Générale*, Dunod: Paris (translated, 1949, *General and Industrial Administration*, Pitman: London).

Ferlie, E. and Pettigrew, A.M. (1990) 'Coping with change in the NHS', *Journal of Social Policy*, vol. 19 (2): 191–220.

Finlow-Bates, T. (1993) 'The swing of the pendulum', *Management Service Quality*, January: 469–472.

Fischer, D.H. (1970) *Historical Fallacies: Towards a Logic of Historical Thought*, Harper and Row: London.

Fischer, S. and Cooper, C.L. (eds) (1990) *On the Move: The Psychology of Change and Transition*, John Wiley: Chichester.

Flood, R.L. (1987) 'Some theoretical considerations of mathematical modelling', *Problems of Constancy and Change, Proceedings of the 31st Conference of the International Society for General Systems Research*, Budapest, vol. 1: 354–360.

—— (1988) 'Unleashing the 'open system' metaphor', *Systems Practice*, vol. 1 (3): 313–318.

Flood, R.L. and Carson, E.R. (1988) *Dealing with Complexity*, Plenum Press: New York.

Flood, R.L. and Jackson, M.C. (1991a) *Creative Problem Solving: Total Systems Intervention*, John Wiley: Chichester.

—— (1991b) 'Total systems intervention: a practical face to critical systems thinking', *Systems Practice*, vol. 4 (3): 197–213.

—— (eds) (1991c) *Critical Systems Thinking*, John Wiley: Chichester.

Flood, R.L., Jackson, M.C. and Keys, P. (eds) (1989) *Systems Prospects – The Next Ten Years of Systems Research*, Plenum Press: New York.

Flood, R.L. and Robinson, S.A. (1988) 'The utility of analogy in systems research: a reappraisal', *Proceedings of the 4th International Conference on Systems, Infomatics and Cybernetics*, Baden-Baden: Germany.

Flood, R.L. and Ulrich, W. (1990) 'Testament to conversations on critical systems thinking between two systems practitioners', *Systems Practice*, vol. 3:

Ford, J.D. and Backoff, R.W. (1987) 'Organisational change in and out of dualities and paradox', in R. Quinn and K. Cameron (eds) *Paradox and Transformation*, Ballinger Press: Cambridge, MA, pp.81–121.

Ford, J.D. and Ford, L.W. (1994) 'Logics of identity, contradiction and attraction in change', *Academy of Management Review*, vol. 19 (4): 756–785.

Forrest, S. (ed.) (1991) *Emergent Computation: Self-Organizing, Collective, and Cooperative Phenomena in Natural and Artificial Computing Networks*, MIT Press: Cambridge, MA.

Forrester, J.W. (1971) 'The counter-intuitive behaviour of social systems', *Technology Review*, January: 52–68.

—— (1994) 'Systems dynamics, systems thinking and soft OR', *System Dynamics Review*, vol. 10 (2–3): 245–256.

Fortune, J. and Peters, G. (1995) *Learning from Failure: The Systems Approach*, John Wiley: Chichester.

Foucault, M. (1972) *The Archaeology of Knowledge*, Tavistock Publications: London.

Francis, A. and Tharakan, P.K. (eds) (1989) *The Competitiveness of European Industry*, Routledge: London.

French, W.L. and Bell, C.H. (1984) *Organisation Development: Behavioural Science Interventions for Organisation Improvement*, Prentice-Hall: Englewood Cliffs, NJ.

—— (1990) *Organization Development*, Prentice-Hall: Englewood Cliffs, NJ.

Gao, S.J. (1992) 'Systems evolution: the conceptual framework and a formal model', PhD thesis, City University: London.

Garcia, L. (1991) *The Fractal Explorer*, Dynamic Press: Santa Cruz, CA.

Gass, M.A. (1995) *Book of Metaphors*, Association for Experimental Education, Kendal and Hunt: Dubuque, IA.

Gaustello, S.J. (1995) *Chaos, Catastrophe and Human Affairs: Applications of Nonlinear Dynamics to Work, Organisations and Social Evolution*, Lawrence Erblaum Associates: Mahwah, NJ.

Geertz, C. (1973) *The Interpretation of Culture*, Basic Books: New York.

General Systems (1988) *Yearbook of the International Society for the Systems Sciences*, vol. xxxi.

George, C.S. (1968) *The History of Management Thought*, Prentice-Hall: Englewood Cliffs, NJ.

Gerard, R.W. (1957) 'Units and concepts of biology', *Science*, vol. 125: 429–433.

Gerking, S.D. (1974) *Biological Systems*, W.B. Saunders: Philadelphia.

Gersick, C.J. (1988) 'Time and transitions in work teams', *Academy of Management Review*, vol. 31: 9–41.

—— (1991) 'Revolutionary Change Theories: A Multilevel Exploration of the Punctuated Equilibrium Paradigm', *Academy of Management Review*, vol. 16 (1): 10–36.

Gersick, C.J. and Davis, M.D. (1989) 'Task forces', in J.R. Hackman (ed.) *Groups that Work and Those that Don't*, Jossey-Bass: San Francisco, pp. 146–153.

Gerson, E.M. (1976) 'On quality of life', *American Sociological Review*, vol. 41: 793–806.

Gibbs, J.W. (1902) *Elementary Principles in Statistical Mechanics*, Yale University Press: New Haven, CT.

Gilbert, G.K. (1896) 'The origin of hypothesis illustrated by the discussion of topographic method', *Science*, vol. 3: 1–13.

Gilbreth, F.B. and Gilbreth, L.M. (1914) *Applied Motion Study*, Sturgis and Walton: New York.

Glansdorff, P. and Prigogine, I. (1971) *Thermodynamic Theory of Structure, Stability and Fluctuations*, Wiley-Interscience: New York.

Gleick, J. (1987) *Chaos*, Sphere: London.

Glick, W.H., Huber, G.P., Miller, C.C., Doty, D.H. and Sutcliffe, K.M. (1990) 'Studying changes in organisational design and effectiveness: retrospective event histories and periodic assessments', *Organisational Science*, vol. 1 (3): 293–312.

Goerner, S. (1994) 'Chaos and the evolving ecological universe', *World Futures*, vol. 7: 1–272.

Goertzel, B. (1993) *The Evolving Mind*, Gordon and Breach: Berkshire.

Goldberg, D.E. (1989) *Genetic Algorithms in Search, Optimization, and Machine Learning*, Addison-Wesley: Reading, MA.

Goldfried, M.R. (1980) 'Towards the delineation of therapeutic change principles', *American Psychologist*, vol. 35: 991–999.

Goldstein, J. (1988) 'A Far-from-equilibrium systems approach to resistance to change', *Organisational Dynamics*, vol. 17: 16–26.

Golembiewski, R.T., Billingslev, K. and Yeager, S. (1976) Measuring change and persistence in human affairs: types of change generated by OD designs, *Journal of Applied Behavioural Science*, vol. 12 (2):133–157.

Goodman, P.S. and associates (eds) (1982) *Change in Organizations*, Jossey-Bass: San Francisco.

Goodman, P.S. and Kurke, L. (1982) 'Studies of change in organisations: a status report', in P.S. Goodman (ed.) *Change in Organizations*, Jossey-Bass: San Francisco, pp. 1–46.

Gossop, M. (1989) *Relapse and Addictive Behaviour*, Routledge: London.

Gould, S.J. (1977) *Ever Since Darwin*, W.W. Norton: New York.

Goullart, F.J. and Kelly, J.N. (1995) *Transforming the Organisation*, McGraw-Hill: New York.

Greenwood, R. and Hinings, C.R. (1986) *Organisational Design Types, Tracks and the Dynamics of Change*, Department of Organizational Analysis: University of Alberta, Canada.

Greer, S. (1969) *The Logic of Social Enquiry*, Aldine: Chicago.

Greiner, L. (1965) unpublished PhD dissertation, Harvard University.

—— (1972) 'Evolution and revolution as organisations grow', *Harvard Business Review*, vol. 50: 39–46.

Grene, M. (1967) 'Biology and the Problem of Levels of Reality', *New Scholasticism*, vol. 41: 427–449.

—— (1968) *Approaches to Philosophical Biology*, Basic Books: New York.

Grinyer, P. and McKiernan, P. (1990) 'Generating major change in stagnating companies', *Strategic Management Journal*, vol. 11: 131–146.

Gronhaug, K. and Kaufmann, G. (1988) 'Problem solving and creativity', in *Innovation: A Cross Disciplinary Perspective*, Norwegian University Press: Oslo, pp. 87–139.

Guckenheimer, J. and Holmes, P. (1983) *Nonlinear Oscillations, Dynamical Systems and Bifurcations of Vector Fields*, Springer-Verlag: New York.

Gulick, L. and Urwick, L. (1937) *Papers in the Science of Administration*, Institute of Public Administration: New York.

Haas, E.B. (1990) *When Knowledge is Power: Three Models of Change in International Organisations*, University of California Press: Berkeley, CA.

Haken, H. (1977) *Synergetics: An Introduction – Non-Equilibrium Phase Transitions and Self-Organisation in Physics, Chemistry and Biology*, 2nd edn, Springer Verlag: Berlin.

Hall, A.D. (1962) *A Methodology for Systems Engineers*, Van Nostrand: New York.

Hall, B.P. (1994) *Values Shift*, Twin Lights: Rockport, MA.

Hall, R.I. (1976) 'A system pathology of an organisation: the rise and fall of the old' *Saturday Evening Post*, *Administrative Science Quarterly*, vol. 21: 185–211.

Hammer, M. and Champy, J. (1993) *Reengineering the Corporation*, Nicholas Brealey: London.

Handy, C. (1981) *Understanding Organisations*, Penguin: London.

—— (1989) *The Age of Unreason*, Business Books: London.

Hanken, H. (1981) 'Synergetics: is self organisation governed by universal principles?', in E. Jantsch (ed.) *The Evolutionary Vision*, Westview Press: Colorado.

—— (1983) *Synergetics: An Introduction*, Springer-Verlag: Berlin.

Hannan, M.T. and Freeman, J. (1977) 'The population ecology of organisations', *American Journal of Sociology*, vol. 82: 929–965.

—— (1984) 'Structural inertia and organisational change', *American Sociological Review*, vol. 49: 149–164.

Hanson, N.R. (1958) *Patterns of Discovery*, Cambridge University Press: Cambridge, 85ff.

—— (1969) *Perceptions and Discovery*, Freeman Cooper: San Francisco.

Hanwell, J.D. (1980) *Atmospheric Processes*, Allen and Unwin: London.

Hardin, G. and Bajema, C. (1978) *Biology – Its Principles and Implications*, Freeman: San Francisco.

Harman, W. (1969) 'The nature of our changing society, unpublished paper', Stanford Research Institute.

Harris, C.W. (1963) *Problems in Measuring Change*, University of Wisconsin Press: Madison.

Harrison, R. (1970) 'Choosing the depth of organisational intervention', *Journal of Applied Behavioral Science*, vol. 6 (April–June): 181–202.

Harvey, D. (1988) *New Parents*, Hamlyn: London.

Haslett, T. (1994) 'Implications of systems thinking for research and practice in management', *Proceedings of the 38th Annual Meeting of the International Society for the Systems Sciences*, Pacific Grove, CA, vol. 2: 1141–1156.

Hayek, F. (1988) *The Fatal Conceit: The Errors of Socialism*, University of Chicago Press: Chicago.

Hazzard, B.J. (1973) *Organicum*, Pergamon Press: Oxford.

Hedberg, B., Nystrom, P. and Starbuck, W. (1976) 'Camping on seesaws: prescriptions for a self-designing organisation', *Administrative Science Quarterly*, vol. 21: 41–65.

Hellreigal, D., Slocum, J.W. and Woodman, R.W. (1986) *Organisational Behaviour*, 4th edn, West Publishing.

Henderson, L.J. (1970) *The Social System: Selected Writings*, B. Barber (ed.), University of Chicago Press: Chicago, pp. 136–139.

Henry, J. (ed.) (1991) *Creative Management*, Sage: London.

Henry, J. and Walker, D. (eds) (1991) *Managing Innovation*, Sage: London.

Heraclitus (500 BC) quoted in B. Russell (1946) *A History of Western Philosophy*, Allen and Unwin: London, p. 63.

Hernes, G. (1976) 'Structural change in social processes', *American Journal of Sociology*, vol. 82 (3): 513–545.

Hesse, M.B. (1966) *Models and Analogies in Science*, University of Notre Dame Press: Indiana.

Hilton, K. (1979) *Process and Pattern in Physical Geography*, University Tutorial Press: Slough.

Hirsch, M.W. (1984) 'The dynamical approach to differential equations', *Bulletin of American Mathematical Society*, vol. 87 pp. 1–64.

Hoffman, L. (1981) *Foundations of Family Therapy*, Basic Books: New York.

Hofstede, G. (1991) *Cultures and Organisations: Intercultural Cooperation and its Importance to Survival*, Harper and Collins: Glasgow.

Holy Bible (1978) 'New International Version', Luke, Chapter 6, verse 41, Hodder and Stoughton: Kent.

Hooke, R. (1961) *Micrographia or Some Physiological Description of Minute Bodies made by Magnifying Glasses with Observations and Enquiries Thereupon*, reproduced 1st edn, Facsimile: London.

Hoos, I.R. (1976) 'Engineers as analysts of social systems – a critical enquiry', *Journal of Systems Engineering*, vol. 4 (2), reproduced in Beishon, J. and Peters, G. (eds) (1981) *Systems Behaviour*, Open University Systems Group, Harper and Row, pp. 315–321.

Hsu, L.S. (1932) *The Political Philosophy of Confucianism*, E.P. Dutton: New York.

Huber, G.P. (1991) 'Organizational learning: the contributing processes and the literatures', *Organization Science*, vol. 2: 88–115.

Huber, G.P. and Glick, W.H. (eds) (1993) *Organizational Change and Redesign*, Oxford University Press: Oxford.

Huczynski, A. (1987) *Encyclopedia of Organisational Change Methods*, Gower: Aldershot.

Jackson, M.C. (1985) 'Social systems theory and practice: the need for a critical approach', *International Journal of General Systems Theory*, vol. 10:

Jacobs, J. (1992) *Systems of Survival: A Dialogue on the Moral Foundations of Commerce and Politics*, Bury Free Press: Bury St. Edmunds.

Jaeger, W. (1947) *The Theology of the Early Greek Philosophers*, Clarendon Press: Oxford.

Jammer, M. (1966) *Conceptual Developments in Quantum Mechanics*, McGraw-Hill: New York.

—— (1974) *The Philosophy of Quantum Mechanics*, John Wiley: New York.

Janis, I.L. and Mann, L. (1977) *Decision Making: A Psychological Analysis of Conflict, Choice and Commitment*, Free Press: Chicago.

Jantsch, E. (1980a) *The Self Organising Universe*, Pergamon Press: Oxford.

—— (1980b) 'Unifying principles of evolution', paper presented at the AAAS Selected Symposium 61, 3–8 January, San Francisco.

—— (ed.) (1981) *The Evolutionary Vision*, Westview Press: Colorado.

Jaques, E. (1951) *The Changing Culture of a Factory*, Tavistock Institute: London.

Jaques, E., Gibson, R.O. and Isaac, D.J. (eds) (1978) *Levels of Abstraction in Logic and Human Action*, Heinemann: London.

Jen, E. (ed.) (1990) (1989) *Lectures in Complex Systems*, Santa Fe Institute Studies in the Sciences of Complexity, Lectures vol. 2, Addison-Wesley: Redwood City, CA.

Jenkins, G.M. (1969) 'The systems approach', *Journal of Systems Engineering*, vol. 1 (1).

Johns, E.A. (1970) *The Sociology of Organisational Change*, Pergamon Press: Oxford.

Jones, L. (1982) 'Defining systems boundaries in practice: some proposals and guidelines', *Journal of Applied Systems Analysis*, vol. 9: 41–55.

Josephson, B.D. (1990) personal communication.

Josephson, B.D., Conrad, M. and Home, D. (1985) *Beyond Quantum Theory: A Realist Psycho-Biological Interpretation of Physical Reality*, Cavendish Laboratory, Cambridge University: Cambridge.

Judson, H.F. (1980) *The Search for Solutions*, Holt Rinehart and Winston: New York, p. 109.

Juran, J.M. (1988) *Quality Control Handbook*, McGraw-Hill: New York.

Jurkovich, R. (1974) 'A core typology of organisational environment', *Administrative Science Quarterly*, vol. 19 (3): 380–394.

Kahn, R.L. (1974) 'Organisational development: some problems and proposals', *Journal of Applied Behavioural Science*, vol. 10: 487.

Kamall, S.S. (1994) 'Management of radical change: a case study of hungarian tele-communications', PhD thesis, City University: London.

Kamphuis, R.W., Watson, R.C. and Watson, J.W. (eds) (1988) *Black Monday and the Future of Financial Markets*, Dow-Jones Irwin, Mid America Institute: Homewood, IL.

Kanter, R.M. (1984) *The Change Masters*, Allen and Unwin: London.

—— (1989) *When Giants Learn to Dance*, Allen and Unwin: London.

Kaplan, R.B. and Murdock, L. (1991) 'Core process redesign', *McKinsey Quarterly*, vol. 2: 246–262.

Kaplan, R.S. and Norton, D.P. (1992) 'Measures that drive performance', *Harvard Business Review*, January–February:

——*The Balanced Scorecard*, Harvard Business School Press: Cambridge, MA.

Kast, F.E. and Rosenzweig, J.E. (1970) *Organisation and Management: A Systems Approach*, McGraw-Hill: London.

—— (eds) (1976) *Experiential Exercises and Cases in Management*, McGraw-Hill: New York, pp. 345–348.

Katz, D. and Kahn, R.L. (1966) *The Social Psychology of Organisations*, John Wiley: New York.

Kauffman, S.A. (1991) 'Anti-chaos and adaptation', *Scientific America*, vol. 265 (2): 64–70.

—— (1992) *Origins of Order: Self-Organisation and Selection in Evolution*, Oxford University Press: Oxford.

Kellert, S.H. (1995) 'When is the economy not like the weather? The problem of extending chaos theory to the social sciences', In A. Albert (ed.) *Chaos and Society*, IOS Press: Amsterdam.

Keohane, R.O. and Nye, J.S. (1989) *Power and Interdependence*, Scott Foresman: Glenview, IL.

Kiel, D. and Elliott, E. (eds) (1995) *Chaos Theory in the Social Sciences: Foundations and Applications*, University of Michigan Press: Ann Arbor, MI.

Kimberly, J.R. and Quinn, R.E. (eds) (1984) *New Futures: The Challenge of Managing Corporate Transitions*, Dow Jones-Irwin: Homewood, IL.

Kirdar, U. (ed.) (1992) *Change: Threat or Opportunity – Political Change*, United Nations Publications: New York.

Kirton, M.J. (1980) 'Adaptors and innovators in organisations', *Human Relations*, vol. 33 (4): 689–713.

—— (1984) 'Adaptors and innovators: why new initiatives get blocked', *Long Range Planning*, vol. 17 (2): 137–143.

Klir, G.J. (1969) *An Approach to General Systems Theory*, Van Nostrand Reinhold: New York.

—— (1985) *Architecture of Systems Problem Solving*, Plenum: New York.

Koestler, A. (1970) *The Act of Creation*, Pan: London.

Koontz, H., O'Donnell, C. and Weihrich, H. (1984) *Management*, 8th edn, McGraw-Hill: Singapore.

Kotter, J.P., Schlesinger, L.A. and Sathe, V. (1986) *Organization: Text, Cases and Readings on the Management of Organisational Design and Change*, Dow Jones-Irwin: Homewood, IL.

Krieger, M. (1992) 'Literary invention, critical fashion and the impulse to theoretical change', in R. Cohen (ed.) *Studies in Historical Change*, University Press of Virginia: pp. 179–206.

Kroeber, A.K. and Kluckhohn, C. (1952) *Culture: A Critical Review of Concepts and Definitions*, Vintage Books: New York.

Krovi, R. (1993) 'Identifying the causes of resistance to IS implementation: a change theory perspective', *Journal of Information and Mangement*, vol. 25: 327–335.

Kuhn, T. (1970) *The Structure of Scientific Revolutions*, University of Chicago Press: Chicago.

—— (1979) 'Metaphor in science', in A. Ortony (ed.) *Metaphor and Thought*, Cambridge University Press: Cambridge.

Kurtz, N.R. (1983) *Introduction to Social Statistics*, McGraw-Hill: London.

Lakoff, M. and Johnson, R. (1980) *Metaphors We Live By*, University of Chicago Press: Chicago.

Land, V.A. (1982) 'Imaging and creativity: an integrating perspective', *Journal of Creative Behaviour*, vol. 16 (1): 5–29.

Landau, L. and Lifshitz, E. (1958) *Quantum Mechanics*, Pergamon Press: Oxford.

Lane, D.C. (1993) 'With a little help from out friends: how third generation system dynamics and issue structuring techniques of 'soft OR' can learn from each other', in E. Zepda and J.A. Machuca (eds) *Systems Dynamics*, Systems Dynamics Society: published in expanded form as CUBS Discussion Paper ITM/93/DCL2, City University: London.

Langton, C.G. (ed.) (1989) *Artificial Life*, Santa Fe Institute Studies in the Sciences of Complexity, *proceedings*, vol. 6, Addison-Wesley: Redwood City, CA.

Langton, C.G., Taylor, C., Farmer, J.D. and Rassmussen, S. (eds) (1992) *Artificial Life II*, Santa Fe Institute Studies in the Sciences of Complexity, proceedings vol. 10, Addison-Wesley: Redwood City, CA.

Lant, T.K. and Mezias, S.J. (1990) 'Managing discontinuous change: a simulation study of organisational learning and entrepreneurship', *Strategic Management Journal*, vol. 11: 147–179.

Lasker, G. (ed.) (1983) *The Relation Between Major World Problems and Systems Learning*, Intersystems Publications: Seaside, CA.

Laszlo, E. (1972) *Introduction to Systems Philosophy: Toward a New Paradigm of Contemporary Thought*, Gordon and Breach, Harper Torchbooks: New York.

—— (1994) *Vision 2020: Reordering Chaos for Global Survival*, Gordon and Breach: Berkshire.

Lauer, L.H. (1971) 'The scientific legitimation of fallacy: neutralizing social change theory', *American Sociological Review*, vol. 36 (5): 881–889.

Lawrence, P.R. and Lorsch, J.W. (1967) *Organisation and Environment*, Harvard Business School: Boston, MA.

Leatherdale, W.H. (1974) *The Role of Analogy, Model and Metaphor in Science*, North Holland: Amsterdam.

Lee, S., Courtney, J.F. and O'Keefe, R.M. (1992) 'A system for organizational learning using cognitive maps', *OMEGA*, vol. 20: 23–36.

Leggett, A.J. (1986) 'Reflections on the quantum measurement paradox', in B.J. Hiley and F.D. Peat (eds) *Quantum Theory and Beyond*, Routledge and Kegan Paul: London.

—— (1987) *The Problems of Physics*, Oxford University Press: Oxford.

Leibniz, G.W. (c1708) 'Animadversiones ad Joh George Wachteri librum de recondita Hebraeorum philosophia', unpublished. English translation in P.P. Wiener *Leibniz Selections*, Scribners: New York, p. 488.

Lektorsky, V.A. and Sadovsky, V.N. (1960) On principles of systems research (related to L. Bertalanffy's GST), *General Systems*, vol. 5: 171–179.

Lenz, R.T. and Engledow, J.L. (1986) 'Environmental analysis: the applicability of current theory', *Strategic Management Journal*, vol. 7: 329–346.

Lepawsky, A. (1949) *Administration*, Knopf: New York, pp. 78–81.

Levinson, D.J. (1978) *The Seasons of a Man's Life*, Knopf: New York.

—— (1986) 'A conception of adult development', *American Psychologist*, vol. 41: 3–13.

Levy, A. (1986) 'Second order planned change: definition and conceptualisation', *Organisational Dynamics*, vol. 15 (1): 5–20.

Lewin, K. (1938) *The Conceptual Representation and Measure of Psychological Forces*, Duke University Press: Durham, NC.

—— (1947) 'Frontiers in group dynamics', *Human Relations*, vol. 6: 2–38.

—— (1951) *Field Theory in Social Science*, Harper and Row: New York.

—— (1958) 'Group decisions and social change', in G.E. Swanson, T.M. Newcombe and E.L. Hartley (eds) *Readings in Social Psychology*, Holt, Rhinehart and Winston: New York.

Likert, R. (1967) *The Human Organisation: Its Management and Value*, McGraw-Hill: New York.

Lilienfeld, R. (1978) *The Rise of Systems Theory*, John Wiley: New York.

Lippitt, R., Watson, J. and Westley, B. (1958) *Dynamics of Planned Change*, Harcourt Brace: New York.

Litwick, R. (1987) quoted in A. Huczynski *Encyclopedia of Organisational Change Methods*, Gower: Aldershot.

Lofgren, L. (1980) 'Knowledge of evolution and evolution of knowledge', in E. Jantsch (ed.) *The Evolutionary Vision*, Westview Press: Colorado, pp.129–151.

Lorenz, E.N. (1963) 'Deterministic non-periodic flow', *Journal of Atmospheric Sciences*, vol. 20: 448–464.

Lundberg, C.C. (1984) 'Strategies for organisational transitioning', in J.R. Kimberly and R.E. Quinn (eds) *New Futures: The Challenge of Managing Corporate Transitions*, Dow Jones-Irwin: Homewood, IL, pp. 60–82.

McCaskey, M.B. (1974) 'A contingency approach to planning', *Academy of Management Journal*, vol. 17 (2): 281–291.

—— (1982) 'Mapping: creating, maintaining and relinquishing conceptual frameworks', in *The Executive Challenge: Managing Ambiguity and Change*, Pitmann: Boston, MA, pp. 14–33.

McGee, J. and Thomas, H. (1985) *Strategic Management Research: A European Perspective*, John Wiley: Chichester.

McGregor, D. (1960) *The Human Side of Enterprise*, McGraw-Hill: New York.

Mach, E. (1885) *The Analysis of Sensations*, Open Court: Chicago.

McKergow, M. (1997) 'Mind your metaphors: lessons from complexity science', *Long Range Planning*, vol. 29: 721–727.

McKinney, J. and Tiryakin, E. (eds) (1970) *Theoretical Sociology: Perspectives and Developments*, Meredith Press: New York.

McNeil, D.H. (1995) 'A survey of applied systemology', *Systems Research*, vol. 12 (2): 133–145.

Mandelbrot, B. (1977) *The Fractal Geometry of Nature*, W.H. Freeman: New York.

Mangham, I.L. (1986) *Power and Performance in Organizations: An Exploration of Executive Process*, Blackwell: Oxford.

March, J.G. (1962) 'The business firm as a political coalition', *Journal of Politics*, vol. 24: 662–678.

—— (1981) 'Footnotes to organizational change', *Administrative Science Quarterly*, vol. 26: 563–577.

—— (1994) 'The evolution of evolution', in J.A. Baum and J.V. Singh (eds) *Evolutionary Dynamics of Organisations*, Oxford University Press: Oxford.

Martin, J. (1989) *Information Engineering: Volumes I–III*, Prentice Hall: Englewood Cliffs, NJ.

Maslow, A.H. (1943) 'A theory of human motivation', *Psychology Review*, vol. 50: 370–396.

Mason, R.O. and Mitroff, I.I. (1981) *Challenging Strategic Planning Assumptions*, John Wiley: Chichester.

Maturana, H.R. and Varela, F.J. (1972) *Autopoiesis and Cognition*, Reidel Publishing: Dordrecht.

—— (1975) *Autopoietic Systems*, Report BCL 9.4 Urbana IL, Biological Computer Laboratory, University of Illinois.

—— (1987) *The Tree of Knowledge*, Shambhala Publications: Massachusetts.

Mayo, E. (1933) *The Human Problems of Industrial Civilization*, Macmillan Press: New York.

Mehra, J. (1979) *The Historical Development of Quantum Theory*, Wiley-Interscience: New York.

Melin, L. (1987) 'The field-of-force metaphor: a study of industrial change', *International Studies of Management and Organisation*, vol. 17 (1): 24–33.

Merali, Y. and Martin, A. (1994) 'Metaphor in information systems teaching and research', *Systemist*, vol. 16 (1): 12–19.

Mesarovic, M.D. (ed.) (1964) *Views on General Systems Theory*, John Wiley: New York.

Mesarovic, M.D. and Takahara, Y. (1975) *General Systems Theory: Mathematical Foundations*, Academic Press: New York.

—— (1988) *Abstract Systems Theory*, Academic Press: New York.

Meyer, A.D., Goes, J.B. and Brooks, G.R. (1990) 'Environmental jolts and industry revolutions: organisational reponses to discontinuous change', *Strategic Management Journal*, vol. 11: 93–110.

—— (1993) 'Organisations reacting to hyperturbulence', in G.P. Huber and W.H. Glick *Organisational Change and Redesign*, Oxford University Press: Oxford, pp. 66–111.

Milby, J.B. (1981) *Addicitive Behaviour and its Treatment*, Springer: New York.

Miles, R.E. and Snow, C.C. (1986) 'Organisations: new concepts for new forms', *California Management Review*, vol. 28 (3): 62–73.

Miller, D. (1982) 'Evolution and revolution: a quantum view of structural change in organisations', *Journal of Management Science*, vol. 19 (2): 131–151.

—— (1990) *The Icarus Paradox: How Excellent Organisations Can Bring about their Own Downfall*, Harper Business Press: New York.

Miller, D. and Friesen, P.H. (1980a) 'Archetypes of organisational transitions', *Administrative Science Quarterly*, vol. 25: 269–305.

—— (1980b) 'Momentum and revolution in organizational adaptation', *Academy of Management Journal*, vol. 23: 591–614.

—— (1984) *Organisations: A Quantum View*, Prentice Hall: Englewood Cliffs, NJ.

Miller, E.J. and Rice, A.K. (1967) *Systems of Organisation*, Tavistock Institute: London.

Miller, J.G. (1978) *Living Systems*, McGraw-Hill: New York.

Miller, W.R. (1980) *The Addictive Behaviours: Treatment of Alcoholism, Drug Abuse, Smoking and Obesity*, Pergamon Press: Oxford.

—— (1993) 'What really drives change?', *Addiction*, vol. 88 (11): 1479–1480.

Milnor, J. (1985) 'On the concept of attractor', *Commun. Math. Phys.*, vol. 99: 177–195.

Mintzberg, H. (1979) *The Structure of Organisations*, Prentice Hall: Englewood Cliffs, NJ.

Mintzberg, H. and Quinn, J.B. (1996) *The Strategy Process*, Prentice Hall International: London.

Moeller, T. (1959) *Inorganic Chemistry*, John Wiley: New York.

Mooney, J.D. (1947) *The Principles of Organization*, Harper: New York.

Mooney, J.D. and Reiley, A.C. (1931) *Onward Industry*, Harper: New York.

Moore, B. (1966) *Social Origins of Dictatorship and Democracy*, Penguin: Boston, MA.

Moore, W.E. (1960) 'A reconsideration of theories of social change', *American Sociological Review*, vol. 25: 810–818.

—— (1963) *Social Change*, Prentice Hall: Englewood Cliffs, NJ.

Morgan, G. (1980) 'Paradigms, metaphors and puzzle solving in organisation theory', *Administrative Science Quarterly*, vol. 25 (4): 605–622.

—— (1981) 'The schismatic metaphor and its implications for organisational analysis', *Organisation Studies*, vol. 2: 23–44.

—— (1983) 'More on metaphor: why we cannot control tropes in administrative science', *Administrative Science Quarterly*, vol. 28: 601–607.

—— (1986) *Images of Organisations*, Sage: London.

—— (1988) *Riding the Waves of Change: Developing Managerial Competencies for a Turbulent World*, Jossey-Bass: San Francisco, pp. 1–15.

—— (1993) *Imaginization*, Sage: London.

Morgan, G. and Ramirez, R. (1984) 'Action learning: a holographic metaphor for guiding social change', *Human Relations*, vol. 37: 1–28.

Mullins, L.J. (1989) *Management and Organisational Behaviour*, Pitman: London.

Myers, C.S. (1934) *An Account of the Work Carried Out at the National Institute of Industrial Psychology During the Years 1921–34*, NIPP: London.

Nadler, D.A. (1988) 'Concepts for the management of organisational change', in M.L. Tushman and W.L. Moore (eds) *Readings in the Management of Innovation*, 2nd edn, Ballinger Publishing: New York, pp. 718–731.

National Science Foundation (1972) Report of the National Science Board, *The Role of Engineers and Scientists in a National Policy for Technology*, NSF: Washington, DC.

Naughton, J. (1979) Review of Lilienfeld, R. (1978), *Futures*, vol. 11 (2): 165–166.

Nelson, R.R. and Winter, S.G. (1982) *An Evolutionary Theory of Economic Change*, Belknap Press, Harvard University: Cambridge, MA.

Nesselroade, J.R. (1991) 'Interindividual differences in intraindividual change', in L.M. Collins and J.L. Horn (eds) *Best Methods for the Analysis of Change*, American Psychology Association: New York, pp. 92–105.

Newell, A. and Simon, H.A. (1972) *Human Problem Solving*, Prentice Hall: Englewood Cliffs, NJ.

Nicolis, G. and Prigogine, I. (1977) *Self-Organiastion in Non-Equilibrium Systems: From Dissipative Structures to Order through Fluctuations*, Wiley-Interscience: New York.

—— (1989) *Exploring Complexity*, W.H. Freeman: New York.

Nisbet, R.A. (1970) 'Developmentalism: a critical analysis', in J. McKinney and E. Tiryakin (eds) *Theoretical Sociology: Perspectives and Developments*, Meredith: New York, pp. 167–204.

Nonaka, I. (1988) 'Creating organizational order out of chaos: self-renewal in Japanese firms', *California Management Review*, vol. 30 (3): 57–93.

Oech, R. von (1990) *A Wack on the Side of the Head*, Thorsons-Harper Collins: London.

Oliga, J.C. (1988) 'Methodological foundations of systems methodologies', *Systems Practice*, vol. 1: (1).

—— (1990) 'Power–ideology matrix in social systems control', *Systems Practice*, vol. 3:

Olsen, M. (1982) *The Rise and Decline of Nations*, Yale University Press: New Haven, CT.

Open University (1971) *Cells and Organisms*, Open University Press: Milton Keynes.

—— (1976) *Characteristics of Organic Chemistry*, Open University Press: Milton Keynes.

Oppenheimer, R. (1955) 'Prospects in the arts and sciences', *Perspectives USA*, vol. 2: 9–11.

—— (1956) 'Analogy in science', *American Psychologist*, vol. 11: 130.

Ortony, A. (ed.) (1979) *Metaphor and Thought*, Cambridge University Press: Cambridge.

Otto, J.H. and Towle, A. (1969) *Modern Biology*, Holt Rinehart and Winston: New York.

Ould, M. (1995) *Business Process: Modelling and Analysis for Re-engineering*, John Wiley: Chichester.

Overman, E.S. (1996) 'The new science management: chaos and quantum theory and method', *Journal of Public Administration Research and Theory*, vol. 6: 75–89.

Oxford Dictionary (1984) ed. R.E. Allen, 7th edn, Oxford University Press: Oxford.

Pacault, A. and Vidal, C. (eds) (1979) *Synergetics Far From Equilibrium*, Springer Books: New York.

Parker, D. and Stacey, R. (1994) *Chaos, Management and Economics*, Institute of Economic Affairs: London.

Parmenides (450 BC) as discussed in K. Popper, 'On the nature of philosophical problems and their roots in science', *British Journal for the Philosophy of Science*, vol. 3 (10): 141.

Parsons, T. (1960) *Structure and Process in Modern Societies*, Free Press: Chicago.

Partington, J.R. (1944) *A Text Book of Inorganic Chemistry*, 5th edn, Macmillan: London.

Pascale, R.T. (1991) *Managing on the Edge*, Simon and Schuster: New York.

Pattee, H.H. (1973) *Hierarchy Theory: The Challenge of Complex Systems*, Braziller: New York.

—— (1981) 'Symbol structure complementarity in biological evolution', in E. Jantsch (ed.) *The Evolutionary Vision*, Westview Press: Colorado, pp. 117–128.

Pearce, D. (1994) 'Complexity theory and economics', *Agenda*, vol.1 (1): 101–110.

Pearman, R. (1995) *Business Process Modelling and Simulation*, Casewise: London.

Peitgen, H.O. and Richter, P.H. (1986) *The Beauty of Fractals*, Springer-Verlag: Berlin.

Pennings, J.M. (ed.) (1985) *Organizational Strategy and Change*, Jossey-Bass: San Francisco.

Penrose, R. (1989) *The Emperor's New Mind*, Oxford University Press: Oxford.

Peppard, J.W. (1994) 'Organisational change through information technology and business process re-engineering', paper presented at OASIG Conference on BPR, 29 September, Department of Trade and Industry: London.

Peppard, J. and Preece, I. (1994) 'The content, context and process of BPR', in G. Burke and J. Peppard (ed.) *Exploring Business Process Engineering*, Kogan Page: London.

Pepper, S.C. (1954) *World Hypotheses*, University of California Press: Berkeley, CA.

Peters, T.J. and Waterman, R.H. (1982) *In Search of Excellence*, Harper and Row: London.

Pettigrew, A.M (1987a) *The Management of Strategic Change*, Blackwell: Oxford.

—— (1987b) 'Theoretical, methodological and empirical issues in studying change', *Journal of Management Studies*, vol. 24: 420–426.

—— (1990a) 'Longitudinal field research on change: theory and practice', *Organisational Science*, vol. 3 (1): 267–292.

—— (1990b) 'Studying strategic choice and strategic change', *Organisation Studies*, vol. 11 (1): 6–11.

—— (1991) *Managing Change for Competative Success*, Blackwell: Oxford.

—— (1992) *Shaping Strategic Change*, Sage: London.

Pfeffer, J. (1981) *Power in Organisations*, Pitman: Marshfield, MA.

Poincare, H. (1952) 'Science and hypothesis', in *The Foundations of Science*, Science Press: New York, republication of the first English translation of 1905.

Polkinghorne, J.C. (1984) *The Quantum World*, Longman: Harlow.

Pollard, S. (1965) *The Genesis of Modern Management*, Pelican: Harmondsworth.

Pondy, L.R., Boland, R.J. and Thomas, H. (1988) *Managing Ambiguity and Change*, John Wiley: Chichester.

Popper, K.R. (1976) *Unended Quest*, Fontana Books: London, pp. 129–130.

—— (1982) *The Open Universe*, Hutchinson: London.

Porras, J.I. and Robertson, P.J. (1987) 'Organisational development theory: a typology and evaluation', *Research in Organisational Change and Development*, vol. 1: 1–57.

Porter, L.W., Lawler, E.G. and Hackman, J.R. (1975) *Behaviour in Organisations*, McGraw-Hill: New York.

Powers, J. (1982) *Philosophy and the New Physics*, Methuen: London.

Prahalad, C.K. and Hamel, G. (1990) 'The core competence of the corporation', *Harvard Business Review*, May–June: 79–91.

Prigogine, I. (1980) *From Being to Becoming: Time and Complexity in the Physical Sciences*, W.H. Freeman: New York, pp. 203–204.

—— (1981) 'Time, irreversibility and randomness', paper presented at the AAAS Selected Symposium 61, 3–8 January 1980, San Francisco.

Prigogine, I. and Stengers, I. (1984) *Order Out of Chaos: Man's New Dialogue with Nature*, Bantam: Toronto.

Puccia, C.J. and Levins, R. (1985) *Qualitative Modelling of Complex Systems*, Havard University Press: Cambridge, MA.

Putney, S. (1972) *The Conquest of Society*, Wadsworth: London.

Quinn, R.E. and Anderson, D.E. (1984) 'Formalisation as crisis: transition planning for a young organisation', in J.R. Kimberly and R.E. Quinn (eds) *New Futures: The Challenge of Managing Corporate Transitions*, Dow Jones-Irwin: Homewood, IL.

Quinn, R.E. and Cameron, K. (eds) (1987) *Paradox and Transformation: Towards a Theory of Change in Organization and Management*, Ballinger: Cambridge, MA.

Radhakrishnan, S. (1925) quoted in J. Pilkington (1985) *Into Thin Air*, Allen and Unwin: London.

Railston, W. (1953) *Physics*, Chaucer Press: Suffolk.

Ranson, S., Hinnings, B. and Greenwood, R. (1980) 'The structure of organisational structures', *Administrative Science Quarterly*, vol. 25: 1–17.

Rapoport, A. (1966) 'Mathematical aspects of general systems theory', *General Systems Yearbook*, vol. 11: 3–11.

—— (1988) 'The relevance of the systemic outlook to our present predicament', *Yearbook of the International Society for the Systems Sciences*, vol. xxxi: 5–12.

—— (1995) 'Systems thinking, government policy and decision making', *Proceedings of the 39th Annual Meeting of the International Society for the Systems Sciences*, Free University: Amsterdam.

Rawcliffe, C.T. and Rawson, D.H. (1969) *Principles of Inorganic and Theoretical Chemistry*, Heineman: London.

Rickards, T and Jones, L. (1987) 'Creativity audit: a diagnostic approach to overcoming blocks', *Academy of Management Journal*, vol. 2 (1): 17–21.

Robb, F.F. (1985) 'Cybernetics in management thinking', *Systems Research*, vol. 1 (1): 5–23.

Robbins, S.P. (1983) *Organization Theory*, Prentice Hall: Englewood Cliffs, NJ.

Robbins, S. and Oliva, T.A. (1984) 'Usage of GST core concepts by discipline, time period and publication category', *Behavioural Sciences*, vol. 29: 28–39.

Roberts, J.D. and Caserio, M.C. (1979) *Basic Principles of Organic Chemistry*, 2nd edn, Addison-Wesley: Reading, MA.

Robinson, S.A. (1990) 'The utility of analogy in systems sciences', PhD thesis, City University: London.

Rockart, J.F. and Short, J.E. (1989) 'IT in the 1990's: managing organisational interdependence', *Sloan Management Review*, vol. 30: 7–17.

Roethlisberger, F.J. and Dickson, W.J. (1939) *Management and the Worker*, Harvard University Press: Cambridge, MA.

Rosenberg, H.M. (1978) *The Solid State*, Oxford University Press: Oxford.

Rubin, I. (1967) 'Increasing self acceptance', *Journal of Personality and Social Psychology*, vol. 5: 233–238.

Ruelle, D. (1989) *Strange Attractors and Non-Linear Evolution*, Cambridge University Press: Cambridge.

Rundall, T.G. and McClain, J.O. (1982) 'Environmental selection and physician supply', *American Journal of Sociology*, vol. 87: 1090–1112.

Russell, B. (1946) *A History of Western Philosophy*, Allen and Unwin: London.

Sahal, D. (1979) 'A unified theory of self-organisation', *Journal of Cybernetics*, vol. 9: 127–142.

Salomons, R.C. (1992) *Ethics and Excellence: Corporation and Integrity in Business*, John Wiley: New York.

Sambursky, S. (1963) *The Physical World of the Greeks*, trans. M. Dagut, Routledge and Kegan Paul: London.

Sathe, V. (1985) 'How to decipher and change organisational culture', in R.H. Kilman (ed.) *Managing Corporate Cultures*, Jossey-Bass: San Francisco.

Scarbrough, H. and Corbett, J.M. (1992) *Technology and Organisation: Power, Meaning and Design*, Routledge: London.

Schein, E.H. (1964) 'The mechanism of change', in W. Bennis, E. Schein, F. Steele and D. Berlew (eds) *Interpersonal Dynamics*, Dorsey Books: Homewood, IL, pp. 362–378.

—— (1980) *Organisational Psychology*, Prentice Hall: Englewood Cliffs, NJ.

—— (1983) *Organisational Culture: A Dynamic Model*, Working Paper No. 1412-83, Massachusetts Institute of Technology, February.

—— (1987) *Process Consultation: Lessons for Managers and Consultants*, vol. 2, Addison-Wesley: Reading, MA.

Schlipp, P.A. (ed.) (1949) *Albert Einstein: Philosopher–Scientist*, Evanston: London, p. 228.

Schmuck, R. and Miles, M.B. (1976) *Organisational Development in Schools*, National Press Books: Palo Alto, CA.

Schoderbek, P.P., Schoderbek, C.G. and Kefalas, A.G. (1990) *Management Systems: Conceptual Considerations*, 4th edn, BPI-Irwin: Boston, MA.

Scholes, R.J. (1990) 'Change in nature and the nature of change: interactions between terrestrial ecosystems and the atmosphere', *South African Journal of Science*, vol. 86: 350–354.

Schon, D.A. (1971) *Beyond the Stable State*, Random House: New York.

—— (1979) 'Creative metaphor: a perspective on problem setting in social policy', in A. Ortony (ed.) *Metaphor and Thought*, Cambridge University Press: Cambridge, pp. 254–283.

Schrodinger, E. (1944) *What is Life?*, Cambridge University Press: Cambridge.

Scott, A. (1988) *Vital Principles*, Blackwell: New York.

Scott, W.G. and Mitchell, T.R. (1976) *Organisation Theory: A Structural and Behavioural Analysis*, Richard D. Irwin: Homewood, IL.

Scott, W.R. (1987) *Organisations: Rational, Natural and Open Systems*, Prentice Hall: Englewood Cliffs, NJ.

Seashore, S.E. and Bowers, D.G. (1970) 'Durability of organizational change', *American Psychologist*, vol. 25: 227–333.

Senge, P.M. (1990) *The Fifth Discipline*, Century Business Press: London.

Sheldon, A. (1980) 'Organisational paradigms: a theory of organisational change', *Organisational Dynamics*, vol. 8 (3): 61–71.

Shepard, H. and Blake, R. (1962) 'Changing behaviour through cognition change', *Human Organisation*, vol. 21 (2):

Shlesinger, M.F. (1987) quoted in J. Gelick, *Chaos*, Cardinal Books: London, p. 5.

Shurig, R. (1986) 'Morphology: a knowledge tool', *Systems Research*, vol. 3 (1): 9–19.

Sienko, M.J. and Plane, R.A. (1979) *Chemistry: Principles and Applications*, McGraw-Hill: New York.

Simon, H.A. (1947) *Administrative Behaviour: A Study of Decision Making Processes in Administrative Organizations*, Macmillan: New York.

—— (1960) *The New Science of Management Decision*, Harper and Row: New York.

Simons, R. (1995) 'Control in an age of empowerment', *Harvard Business Review*, vol. 73 (2): 80–88.

Sinkula, J.M. (1994) 'Market information processing organisational learning', *Journal of Marketing*, vol. 58: 35–45.

Skibbins, G.J. (1974) *Organisational Evolution*, Amacom: New York.

Skolmli, J.T. (1989) 'New screen based stock market and its supporting systems', MSc thesis (ref. 910281), City University Business School: London.

Smale, S. (1967) 'Differentiable dynamical systems', *Bulletin of American Mathematical Society*, vol. 73: 747–817.

—— (1980) *The Mathematics of Time: Essays on Dynamical Systems, Economic Processes, and Related Topics*, Springer-Verlag: New York.

Smith, C. (1986) 'Transformation and regeneration in social systems: a dissipative structure perspective', *Systems Research*, vol. 3: 203–213.

Smith, K.K. (1982) 'Philosophical problems in thinking about organizational change', in P.S. Goodman and associates (eds) *Change in Organizations*, Jossey-Bass: San Francisco, pp. 316–374.

Smith, P.B. (1980) *Group Processes and Personal Change*, Harper and Row: New York.

Smith, M., Beck, J., Cooper, C.L., Cox, C., Ottaway, D. and Talbot, R. (1982) *Introducing Organisational Behaviour*, Macmillan: London.

Smith, C. and Gemmill, G. (1991) Change in small groups: a dissipative structure perspective, *Human Relations*, vol. 44: 697–716.

Sofer, C. (1961) *The Organisation from Within*, Tavistock Institute: London.

Sprague, R.H. and McNurlin, B.C. (1993) *Information Systems Management in Practice*, Prentice Hall: Englewood Cliffs, NJ.

Stacey, R.D. (1992) *Managing Chaos*, Kogan Page: London.

—— (1993) *Strategic Management and Organisational Dynamics*, Pitman: London.

Stapp, H.P. (1982) *Journal of Found. Phys.*, vol. 12: 363–399.

—— (1985) *Journal of Found. Phys.*, Vol. 15: 35–47.

Starkey, K. and McKinlay, A. (1988) *Organisational Innovation*, ESRC: Avebury.

Stein, D.L. (ed.) (1989) *Lectures in the Sciences of Complexity*, Addison-Wesley: Redwood City, CA.

Sterman, J.D. (1988) 'Deterministic chaos in models of human behaviour', *System Dynamics Review*, vol. 4 (1–2): 148–178.

—— (1994) 'Learning in and about complex systems', *Systems Dynamics Review*, vol. 10 (2–3): 291–330.

Stickland, F. (1996) 'Business process change: a systems thinking perspective', *World Futures*, vol. 47: 69–77.

Stickland, F. and Reavill, L. (1995) 'Understanding the nature of system change: an interdisciplinary approach', *Systems Research*, vol. 12 (2): 147–154.

Stowell, F.A. and Allen, G.A. (1988) 'Cooperation, power and the impact of information systems', *Systems Practice*, vol. 1 (2): 181–192.

Swanson, G.E., Newcomb, T.E. and Hartley, E.L. (eds) (1958) *Readings in Social Psychology*, Holt Rinehart and Winston: New York.

Swenson, R. (1989) 'Emergent attractors and the law of maximum entropy production: foundations to a theory of general evolution', *Systems Research*, vol. 6 (3): 187–189.

Taguchi, G. (1986) *Introduction to Quality Engineering*, Asian Production Organisation: Dearborn, MI.

Tajfel, H. and Fraser, C. (1981) *Introducing Social Psychology*, Penguin: London, Chapter 17.

Tanck, H.J. (1972) *Meteorology*, Transworld Publishers: Reading.

Taylor, A.E. (1921) *Elements of Metaphysics*, Methuen: London.

Taylor, F.W. (1903) *Shop Management*, Harper: New York.

—— (1911) *The Principles of Scientific Management*, Harper: New York.

Terborg, J.A., Howard, G.S. and Maxwell, S.E. (1980) 'Evaluating planned organisational change: a method for assessing alpha, beta, and gamma change', *Academy of Management Review*, vol. 5: 109–121.

Termier, H. and Termier, G. (1958) *The Geological Drama*, Hutchinson: London, p. 13.

Teweles, E.S., Bradley, T.M. and Teweles, T.M. (1992) *The Stock Market*, John Wiley: Chichester.

Thiertat, R.A. and Forgues, B. (1995) 'Chaos theory and organisation', *Organisation Science*, vol. 6: 19–31.

Thom, R. (1975) *Structural Stability and Morphogenesis: An Outline of a General Theory of Models*, trans. D.H. Fowler, Benjamin: Reading, MA.

Thomas, J.M. and Bennis, W.G. (eds) (1972) *The Management of Change and Conflict*, Penguin: London.

Thomas, W.I. (1937) *Primitive Behaviour: An Introduction to the Social Sciences*, McGraw-Hill: New York.

Thompson, J. (1967) *Organisations in Action*, McGraw-Hill: New York.

Toffler, A. (1970) *Future Shock*, Pan: New York.

Tomita, G. (1986) 'Periodically forced nonlinear oscillators', in A. Holden (ed.) *Chaos*, Manchester University Press: Manchester, pp. 211–236.

Torbert, W.R. (1989) Leading organisational transformation, *Research in Organisational Change and Development*, vol. 3: 83–116.

Toro, M. and Aracil, J. (1988) 'Qualitative analysis of system dynamics ecological models', *System Dynamics Review*, vol. 4 (1–2): 56–80.

Tozer, E.E. (1991) *Planning for Effective Business Information Systems*, Pergamon Press: Oxford.

Trifogli, C. (1993) 'Giles of Rome on the instant of change', *Synthese*, vol. 96: 93–114.

Troncale, L. (1985) 'Duality/complementarity as a general systems isomorphy', *Proceedings of the International Conference on Systems Inquiry*, vol. 1: 186–199.

—— (1988) 'Tools for application of systems theory: preliminary design of a knowledge based computer system on GST', *Proceedings of 32nd Annual Conference ISGSR*, 23–27 May, St. Louis.

Tsoukas, H. (1991) 'The missing link: a transformational view of metaphors in organizational science', *Academy of Management Review*, vol. 16 (3): 566–585.

Tushman, M.L. and Moore, W.L. (1988) *Readings in the Management of Innovation*, 2nd edn, Ballinger: Cambridge, MA.

Ulrich, W. (1987) 'Critical heuristics of social systems design', *European Journal of Operational Research*, vol. 31:

—— (1988) 'Systems thinking, systems practice and practical philosophy: a program of research', *Systems Practice*, vol. 1:

Utterback, J. and Abernathy, W. (1975) 'A dynamic model of process and product innovation', *Omega*, vol. 3 (6): 639–656.

Vaill, P.B. (1989) *Managing as a Performing Art*, Jossey-Bass: San Francisco.

Van de Ven, A.H. (1980) *Measuring and Assessing Organisations*, John Wiley: Chichester.

—— (1987) 'Review essay: four requirements for processual analysis', in A. Pettigrew (ed.) *The Management of Strategic Change*, Blackwell: Oxford, pp. 330–341.

Van de Ven, A.H. and Poole, M.S. (1987) 'Paradoxical requirements for a theory of organisational change', in R. Quinn and K. Cameron (eds) *Paradox and Transformation*, Ballinger Press: Cambridge, MA.

Van den Daele, L.D. (1969) 'Qualitative models in developmental analysis', *Developmental Psychology*, vol. 1 (4): 303–310.

—— (1974) 'Infrastructure and transition in developmental analysis', *Human Development*, vol. 17: 1–23.

Van Gigch, J.P. (1974) *Applied General Systems Theory*, Harper and Row: New York.

Van Gundy, A.B. (1988) *Techniques of Structured Problem Solving*, 2nd edn, Van Nostrand Reinhold: New York.

Van Maanen, J. and Barley, S.R. (1984) 'Occupational communities: culture and control in organisations', in B. Straw and L.L Cummings (eds) *Research in Organisational Behaviour*, JAI Press: Greenwich, CT.

Van Meter, D.S. (1974) 'Alternative methods of measuring change', *Political Methodology*, vol. 1: 125–139.

Varela, F.J. (1979) *Principles of Biological Autonomy*, New Holland: New York.

Vickers, G. (1965) *The Art of Judgement*, Basic Books: New York.

—— (1980a) 'Some implications of systems thinking', in J. Beishon and G. Peters (eds) *Systems Behaviour*, Harper and Row: Open University: Milton Keynes, pp. 19–25.

—— (1980b) *Responsibility – Its Sources and Limits*, Intersystems Publications: Seaside, CA.

—— (1983) *Human Systems are Different*, Harper and Row: London.

Villars, C.N. (1983) *Journal of Psychoenergetics*, vol. 5: 1–10, 129–139.

Villee, C.A. and Deithier, V.G. (1976) *Biological Principles and Processes*, 2nd edn, W.B. Saunders: Philadelphia.

Waddington, C.H. (1968) *Towards a Theoretical Biology*, Aldine: Chicago, pp. 1–31.

—— (1976) 'Evolution in the sub-human world', in E. Jantsch and C. Waddington *Evolution and Consciousness: Human Systems in Transition*, Addison-Wesley: Reading, MA.

Waelchli, F. (1992) 'Eleven theses of general systems theory', *Systems Research*, vol. 9 (4): 3–8.

Wager, W.W. (1971) *Building the City of Man*, Grossman: New York, p. 4.

Wake, D.B., Roth, G. and Wake, M.H. (1983) 'On the problem of stasis in organismal evolution', *Journal of Theoretical Biology*, vol. 101: 211–224.

Waldram, J.R. (1985) *Theory of Thermodynamics*, Cambridge University Press: Cambridge.

Waldrop, M.M. (1992) *Complexity: The Emerging Science at the Edge of Chaos*, Penguin: London, p. 356.

Walsham, G. (1991) 'Organisational metaphors and information systems research', *Journal of Information Systems*, vol. 1 (2): 83–94.

Warfield, J.N. (1976) *Societal Systems: Planning, Policy and Complexity*, John Wiley: New York.

—— (1982) *Consensus Methodologies*, Centre for Interactive Management: Charlottesville, VA.

Warfield, J.N. and Cardenas, A.R. (1993) *A Handbook of Interactive Management*, IASIS: George Mason University, Virginia.

Wark, K. (1988) *Thermodynamics*, 5th edn, McGraw-Hill: New York.

Waterman, R.H. Peters, T.J. and Philips, J.R. (1980) *Structure is Not Organisation*, Business Horizons, Indiana University Foundation for the School of Business.

Watt, K.E. and Craig, P.P. (1986) 'Systems stability principles', *Systems Research*, vol. 3: 191–201.

Watzlawick, P., Weakland, J.H. and Fisch, R. (1974) *Change: Principles of Problem Formation and Resolution*, W.W. Norton: New York.

Weber, M. (1947) *The Theory of Social and Economic Organisations*, trans. A.M. Henderson and T. Parsons, Free Press: New York.

Weick, K.E. (1969) *The Social Psychology of Organising*, Addison-Wesley: Reading, MA.

—— (1979) *The Social Psychology of Organisation*, Random House: New York.

—— (1993) 'Organisational redesign as improvisation', in G.P. Huber and W.H. Glick *Organisational Change and Redesign*, Oxford University Press: Oxford, pp. 346–379.

Weiss, P. (1947) 'The place of physiology in the biological sciences', *Federation Proceedings*, vol. 6: 523–525.

West, B.J. (1985) *An Essay on the Importance of Being Nonlinear*, Springer-Verlag: Berlin.

Wheatley, M.J. (1992) *Leadership and the New Science*, Berrett-Koehler: San Francisco.

Whitaker, I. (1965) 'The nature and value of functionalism in sociology', in *Functionalism in the Social Sciences*, Monograph 5, American Academy of Political and Social Science, February.

Whitehead, A.N. (1925) *Science and the Modern World*, Macmillan: New York.

Whitfield, P. (1975) *Creativity in Industry*, Penguin: London.

Whyte, L.L. (1970) 'The structural hierarchy in organisms', in Jones and Brandl (eds) *Unity and Diversity in Systems*, Braziller: New York.

Widaman, K.F. (1991) 'Qualitative transitions amid quantitative development: a challenge for measuring and representing change', in L.M. Collins and J.L. Horn (eds) *Best Methods for the Analysis of Change*, American Psychology Association: New York, pp. 204–217.

Wigner, E.P. (1964) 'Events, laws of nature and invariance principles', the Nobel lecture, *Science*, vol. 145: 995–999.

Wilber, K. (1983) *A Sociable God: Toward a New Understanding of Religion*, New Science Library: Boulder, CO.

Wilby, J. (1994) 'A critique of hierarchy theory', *Systems Practice*, vol. 7 (6): 653–670.

Wilden, A. (1980) *Systems and Structures: Essays in Communication and Exchange*, Tavistock: New York.

Williams, J.E., Metcalfe, H.C., Trinklein, F.E. and Lefler, R.W. (1968) *Modern Physics*, Holt Rinehart and Winston: New York.

Wilson, B. (1990) *Systems: Concepts, Methodologies and Applications*, 2nd edn, John Wiley: Chichester.

Wilson, D.C. (1992) *A Strategy of Change: Concepts and Controversies in the Management of Change*, Routledge: London.

Wilson R.J. (1979) *Introduction to Graph Theory*, Longman: Harlow.

Wimsatt, W.C. (1980) 'Reductionists research strategies', *Scientific Discovery Case Studies*, Reidel: Dordrecht.

Wolfram, S. (ed.) (1986) *Theory and Applications of Cellular Automata*, World Scientific: Singapore.

Wolstenholme, E.F. (1990) *System Enquiry: A System Dynamics Approach*, John Wiley: Chichester.

Woodman, R.W. (1989) 'Evaluation research on organisational change: arguments for a "combined paradigm" approach', *Organisational Change and Development*, vol. 3: 161–180.

Woodward, J. (1965) *Industrial Organisation: Theory and Practice*, Oxford University Press: Oxford.

Wren, D.A. (1979) *The Evolution of Management Thought*, John Wiley: New York.

Zald, M. and Berger, M. (1978) 'Social movements in organisations', *American Journal of Sociology*, vol. 83: 823–861.

Zaltman, G. and Duncan, R. (1977) *Strategies for Planned Change*, Wiley-Interscience: New York.

Zand, D.E. and Sorensen, R.E. (1975) 'Theory of change and effective use of management science', *Administrative Science Quarterly*, vol. 20: 532–545.

Zeeman, E.C. (1977) *Catastrophe Theory: Selected Papers 1972–1977*, Addison-Wesley: Reading, MA.

—— (1986) 'Dynamics of Darwinian evolution', in S. Diner, D. Fargue and G. Lochak (eds) *Dynamical Systems: A Renewal of Mechanism*, World Scientific: Singapore, pp. 155–165.

—— (1988) 'On the classification of dynamical systems', *Bulletin of the London Mathematical Society*, vol. 20: 545–557.

Zeleny, M. and Pierre, N.A. (1976) 'Simulation of self-renewing systems', in E. Jantsch and C.H. Waddington (eds) *Evolution and Consciousness: Human Systems in Transtion*, Addison-Wesley: Reading, MA.

Zey-Ferrell, M. (1979) *Dimensions of Organizations*, Goodyeat: Santa Monica, CA, pp. 90–91.

Zimmerman, B.J. (1992) *Chaos and Self-Renewing Organisations: Designing Transformation Processes for Co-evolution*, Faculty of Administrative Studies, York University: Ontario.

Zimmerman, B.J. and Hurst, D.K. (1993) 'Breaking the boundaries: the fractal organization', *Journal of Management Inquiry*, vol. 2 (4): 334–355.

Zmud, R.W. and Armenakis, A.A. (1978) 'Understanding the measurement of change', *Academy of Management Review*, vol. 3: 661–669.

Zohar, D. (1990) *The Quantum Self*, Bloomsbury: London.

Zucker, L.G. (1977) 'The role of institutionalisation in cultural persistence', *American Sociological Review*, vol. 42: 726–743.

Zurek, W.H. (ed.) (1990) *Complexity, Entropy, and the Physics of Information*, Santa Fe Institute Studies in the Sciences of Complexity, proceedings, vol. 8, Addison-Wesley: Redwood City, CA.

Author index

Subject index